Mountain Biking
Idaho

Stephen Stuebner

FALCON®
HELENA, MONTANA

A FALCON GUIDE ®

Falcon® Publishing is continually expanding its list of recreation guidebooks. All books include detailed descriptions, accurate maps, and all the information necessary for enjoyable trips. You can order extra copies of this book and get information and prices for other Falcon® guidebooks by writing Falcon, P.O. Box 1718, Helena, MT 59624 or calling toll free 1-800-582-2665. Also, please ask for a free copy of our current catalog. Visit our website at www.FalconOutdoors.com or contact us by e-mail at falcon@falcon.com.

Library of Congress Cataloging-in-Publication Data

Stuebner, Stephen.
    Mountain biking Idaho / by Stephen Stuebner.
        p.   cm. — (A Falcon guide)
    ISBN 1-56044-744-3 (pbk.)
    1. All terrain cycling—Idaho—Guidebooks. 2. Trails—Idaho—Guidebooks.
    3. Idaho—Guidebooks. I. Title. II. Series
    GV1045.5.I25S88   1999
    917.9604'33--dc21   98-52472
                                                                              CIP

CAUTION

Outdoor recreational activities are by their very nature potentially hazardous. All participants in such activities must assume the responsibility for their own actions and safety. The information contained in this guidebook cannot replace sound judgment and good decision-making skills that help reduce risk exposure, nor does the scope of this book allow for disclosure of all the potential hazards and risks involved in such activities.

Learn as much as possible about the outdoor recreational activities in which you participate, prepare for the unexpected, and be cautious. The reward will be a safer and more enjoyable experience.

♻ Text pages printed on recycled paper.

Contents

Map Legend

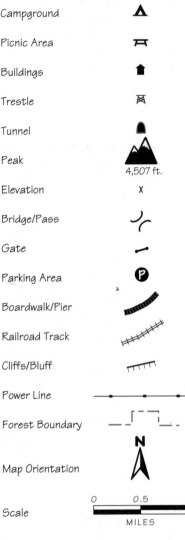

Interstate	
U.S. Highway	
State or Other Principal Road	
Forest Road	
Interstate Highway	
Paved Road	
Gravel Road	
Unimproved Road	
Trail (singletrack)	
Trailhead	
Trail Marker	
Waterway	
Intermittent Waterway	
Lake/Reservoir	
Meadow/Swamp	

Campground

Picnic Area

Buildings

Trestle

Tunnel

Peak
4,507 ft.

Elevation
X

Bridge/Pass

Gate

Parking Area

Boardwalk/Pier

Railroad Track

Cliffs/Bluff

Power Line

Forest Boundary

Map Orientation

N

Scale

0	0.5	1

MILES

Idaho Locator Map

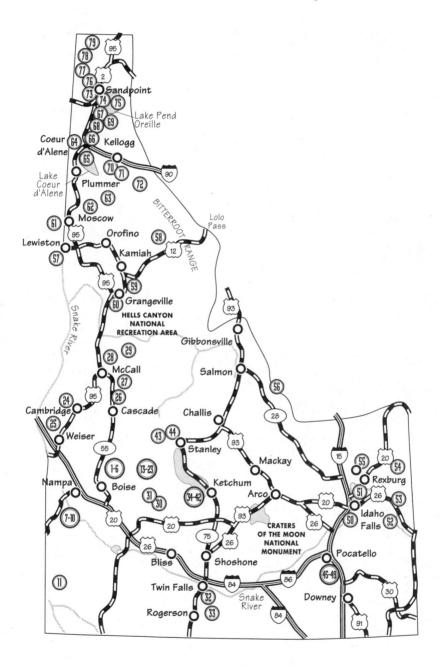

Welcome to Idaho

On a clear, crisp fall day, I pedaled up a doubletrack trail in the East Fork of Baker Creek, north of Sun Valley. As always, I did the ride to get a workout, soak in the colors, sniff the fresh fragrance of fall, and generally have a good time. Just a couple miles of moderate climbing on the East Fork Road puts you on a high open ridge in the rounded and rolling Smoky Mountains. I rode around the last switchback on the uphill grade, and my heart filled with awe as I watched the front side of the 11,000-foot Boulder Mountains rise up so impressively from the valley below. On a grassy mountain slope about 1,000 feet below my feet, I happened to notice a cluster of cow elk and their young lying there in a swale. Ah, life is good.

There, on the broad ridge, surrounded by beauty, I sat down and pondered. In truth, this was more than a routine mountain bike ride. I was on a vision quest of sorts, thinking about the immensity of the great state of Idaho. It's a place that's uncommonly rich with public land—11 national forests encompassing 20 million acres, 12 million acres of Bureau of Land Management (BLM) land, and 2 million acres of state land—all endowed with elaborate networks of roads, jeep trails, and singletrack. At last count, Idaho had 19,000 miles of jeep trails and singletrack. Whew! Beyond that, Idaho is blessed with an amazingly diverse landscape—from incised rocky canyons in the Owyhee desert, to an eclectic mix of densely forested mountains throughout the state, to the much wetter lakes region in the Panhandle. It's as though you can visit the landscapes of southern Utah, British Columbia, and Lake Tahoe in one largely undiscovered place, Idaho.

So how could I craft a statewide mountain bike book and do it all justice? It was a daunting and humbling thought.

As the author of several regional mountain bike guides on Idaho, I brought a similar guiding principle to the challenge before me: You've got to have something for everyone. Some folks like to ride urban paved trails. Some folks don't like to climb—they'd prefer to take a lift, a chairlift that is, and ride down a real mountain trail. And, of course, there are the hard-cores, too, who expect to get punished by long, taxing climbs, followed by the longest descent possible on the sweetest singletrack known to man.

Here you'll find all of that and more. Idaho is blessed with a growing number of rail-trails—railroad tracks converted to gravel trails—which follow an easy grade and take you to previously inaccessible places. The coolest rail-trail of them all, the Route of the Hiawatha, follows a 2 percent downhill grade for 12.7 miles through eight dark tunnels and over seven high trestles in the Upper St. Joe River country. In its first year of operation in 1998, more than 8,000 people visited the Route of the Hiawatha.

I'm a history buff, too. Near Boise, you can ride along the same bumpy desert terrain that more than 200,000 Oregon Trail emigrants crossed as they approached water and shade in the Boise Valley after weeks of hot and arduous travels across the Snake River Plain. Near Lolo Pass in north-central Idaho, riders can retrace the overland route followed by Lewis and Clark's Corps of Discovery on the north ridgetops of the Lochsa River canyon. Here, Lewis and Clark faced the single most difficult challenge of their journey to the sea, trudging through jackstrawed timber and snow in late September. Wild game was so scarce they were forced to eat horsemeat to survive. The Lolo Motorway, a single-lane primitive dirt road built in the 1930s by the Civilian Conservation Corps, follows the same ridgetops up and down, up and down, for 73 miles. I provide a detailed guide of the entire route, spread over three days. Put together a group of friends, pack up your camping gear, and enjoy a most memorable trip while learning a bit about Western frontier history.

If you like to ride at ski areas, I provide a guide to them all: Schweitzer Mountain and Silver Mountain in the Panhandle, world-famous Sun Valley with 20 miles of brand-new singletrack, Brundage Mountain's serpentlike elk trail, Bogus Basin, and Kelly Canyon.

Never before has any guidebook in Idaho provided a comprehensive guide to all of the urban paved recreation trails throughout the state. It's all here: the North Idaho Centennial Trail, the Wood River Trail in Sun Valley, the Boise River Greenbelt in Boise, the Lewiston Levies, the Bill Chipman Palouse Trail between Moscow and Pullman, the Idaho Falls Greenbelt, the Victor–Driggs Paved Trail, and the Sagle Community Trail between Sagle and Sandpoint.

In every corner of Idaho, a magnificent system of mountain trails awaits you. In the first edition of this book, we present the crème de la crème of the best mountain trail loops in Idaho. Thanks to the generosity and assistance of local riders in Sandpoint, Coeur d'Alene, Moscow, Idaho Falls, Pocatello, and Twin Falls, you can experience their all-time favorite rides. Instead of trying to pioneer my own routes in these areas, I relied on veteran riders to show me the best of the best.

If you're an Idaho resident and you haven't ventured outside the scope of your regional trail system, you must take at least one vacation a year and check the others out. As one who normally makes one trip a year to Moab, I'll be taking future mountain bike vacations with my family and friends to revisit Idaho rides like the South Hills Singletrack Nirvana near Twin Falls, the Lakeshore Trail at Priest Lake, the Piah Creek Loop near Moscow, and the Mink Creek area in Pocatello.

North Idaho riders must travel south to experience what I call "Idaho classics"—the Fisher-Williams Loop in the White Clouds, the Greenhorn-Mahoney Loop near Hailey, Ruby Meadows–Loon Lake Loop near McCall, and the Deadwood–Julie Creek Loop near Lowman. Or take the Warm Springs Plunge ultimate hot springs ride that finishes off with a 102-degree soothing soak at the Bonneville Hot Springs. In the springtime, when the mountains are still choked with snow, consider a trip to the big wide open, the Owyhee Mountains, and ride the Wilson Creek Mini-Moab Loop. Or see if your legs can climb a mucho-steep ascent to the Stick in the Sky. In May, hundreds of golden eagles, red-tailed hawks, and prairie falcons nest in the Snake River Birds of Prey National Conservation Area. An April or

May trip on the Swan Falls Petroglyph Tour will show you some rock inscriptions while raptors soar overhead.

Add value to your mountain bike camp-out by reserving a backcountry yurt in the Sun Valley or Idaho City—and do it up in luxurious quarters. On Ride 40, I describe an epic loop journey up the East Fork Road, past that beautiful view of the Boulders, to a remote yurt deep in the Smokies near Fox Peak. Vehicle access in midsummer allows you to shuttle in camping supplies by vehicle for an unforgettable star-filled night. The Coyote yurt, owned and managed by Sun Valley Trekking, is outfitted with a double-burner stove, pots and pans, and bunks. All you need is food and sleeping bags. Then, on the next day, you'll ride more than 10 miles of singletrack down a ridge and slalom through aspen trees into Adams Gulch near Ketchum. What a trip!

North of Idaho City, volunteers have built three yurts amid a network of 50 miles of roads and trails. These yurts are brand spanking new, and they're equipped with double-burner stoves, pots and pans, and bunks. You can drive in supplies (and young children) to these yurts as well, and ride relatively modest terrain (no ridiculously steep rides here) in the Banner Ridge area. Dense pine and fir forests in this area play host to a large elk and black bear population. Don't worry, those bears have plenty to feast on in the woods. You'll just see bear sign on the trail, and you might get a chance sighting on a ride.

Now you have an idea what this guide has to offer. But before you head out on the trail, please observe a few words of caution.

Mountain bikers have awesome access to singletrack trails in Idaho because we don't have millions of people living here, but also because the people who enjoy mountain trails—horseback riders, hikers, backpackers, motorcycle riders, ATV riders, and mountain bikers—know something about backcountry ethics. That's our backcountry code, the notion of sharing trails with other people. Please take special care to ride trails in a manner in which you can yield to other folks coming up the trail. Take a moment to say "howdy" and chat. As a founding member of the Southwest Idaho Mountain Biking Association (SWIMBA) in Boise and a board member of the Idaho Trails Council, a statewide trail advocacy group, I know that we will have a long future enjoying our gorgeous singletrack trails by observing the backcountry code. Please: Contrary to the images regularly displayed in mountain bike magazines, mountain trails on public lands are not race courses. One bad encounter on the trail will give that person a permanent negative impression of all mountain bikers.

OK, enough of that. I know that if you have one-tenth as much fun as I did riding the trails in this book, you are guaranteed to have a great time. Be sure to pack along enough food and water, and carry a few basic tools to cope with breakdowns. To complete this book, I had to ride more than 2,000 miles of mountain trails in the past year. So it shouldn't be surprising that I broke three chains, wore out the tread on three back tires and two front tires, popped ten spokes, wore out the springs in two XTR derailleurs and two XTR rapid-fire shifters, and destroyed more cyclecomputers than I'd care to remember. They'd fall off the handlebar mount and get crushed on the road, they'd fly off the roof rack, they'd go blank in the cold (very maddening), or the batteries simply wore out. I'm also on my second bike in two years, but that's because I drove my old purple Fat City Monster Fat into the roof of my garage. My point is, if you ride a lot, you are going to have equipment breakdowns. If you have the right stuff in your tool kit, it makes a huge difference—like the difference between continuing a ride or hiking out.

So here you go, my fellow cyclists, a guide to 80 trails in Idaho. The only challenge remaining is deciding where to go first. Enjoy!

Stephen Stuebner, October 1998

Mountain Bike Manners

Remember, all mountain bikers will be judged by your conduct . . .

Let's face it. The future of mountain biking is directly related to our conduct—our impact on trails and our relations with other trail users. It's called backcountry ethics.

Now comes the question—how can we put this gently?—Do you know about backcountry ethics? Or, as *Mountain Bike Action* editors put it, "Are you an off-road idiot? Are you a bicycling bonehead? Are you a toxic trail user?"

"No way!" you might reply. "I'm not like all those yee-hah, subhumanoid adrenaline sniffers that *Geraldo* and *60 Minutes* feature in their *Two-Wheeled Terrors* videos. Those legless bivalves don't deserve to live, much less to call themselves mountain bikers!"

OK. Let's not get into the blame game. But before you take off on your next mountain bike ride, read about mountain biking's biggest enemies—easily avoidable behaviors that have led to trail closures in more populated areas—and learn how to set a positive example for your sport. It doesn't matter if you've been a bicycling bonehead before; no one will ever know. Just learn how to do it right.

Meet your enemies, as described by *Mountain Bike Action* editor Richard Cunningham, and reprinted here with his permission, with subnotes by the author:

Enemy No. 1: Mr. Control (a.k.a. Mr. Speedball)

Mr. Control rides at top speed everywhere, slowing only slightly to pass other trail users. He thinks that uttering a sharp "On your left!" as he blows by is a polite exchange of good will. Hikers or other cyclists have told him that he's causing others to freak out and that it would be best if he stopped or slowed to walking speed to let others pass quietly. Mr. Control blows 'em off. . . Mr. Control is a mental case.

Bottom line: Ride under control and be prepared to slow down for *all* trail users coming up the trail. Bend over backward to be polite and show fellow trail users that mountain bikers can, indeed, show respect for other folks and share the trail.

Remember: One bad encounter with a hiker, jogger, or equestrian will leave a permanent negative impression about all mountain bikers.

Enemy No. 2: Rear Brake Rodney

Rear Brake Rodney is the most common backcountry bonehead. Forsaking the laws of physics, Rodney refuses to use his front brake. This dude is the skid kid. Rod refuses to believe that most of the weight of his bike transfers to the front wheel under braking, making his rear stopper ineffective. Instead, Rodney the Ridiculous excavates the trail surface, locking up his rear wheel, skidding into every curve and carving a rut down the center of down-hill singletracks. . . .

The most lame excuse is that locking the rear end up is a faster or more controllable way to ride. . . . Mastering the front brake is a fat-tire essential. Locking up the brakes is uncool on singletracks. Besides the fact that it digs up the trail, Rear Brake Rodney leaves ugly stripes that scream, "Follow this broken line to discover another out-of-control cyclist." The front brake is the most important tool for technical riding, especially on steep downhills (ask any pro). Learn how to use it. (Rear Brake Rodney's prison sentence should be to adopt and maintain a singletrack that his fellow skidders use. That'll cure him.)

Tip: When descending a steep trail, put about 65 percent of your braking power on your front brake lever, 35 percent on your back, and "feather" the back brake as you descend. It also helps to lower your seat and shift your butt over the back tire. "Feathering" the back brake means gripping and releasing the brake, in rapid fashion. Try it: You'll notice that the skidding stops and you have much more control. If you've done all of the above and you're still skidding, the hill is too steep. Get off and walk.

Enemy No. 3: Predators in Paradise

Twenty-odd fat-tire cyclists, decked out in team jerseys, racing flat out, side-by-side, is awesome in a closed race course. Put these predators in a local park on a peaceful afternoon and it's a recipe for hateful confrontation. Race training groups suffer from a subhuman pack mentality. If the front of the group burns past a couple of equestrians, invariably the rest will follow. Keeping everyone's speed down in sensitive areas is next to impossible.

Bottom line: Ride in small groups and never race on commonly used trails.

Enemy No. 4: Mr. Conveniently Handicapped

No, this isn't the person who returns from a track meet and parks in a handicapped space to dash into the shopping mall for a latté. This dude is far worse, lower than gum on the floor of a subway station. Mr. Conveniently Handicapped is a local dude who rides illegally past every "No Bicycles" and "Trail Closed" sign in the surrounding parks. All of his friends, and most of the park rangers, have spoken to him about the regulations, but somehow Mr. Convenient thinks the rules are for someone else.

Bottom line: Please heed trail closure signs.

Enemy No. 5: Vernon the Velo-Skier

Every Saturday Vernon and a handful of his buddies load up a couple pickup trucks with bikes and beer, then head to the local mountains for some serious downhill fun. They ride only one trail that used to be a popular hiking trail. One thing's for certain—there's absolutely no climbing involved. Vernon and his buds are Velo-Skiers. Once the caravan reaches the lower trailhead, someone shuttles the whole crew to the top. Vern and his buddies race each other to the bottom, then repeat their gravity game until dark-thirty or they run out of beer and baloney sandwiches. Vern and his buds rule this trail. What will happen if Vern and his buddies keep downhill skiing on the same trail? Authorities will close it to mountain bikes for good.

Velo-skiing is cool; honing your downhill skills in a multi-use area isn't. There is a time and place for screamin' fast descents. Now that most ski areas are open for cycling during the summer, there is no reason to terrorize the local parks. If you are too cheap to shell out $10 or $15 for a lift ticket, downhill in motorcycle areas where other users are expecting high-speed encounters.

Enemy No. 6: Adam & Eve's Palsy

Adam and Eve live in the mountains, surrounded by miles of roads and singletracks. Most mountain bikers would think their local trails were heaven. Unfortunately, life at high altitude must have affected their brains. For some reason, they only ride in wilderness areas that are strictly off-limits to bicycles (or any other mechanical devices, for that matter). . . . Wilderness areas are hallowed ground among the most powerful environmental groups; stay out of them! Conversely, the fact that there are places that people can go to escape bicycles and other devices gives us a strong bargaining chip to win access to the remaining backcountry. Don't blow it for the rest of us. Stay away from the forbidden fruit.

Enemy No. 7: Lewis and Clark

These dudes are dangerous dreamers. Armed with a brain the size of a pinhead, these two brothers boast knowledge of every park within 20 miles. In fact, they are self-appointed trailblazers who have pioneered at least half of the nearby singletracks. Trouble is, nobody asked these gophers to start digging. Their "trails" are steep, hard to maintain and don't go anywhere in particular. . . . Like most wannabe trailbreakers, Lewis and Clark simply rode across any interesting space between two roads. Others followed their tracks until a new trail was born.

This is a bad deal for everyone. Before appointing yourself to cut a new trail, talk to the landowners first. Their likely response will be: Don't do it. We've got enough trouble maintaining the trails we have.

Enemy No. 8: City Slackers

These folks are easy to spot. They own pretty nice bikes and dress up in the type of mountain bike gear that the models wear on Jeep TV commercials. . . . Are you a slacker? Your only salvation is to get down to a good fat-tire bike store, hook up with a couple of authentic mountain bikers, then go out and experience the real McCoy.

Enemy No. 9: Calvin Cutter

Redwood remora, singletrack slime, trail tick, berm bait . . . no trailside insult is rude enough to describe Calvin the Switchback Cutter. Why is it so important for some people to shorten their journey by 5 or 10 feet in the middle of the woods? It sounds petty, doesn't it? Yet, hikers, cyclists, and equestrians are all guilty of destroying switchbacks by shortcutting the last few steps.

Enemy No. 10: Barbara Badger

Barbara the Badger has been mountain biking for a long time. She has done her share of trail maintenance, worked to mend fences with local mountain bike factions, and gets in a few races each year. In the past she has been extremely courteous, but lately, one too many confrontations with hateful hikers has made her bitter.

As a result, Barbara and her cycling partners have given up any pretense of being nice to hikers. Now, instead of a casual trailside greeting, she manages a tight-lipped smile. Rather than stopping to allow others to pass by easily, she slows to an acceptable pace and goes on her merry way. Barbara still cares about joint trail use, but she has lost faith in the system and has begun to give up trying to be nice at all.

Giving up is the worst enemy mountain bikers have to fight. Don't waste your good nature on some backcountry sourpuss. If someone gives you grief, smile, give 'em a quick, "See ya later," then leave. Peer pressure and good faith are the most powerful tools we have to overcome ignorance.

IMBA RULES OF THE TRAIL

In addition to recognizing these off-road enemies and learning from their behavior, it's also a good idea to remember the International Mountain Bicycling Association's (IMBA) rules of the trail. The IMBA is a nonprofit advocacy organization dedicated to promoting mountain biking that's environmentally sound and socially responsible. IMBA's work keeps trails open and in good condition for everyone.

These rules of the trail are reprinted with permission from IMBA.

1. Ride on open trails only. Respect trail and road closures (ask if not sure), avoid possible trespass on land, obtain permits and authorization as may be required. Federal and state wilderness areas are closed to cycling. The way you ride will influence trail management decisions and policies.

2. Leave no trace. Be sensitive to the dirt beneath you. Even on open (legal) trails, avoid riding immediately after heavy rains or when the trail surface is soft and muddy. In some locations, muddy trails are unavoidable. Recognize different types of soils and trail construction. Practice low impact cycling. This also means staying on existing trails and not creating new ones. Be sure to pack out at least as much as you pack in.

3. Control your bicycle. Inattention for even a second can cause problems. Obey all bicycle speed regulations and recommendations.

4. Always yield trail. Give your fellow trail users plenty of advance notice when you're approaching. A friendly greeting (or bell) is considerate and works well; don't startle others. Show your respect when passing by slowing to a walking pace or even stopping, particularly when you meet horses. Anticipate other trail users around corners or in blind spots.

5. Don't scare animals. All animals are startled by an unannounced approach, a sudden movement, or a loud noise. This can be dangerous for you, others, and the animals. Give animals extra room and time to adjust to you. When passing horses use special care and follow the directions from the horseback riders (ask if uncertain). Running cattle or disturbing wildlife is a serious offense. Leave gates as you found them or as marked.

6. Plan ahead. Know your equipment, your ability, and the area in which you are riding—and prepare accordingly. Be self-sufficient at all times, keep your equipment in good repair, and carry all necessary supplies for changes in weather or other conditions. A well-executed trip is a satisfaction to you and not a burden or offense to others. Always wear a helmet.

MOUNTAIN BIKING WITH KIDS

When the time comes to raise a family, there's no reason for your mountain bike to collect cobwebs in the garage. After the baby arrives, consider investing in some child-toting gear so your new child can enjoy the outdoors with you.

The latest toys—a baby trailer for infants and toddlers, and a Trail-A-Bike attachment for three-year-olds and up—are tailor-made to maximize your children's safety and pleasure while you and your partner enjoy the outdoors and get some exercise. Then, when your kids can pedal their own bikes (and they start asking for really cool—and expensive—mountain bikes), they'll hit the dirt or the pavement with their legs a-spinnin' and their faces a-grinnin'.

Parents will have to make the call on when it's time to start taking a child cycling. The main concern, initially, is whether a child's neck is stable and strong enough to support the weight of a helmet and endure the shaking action of a bumpy bike path or gravel road. Typically, when children are six to eight months old, their necks may be stable enough for riding in a bike trailer. Just to be on the safe side, you can secure your child in a car seat for extra stability. Please consult your physician about these considerations.

For extra visibility and safety, it's a good idea to buy an orange safety flag pole and attach that to the back corner of the baby buggy.

Here are some tips from veteran cycling parents for baby trailer trips:

1. Be sure your child is properly dressed for the weather—remember that he or she is just sitting there while you're generating body heat. Close the window flap to shield your child from the cold, rain, and wind. Remem ber to apply liberal amounts of baby-specific sunscreen—children sun burn very easily. Have your child wear sunglasses when it's bright.

2. Feed your child before you go on a ride. Bring along extra food and drink.

3. Be prepared to tow some weight: 20 pounds for the buggy, plus your child's body weight, and a ton of miscellaneous stuff like diapers, extra clothes, and toys.

4. Be sure to bring along a variety of highly entertaining toys to keep your child happy and occupied. Noise-making toys work well. Kids may want to read or color, too. A baby buggy provides the advantage of giving a child his or her own space where these activities are possible.

5. Communicate with your child during the ride. Look back on a regular basis to see how he or she is doing. When your child can talk, encour age him or her to tell you how it's going. If you and your partner are riding together on separate bikes, it may be a good idea for the person not towing the trailer to let you know if you're riding too fast or if your child needs attention.

6. Ride conservatively and give yourself plenty of time to stop. Remem ber that your turning radius is going to be much wider and that you're towing extra weight.

7. Always keep the screen cover on the trailer to protect your child from projectiles launched from the back tire.

8. Use hand signals when riding on streets and observe the same traffic laws that pertain to vehicles. Ride with the flow of traffic.

9. Take your child on streets and pathways that are smooth and feel safe. Remember that many people driving cars and trucks don't think you even have a right to be there on the shoulder of the road.

Trail-A-Bike options

Trail-A-Bike attachments are a nifty new way to allow your child to get accustomed to pedaling his or her own bike, shifting gears, and getting a sense for balance and maneuvering. When you're climbing hills, your child can pedal, too. For adults, the Trail-A-Bike is a great invention that allows you to get a sweat-popping workout while bonding with your child.

Avid mountain bikers shouldn't hesitate to take their kids on dirt roads and some doubletrack trails in Idaho, depending on the bump factor. It's up to you to decide where to go and what you're comfortable with. It's prob ably a good idea to scout places where you might want to take your child on a Trail-A-Bike by riding them on your own first.

Gregg Lewis, a long-time mountain biker in Boise, takes his son riding frequently. "Clay loves the rolling dips and the whoop-de-doos," Lewis says. "There are days when he wants to go home and I want to keep going, and there are days when I'm ready to quit and he wants to keep going. I try to meet his needs."

Lewis outfits Clay with a helmet, sunglasses, cycling gloves, cycling shorts, and sturdy hiking boots. The boots protect his son's feet and ankles from getting nailed by rocks and other obstacles. Lewis teaches him how to keep his feet in a parallel position—at nine o'clock and three o'clock—to avoid hitting rocks. Lewis brings along good energy packs and power bars for Clay.

Other tips:
1. Communicate with your child frequently to ensure that he or she is having a good time. It should be a fun, positive experience, not a night mare that will make your child hate cycling forever.
2. Be sure to adjust the seat and handlebars for a good fit.
3. Use a good dose of common sense to know when to walk the bike during climbs and descents, and know when to return home.
4. Start on short rides and work up to longer ones.
5. When you are towing a child, it helps to have your partner ride with you to let you know when you are going too fast or the child is bouncing around too much.

BIKE MAINTENANCE

Tool Kits and Repairs

Anyone who heads into the backcountry for a mountain biking adventure should carry a basic tool kit, patch kit, and hand pump to cope with flat tires and other common breakdowns. Even Greenbelt riders will be glad to have a pump and patch kit with them if they get a flat.

I recommend carrying a few extra tools in your vehicle if you drive to a trailhead; take along the essentials on the ride itself.

Recommended essential tool kit to carry on your bike:

☐ Hand pump
☐ Allen wrenches
☐ Extra slime tube
☐ Patch kit
☐ Tire irons
☐ Spoke wrench
☐ Chain breaker
☐ Chain lube

Many multipurpose tools include Allen wrenches, a chain-breaking tool, crescent wrench, pliers, and other items.

Recommended tool kit to carry in your vehicle:

☐ Hand pump (preferably an upright, powerful one)
☐ Spokes
☐ Grease rags

☐ Extra patch kit
☐ Freewheel remover
☐ Brake cables
☐ Extra bearings
☐ Derailleur cables
☐ Screwdrivers
☐ Extra chain
☐ Crescent wrench

Recommended safety gear:

☐ Rain gear
☐ First-aid kit
☐ Compass or GPS unit
☐ Lighter or matches
☐ Space blanket
☐ Topographic map

To make your mountain bike outings most pleasurable, you should keep your bike in good running condition, either through preventive maintenance at home or at a bike shop. Regular cleanings, cable adjustments, keeping the rims true, replacing bearings, and periodically replacing a worn, stretched-out chain will help avoid major breakdowns on the trail.

Tips on Coping with Breakdowns

Problem: Broken rear derailleur.
Solution: Create a one-speed with your chain tool.
Open up a chainlink with the chain tool, shorten the chain, and bypass the nonfunctional rear derailleur. Put your chain on the middle chain ring in the front and in the middle ring of your rear sprocket. This creates a one-speed bike that you'll be able to ride home.

Problem: Frequent flat tires due to thorns or "goat heads."

Solution: Slime/new tube.

Trails in the drier parts of Idaho often contain goat heads, a noxious plant that spreads seeds with nail-like spikes. In an especially unlucky situation, you can fly off the trail and end up with 20 punctures in your tire tube. There are three ways to combat this problem: 1) Install slime or self-sealing tubes inside your tire; 2) carry a spare tube; 3) carry a patch kit.

Problem: You get a flat, and your friend's pump (the only one you have with you) works only for Presta valves.

Solution: Carry a valve adapter in your tool kit.

Now you can borrow someone's pump regardless of whether it works for Presta or Schrader valves. Or carry your own pump and you won't have to depend on someone else to bail you out. Some pumps have reversible valve fittings. If you don't like Presta valves, have your local bike shop drill bigger holes in your rim that fit Schrader valves.

Do I Need a Helmet?

Most definitely—for a number of reasons. Here are four: It's cheap life insurance; it's the smart thing to do; experienced riders won't immediately peg you as a rookie; and if you fly over your handlebars, your helmet will soften the blow to your brain.

Medical research shows conclusively that wearing a hard-shell helmet reduces the risk of head and brain injury in the event of a crash. Consider this: Between 1993 and 1996, 12 people in Idaho were killed in bicycle-related crashes and 1,266 were involved in bicycle-automobile collisions. Fewer than 10 percent of the riders involved in collisions were wearing a helmet, according to the Idaho Department of Transportation. A medical study of mountain bike accidents in the Seattle area showed that most mountain bikers (80 percent) wore helmets, and that helmets reduced the risk of head injury by 85 percent and the risk of brain injury by 88 percent.

HOW TO USE THIS GUIDE

Most of the information in this book is self-explanatory. But if anything in the ride description doesn't seem to make sense, reread the following explanation of our format. The glossary may also be helpful.

The information is listed in an at-a-glance format and divided into the following sections:

Number and name of the ride: Rides are cross-referenced by number throughout this book. In many cases, parts of rides or entire routes can be linked to other rides for longer trips or variations of a standard route. These opportunities are noted. The ride name reflects the name of the trail. Where more than one name exists, one has been chosen that best reflects the nature of the trail.

Location: The general whereabouts of the ride.

Distance: The length of the ride in miles.

Time: An estimate of how long it takes to complete the ride, for example: 1 to 2 hours. The time listed is the actual riding time and does not include rest stops. Strong, skilled riders may be able to do a given ride in less time, while other riders may take considerably longer. Also bear in mind that severe weather, changes in trail conditions, or mechanical problems may prolong a ride.

Tread: Describes what the tires ride on when they are rubberside down.

Aerobic level: The level of physical effort required to complete the ride: easy, moderate, or strenuous. Here's what I mean by those terms.
    Easy: Flat or gently rolling terrain. No steeps or prolonged climbs.
    Moderate: Some hills. Climbs may be short and fairly steep or long and gradual.
    Strenuous: Frequent or prolonged climbs steep enough to require riding in the lowest gear; requires a high level of aerobic fitness, power, and endurance. Less fit riders may need to walk.
    Remember, these ratings are for the purpose of comparison. Each ride can still have you gulping air, and moderate ones may induce you to walk. Walking a bike is a perfectly legitimate way to transport it. Also remember that this guide is for everyone, from beginners to experts. And bear in mind that technical sections that exceed your ability will be tiring and can make an easy or moderate ride seem strenuous.

Technical difficulty: The level of bike handling skills needed to complete the ride upright and in one piece. Technical difficulty is rated on a scale from 1 to 5 (including plus or minus symbols), with 1 being the easiest and 5 the hardest. Generally, 1 is reserved for good pavement, 2 applies to smooth gravel roads, 3 and 4 are used for rough unimproved roads and singletrack, and 5 is for expert-level singletrack or highly eroded jeep trails (5-, 5, and 5+ apply to the kind of scary stuff that often warrants getting off the bike and hiking). Here are the five levels defined:
    Level 1: Basic bike riding skills needed. The tread is smooth and without obstacles, ruts, or steeps.
    Level 2: Mostly smooth tread; wide, well-groomed singletrack or road/doubletrack with minor ruts or loose gravel or sand.
    Level 3: Irregular tread with some rough sections; singletrack or doubletrack with obvious route choices; some steep sections; occasional obstacles may include small roots, rocks, water bars, ruts, loose gravel or sand, and sharp turns or broad, open switchbacks.
    Level 4: Rough tread with few smooth places; singletrack or rough doubletrack with limited route choices; steep sections, some with obstacles; obstacles are numerous and varied, including rocks, roots, branches, ruts, sidehills, narrow tread, loose gravel or sand, and switchbacks.

Level 5: Continuously broken, rocky, root-infested, or trenched tread; singletrack or extremely rough doubletrack with few route choices; frequent, sudden, and severe changes in gradient; some slopes are so steep that wheels lift off ground; obstacles are nearly continuous and may include boulders, logs, water, large holes, deep ruts, ledges, piles of loose gravel, steep sidehills, encroaching trees, and tight switchbacks.

Highlights: Special features or qualities that make a ride worthwhile.

Hazards: A list of dangers that may be encountered on a ride, including traffic, weather, trail obstacles and conditions, risky stream crossings, obscure trails, and other perils. Remember: Conditions may change at any time. Be alert for storms, new fences, downfall, missing trail signs, mechanical failure, and wild animals. Fatigue, heat, cold, and/or dehydration may impair judgment. Always wear a helmet and other safety equipment such as eye protection. Ride in control at all times.

Land status: A list of managing agencies or landowners. Most of the rides in this book are on national forest land, state park land, or Bureau of Land Management land. But some of the rides also cross portions of private lands. Always leave gates as you found them. And respect the land, regardless of who owns it.

Maps: A list of available maps including U.S. Geological Survey maps that show each ride's area. These maps may be used for a more detailed view though they may not show the ride's route. In some cases, no maps are available for specific rides.

Access: How to find the trailhead or start of the ride.

Notes on the ride: These paragraphs detail the qualities that make a ride unique. You'll find specifics on things you'll see along the way and a general description of natural surroundings.

The ride: This section lists where to go and how to find the way back. Attached to the directions are odometer readings. These are estimates. Not all bike computers are calibrated the same, but they provide a yardstick to measure against.

Variation: Some ride descriptions are followed by variations—longer, shorter, easier, or more difficult routes starting from the same basic trail.

Maps and Graphs
A map and elevation profile accompanies each ride. The maps are clean, easy-to-use navigational tools. Closed trails are not usually shown but may be listed in the ride description. Painstaking effort has been taken to ensure accuracy.

The elevation profiles provide a good look at what's in store by graphically showing altitude change, tread, and ratings. The ratings listed on the profiles are defined in the technical ratings section. The ups and downs of the route are graphed on a grid of elevation (in feet above sea level) on the left and miles across the bottom. Route surface conditions (see map legend) and technical levels are shown on the graphs.

Note that these graphs are not scaled to perfectly reflect actual slopes. They are exaggerated vertically to call attention to the slope of the route. In short, the slope of a line on an elevation profile is generally much steeper than the actual trail surface. Also keep in mind that the ratio of elevation to distance (for vertical exaggeration) varies from graph to graph, so it's best to study each graph individually and make note of the actual distance climbed as well as the rate of climb.

Desert Southwest: Big and Bold

The Boise foothills, the Snake River Birds of Prey National Conservation Area, and the Owyhee Mountains all share a common character in terms of landscape and weather. Described as a "cool desert" by meteorologists, the greater southwest Idaho area offers an eight- to ten-month riding season (depending on snowpack and rain) and sagebrush-dotted grassy landscapes often without much tree cover or shade. In midsummer, the area gets very hot—expect temperatures in the 90s. Rain is rare to nonexistent in July and August.

The Owyhee Mountains and the Snake River canyon feature red and brown vertical-walled canyons, scenery that's somewhat reminiscent of southern Utah. The Owyhees (o-WHY-hees) can be described as "the big wide open." Managed by the Bureau of Land Management, it's a place with several million acres of public land, and cows easily outnumber people. It's rare to run into anyone else on mountain bike trails in the Owyhees.

The Snake River Birds of Prey National Conservation Area, on the other hand, is very popular in the spring and fall, being only 30 minutes from Boise, Nampa, and Caldwell. The same goes for trails in the Boise foothills, known locally as the "Boise Front," where hikers, joggers, horseback riders, motorcycle riders, and ATV riders can be seen on roads and trails on a typical weekend day. These trails are best ridden in midweek, in the middle of the day, to avoid lots of people.

Before heading out to the Owyhee Desert, be sure to load up on supplies (including water) in Boise, Nampa, Caldwell, Eagle, Meridian, or Mountain Home, because services out there are limited to nonexistent. This, of course, is part of the Owyhee charm. A side trip to the Bruneau Sand Dunes may be worthwhile for hiking on mountains of sand, public showers, and camping.

As Idaho's largest city and state capital, Boise is loaded with things to see and do. It has an eclectic variety of restaurants, shops, and art galleries downtown. In midsummer, thousands of people float the Boise River in inner tubes or rafts every day. The World Center for Birds of Prey, just south of town, offers daily tours featuring exotic birds of prey. The Morrison-Knudsen Nature Center and the Discovery Center are always big hits with kids. On summer evenings, the Idaho Shakespeare Festival offers a variety of plays in an outdoor theater. The Bank of America Center in Boise, the Morrison Center at Boise State University, the Idaho Center in Nampa, and Hawks Memorial Stadium offer many concerts every summer.

Boise River Greenbelt

Location:	Boise, Garden City, and Ada County, Idaho.
Distance:	Up to 19 miles, one-way.
Time:	2.5 hours, depending on ride distance and speed of travel.
Tread:	19 miles of paved urban recreation trail.
Aerobic level:	Easy.
Technical difficulty:	1.
Highlights:	Scenic pathway along the cottonwood-lined Boise River; good chance of seeing waterfowl such as great blue herons, and bald eagles in the winter. People-watching can be entertaining on the popular pathway.
Hazards:	Please yield to pedestrians, babies in strollers, in-line skaters, dogs, etc.
Land status:	Boise City Parks System, Garden City Parks and Recreation, Idaho Department of Parks and Recreation, Ada County Parks and Waterways.
Maps:	Boise City Parks System, Garden City Parks and Recreation, Ada County Parks and Waterways.

Access: There are many places to access the Boise River Greenbelt along the length of the pathway. This ride description starts at the west end of the path, near the Glenwood Bridge, and continues east to Discovery State Park below Lucky Peak Dam, pointing out parking areas and parks along the way. To reach the Glenwood Bridge parking area, take Chinden or State Street toward the Western Idaho Fairgrounds by Glenwood Avenue. The fairgrounds is about 3 miles west of downtown Boise. Take Glenwood to a traffic light next to the Boise Hawks Memorial Stadium and turn into a dirt parking area on the fairgrounds side of Glenwood. Park.

Notes on the trail: The Boise River Greenbelt is one of the finest urban trails in Idaho and the Northwest. Except for an occasional major snow-storm, the Greenbelt can be ridden throughout the winter. Watch for birds and wildlife as you ride the path, and be sure to yield to pedestrians walking, jogging, or in-line skating on the path. Slow down as you approach people from behind, and say, "coming up" or "on your left" to let them know you're trying to pass. Due to improvements to the Greenbelt in 1998, the path now runs from the Glenwood Bridge to Discovery State Park without any gaps. A new bridge and pathway from Lake Harbor to Willow Lane

Boise River Greenbelt

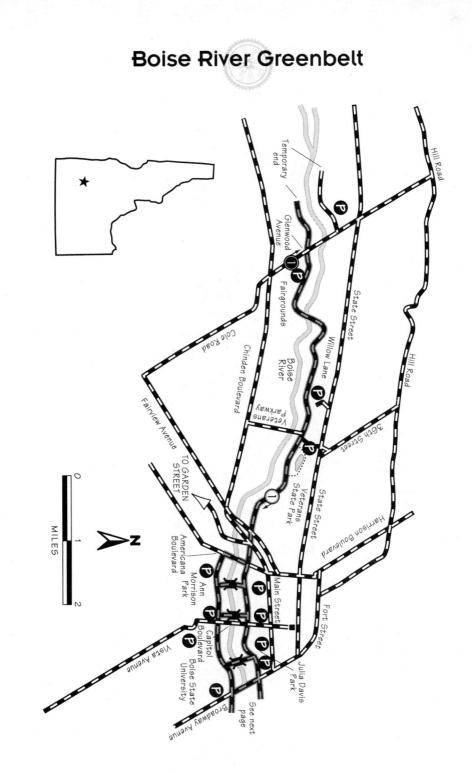

Boise River Greenbelt

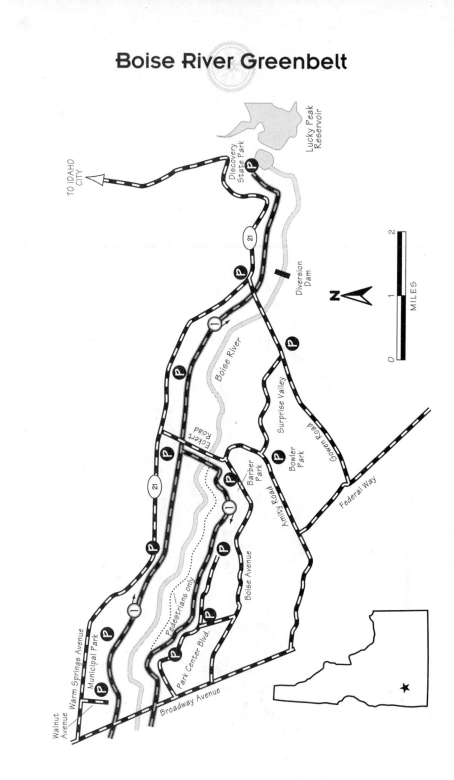

Mark Lisk cruises over one of many nifty bridges on the Boise River Greenbelt. The 17-mile urban pathway knits together many city parks and riverside natural areas throughout the length of Boise.

Park, and an underpass at the Capitol Bridge, allow for continuous travel on the north side of the path. See variations below for loop possibilities. This ride description covers the entire length of the Greenbelt from the extreme west end to Lucky Peak. Future plans call for extending the pathway to Eagle Island Park, which will complete the original vision for the urban pathway. Enjoy!

THE RIDE

0.0 Take the underpass at the Glenwood Bridge and ride west to the temporary dead end of the Greenbelt. It's about 1.2 miles to the end of the pavement (there is no public parking here). A dirt path goes a short way farther until it dead ends at a private fence.

1.2 Turn around and head back to Glenwood.

2.4 Arrive at Glenwood. Continue heading east on the south side of the river. You'll pass by a number of horse stables for Les Bois Park.

3.2 The Greenbelt crosses the Boise River on several steel bridges. At the second bridge, watch for an interpretive sign detailing the history of Pierce Park, a 185-acre amusement park and artificial lake that once occupied the area in the early 1900s.

3.8 Pathway leaves the riverbank behind Lake Harbor and proceeds through the woods (this is a brand new section in deep woods) to Willow Lane Park.

4.1 Bear right at the western edge of Willow Lane Park. Follow the pathway through the city park, which is chock full of softball fields and soccer fields (public parking).

5.0 Wooden bridge crosses water ditch, pathway crosses under Veterans Memorial Parkway and leads into Veterans State Park, another possible access point with ample parking. Here, riders can follow the paved pathway through the park, or take a left at the first wooden bridge leading into Veterans State Park to take a dirt loop around a small lake. The dirt path rejoins the Greenbelt in less than a mile.

5.7 A wooden bridge next to some restrooms marks the end of Veterans Park. The Greenbelt cuts a path in between a large pond and the Boise River.

6.4 Pass under Main Street bridge.

6.5 Pass under Fairview Avenue bridge.

6.6 Pass under Connector bridge.

6.7 Pathway junction with a steel trestle, which provides access to Garden Street, Orchard Avenue, Curtis Road, and the Boise Bench. Bear left to stay on the main Greenbelt. This is a neighborhood cutoff that ends at Garden Street.

7.0 Pass under Americana Street. Now the Greenbelt runs on both sides of the river for several miles.

7.2 Public parking next to Wheels R Fun skate rental center.

7.4 Turn right at the footbridge going into Ann Morrison Park if you wish to ride through the park. The southside pathway provides access to Boise State University. Otherwise, continue heading east on the north side of the river.

7.8 The Greenbelt drops into an underpass below Ninth Street, a pedestrian bridge to Boise State University, and again under Capitol Boulevard.

7.9 Enter the west end of Julia Davis Park, another large city park with public parking.

8.1 Junction with Boise State University pedestrian bridge.

8.6 Broadway Avenue underpass. You'll emerge on the east side of Broadway behind the Ram, a popular sports bar and eatery. Take a break if you like. The Greenbelt passes by several sandy beaches.

9.1 Enter Municipal Park, the last city park along the route (lots of parking). The pathway runs along the river, joins a spur, and heads for Warm Springs Golf Course.

10.0 Greenbelt enters the western end of Warm Springs Golf Course. The path winds through the Back Nine and then beelines on an old railroad right-of-way for the Harris Ranch area.

14.0 Greenbelt junction with Eckert Road. Public parking in gravel pullout. Cyclists can either follow the pathway along Eckert Road to begin a loop back to Boise or continue east toward Lucky Peak.

16.2 Pathway passes behind the Crow Inn, a popular eatery and drinking hole that serves fresh fish.

17.0 Greenbelt passes Diversion Dam, a major diversion point for the Boise River. Public parking is across Idaho Highway 21.

19.0 Greenbelt ends in the eastern end of Discovery State Park, a small park that has public parking, restrooms, and a beach with a swimming area.

Variation: Here's an excellent 9-mile loop ride: Starting from Municipal Park, ride the Greenbelt east through Warm Springs Golf Course to Eckert Road. Turn right on the pathway along Eckert and ride to Barber Park on the south side of the river. Turn right and bear left on the paved pathway that runs on the southern edge of the park. The pathway leaves Barber Park and runs through some new housing developments. Follow signs for the path through the homes. At the end of Park Center Boulevard, follow the bike lane on the right shoulder of the street. Peel right at River Run Drive and follow the bike lane to the Cottonwood Apartments. Here, the Greenbelt merges with the hiking path and the Greenbelt runs back toward Broadway and Boise State University. Cross the river at the Broadway Bridge (treacherous) or the Boise State University pedestrian bridge, and head back to Municipal Park.

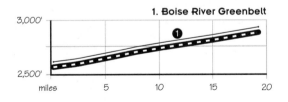

Redtail Ridge Loop

Location:	Lower Dry Creek Valley, west Boise foothills.
Distance:	5.9-mile loop.
Time:	30 minutes to 1 hour.
Tread:	2.1 miles of dirt road, 0.5 miles of doubletrack, 3.3 miles of singletrack.
Aerobic level:	Moderately strenuous on uphill sections.
Technical difficulty:	2.
Highlights:	Sweet singletrack riding in grassy foothills; nifty views of Lower Dry Creek Valley.
Hazards:	Grasshoppers in midsummer may leap and cling on to your legs.
Land status:	Grossman Family Properties (benevolent private landowner encourages public use).
Maps:	Ridge-to-Rivers Trail System map; USGS Boise North, Eagle.

Access: Go to the junction of Cartwright Road and Dry Creek Road in the west foothills of Boise. The easiest way to get there is to head up Bogus Basin Road in the North End of Boise to a signed left-hand turn for Cartwright Road next to a Latter-Day Saints church. Head west on Cartwright Road for 5 miles (over two passes) to the junction. From west Boise, take Hill Road to Seamans Gulch Road (the road to the Ada County landfill). Turn left and follow Seamans over the top of the foothills to Dry Creek Road. Turn right and head for the junction with Cartwright Road in about 2 miles.

Notes on the trail: The Redtail Ridge Loop Trail was built by a host of volunteers (firefighters, SWIMBA, Hidden Springs employees, and the Ridge-to-Rivers trail crew) in the summer of 1997, creating the first trail system open to the public in the west hills of Boise. The Redtail Ridge ride features a fairly steep uphill grade on Cartwright Road and a steep approach to Redtail Ridge, but riders will be richly rewarded with a fun downhill ride on the singletrack portion of the ride. Stronger riders should ride their bikes over the two summits on Cartwright Road to add a major punch to the workout. Beginning riders probably will not be able to handle the uphill sections of the Redtail Ridge ride, but they will enjoy riding the easy loop around the Dry Creek farm (see variation).

Redtail Ridge Loop

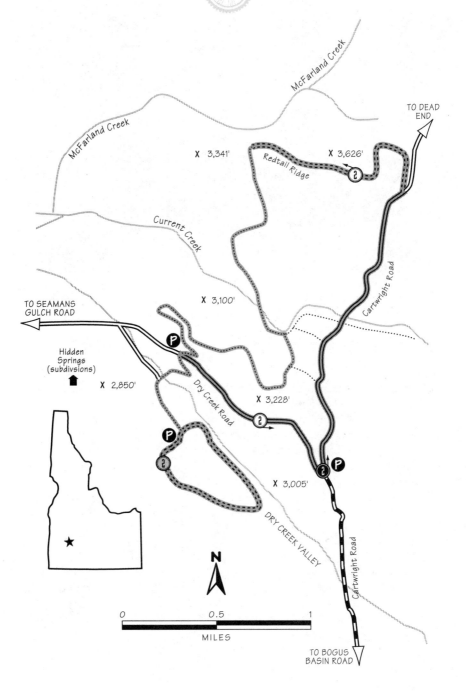

McFarland Creek

McFarland Creek

TO DEAD END

X 3,341'

Redtail Ridge

X 3,626'

Current Creek

Cartwright Road

X 3,100'

TO SEAMANS GULCH ROAD

Hidden Springs (subdivsions)

X 2,850'

Dry Creek Road

X 3,228'

X 3,005'

DRY CREEK VALLEY

Cartwright Road

N

0   0.5   1

MILES

TO BOGUS BASIN ROAD

Volunteers with the Southwest Idaho Mountain Biking Association, including Tom Baskin, Ron Stacy, and Stephen Stuebner (left to right in foreground) work on the beginnings of the Redtail Ridge singletrack in the summer of 1997.

THE RIDE

0.0 Ride up Cartwright Road. The first hill is short, followed by a small downhill section, and then another climb.

1.2 Bear left on an unsigned steep doubletrack road on the left and climb to the top of Redtail Ridge, named for a pair of red-tailed hawks that nest nearby.

1.7 Reach the top of the ridge. Follow the doubletrack on the ridge spine.

2.2 Singletrack trail bends off to the left. It's a nice downhill from here on the winding trail.

3.3 Cross Current Creek. Now the trail climbs at a moderate pace to a set of hills overlooking Dry Creek Valley. Bear right at several junctions to stay with the longer trail.

4.3 Trail drops down to Dry Creek Road. To lengthen the ride a little, bear to the right and stay on the ridge for a little loop around a knoll before dropping down to Dry Creek Road.

5.0 Arrive at Dry Creek Road. Turn left and head back to the junction of Cartwright and Dry Creek.

5.9 Arrive at the junction. If you've still got some energy, try reversing the loop and climb singletrack.

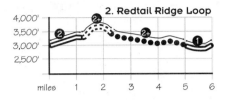

2. Redtail Ridge Loop

Variation: Cross the road at the end of the Redtail Ridge singletrack, and follow the wide singletrack trail into the Hidden Springs Farm. The trail leads to a totally flat (a very rare thing in the Boise foothills) 2-mile loop around the farm. It's a good trail for beginners, families, and kids. After crossing the creek, proceed into the main driveway, turn left, and follow trail signs to a doubletrack road next to Dry Creek. The trail bends to the right after a half mile and tours around the fringe of a farm field. Then it circles back to the public parking area and community center at mile 1.8.

Corrals–Bob's Trail Loop

Location:	2 miles north of downtown Boise.
Distance:	9.9-mile loop.
Time:	1.5 hours.
Tread:	3.5 miles of paved road, 1.2 miles of doubletrack, 5.2 miles of singletrack.
Aerobic level:	Moderate to strenuous on the uphill portion of the Corrals Trail.
Technical difficulty:	2 to 3 on Corrals Trail, 3+ to 4 on Bob's Trail
Highlights:	Challenging technical singletrack ride; fun rolling up and down approach on Corrals Trail.
Hazards:	Many obstacles could cause one to get pitched over the handlebars, cartwheel off the trail, or simply crash on either the downhill portion of Corrals Trail or the entire length of Bob's Trail.
Land status:	Mixture of private and state land. Public use easements provided by private landowners.
Maps:	USGS Boise North, Ridge-to-Rivers Trail System map.

Access: Ride or drive to Highlands School at the intersection of Bogus Basin Road and Curling Drive. Park in the school parking lot. Mileage starts here. There is an alternative parking area 2 miles up Bogus Basin Road, but unless you leave a vehicle at Highlands School, you'll have to climb the hill again to fetch your vehicle.

Corrals—Bob's Trail Loop

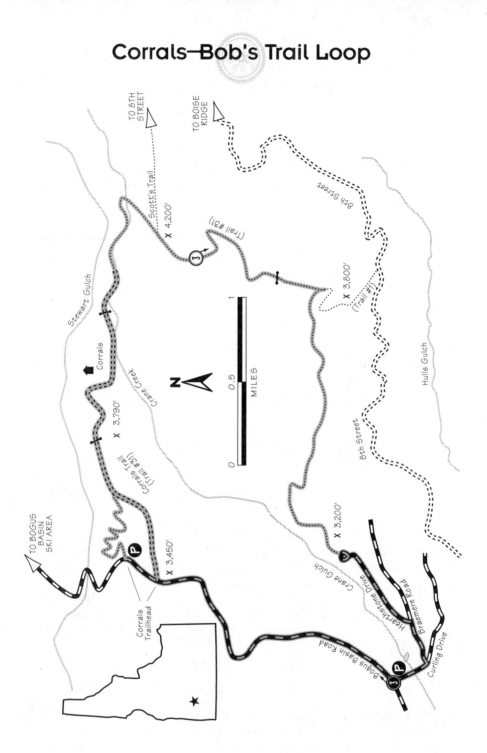

TO 8TH STREET

TO BOISE RIDGE

Scott's Trail

X 4,200'

(Trail #31)

8th Street

X 3,800'

(Trail #1)

Stewart Gulch

Corrals

Hulls Gulch

Crane Creek

X 3,790'

N

MILES

0.5

1

0

Corrals (Trail #35)

8th Street

TO BOGUS BASIN SKI AREA

P

X 3,450'

X 3,200'

Corrals Trailhead

Crane Gulch

Heathstone Drive

Braemere Road

Bogus Basin Road

Curling Drive

P

Notes on the trail: The Corrals–Bob's Trail Loop is one of the most popular rides in the Boise foothills because it promises a good workout on the climb to the Corrals summit and a fun but technically challenging downhill on Bob's Trail. The downhill section from the Corrals summit to Bob's Trail contains many ruts and rocks, too, so take it easy and keep your speed under control. Watch out for walkers, joggers, dogs, equestrians, and other mountain bikers on this route. Locals ride the trail in both directions. The J. R. Simplot family has been very generous to allow public use of this trail. Please respect private property, tread lightly, and don't litter. By the way, Bob's Trail is named for Bob Wood, a mountain bike pioneer who still lives in Boise. The trail was originally developed as a livestock trail by the Simplot family.

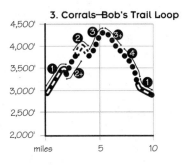

3. Corrals–Bob's Trail Loop

THE RIDE

0.0 Climb up Bogus Basin Road, a paved road that runs for 15 miles to the ski area.

1.8 Gated doubletrack road on right marks the old entrance to the Corrals Trail. Intermediate riders should start the trail here. Advanced riders should continue on the paved road for 0.3 mile to the parking area on the right and the new singletrack approach to Corrals Trail.

2.1 Ride through the parking area to the singletrack trailhead and pedal up the singletrack. It's 0.7 mile of continuous steep climbing to the Corrals doubletrack.

2.8 Junction with Corrals doubletrack. Go straight to merge with the wide dirt road.

3.0 Pass through green gate (normally, it's closed).

3.4 Note the trailhead at the wooden corrals on the left. This is the junction with Hard Guy/Fast Guy Trail. Proceed on the Corral's Trail and enjoy a brisk downhill.

4.0 Encounter a second gate. Lift your bike over the gate and begin a singletrack climb along Crane Creek. Now the trail climbs at a fairly continuous grade to a saddle.

4.9 Final steep section leads to a saddle junction at 5.1. Once on top, take a breather. The trail peeling off to the left is Scott's Trail. Proceed to the right and climb one more short hill to the summit of the Corrals route.

5.3 Corrals Summit. At this point, you've climbed 1,600 vertical feet. Now it's pretty much all downhill to the junction with Bob's Trail. Beware of death holes, cracks, and gullies in the trail ahead.

5.8 Challenging crossing at side draw. Ride uphill a short ways.

6.0 Another steep downhill section features ruts and holes. Exercise caution.

6.5 Climb over BLM gate. Keep riding on the trail (you're on Trail 1 now) and watch for a hairpin turn to the right (Bob's Trail) and a well-vegetated gully.

6.9 Junction with Bob's Trail 30. Turn right, and follow the narrow path as it snakes along next to the East Fork of Crane Creek. Be prepared for a technical trail with many obstacles. At least the grade is mostly downhill. I had a nasty spill into a big grove of poison ivy in here one time, so try to stay in control.

7.3 After an initial descent, a ridable creek-crossing signals it's time to drop into your little ring for a steep, rocky climb. First-time riders typically have to walk this section.

7.4 Walk over big rock drop. Several more smaller and ridable rock drops lie ahead.

7.7 Two creek crossings (ridable).

8.2 Trail encounters the crest of a new 50-foot-high dam that was built for flood-control purposes in the fall of 1997. Follow the trail as it descends the right side of the earthen dam, crosses some hazardous wide crevices near the toe, and drops into the old trail tread in the creek bottom.

8.4 Trail crosses creek five times in the next 100 yards. Negotiate a maze of big rocks.

8.5 Last creek crossing (ridable).

8.8 Bob's Trail ends at a cul-de-sac. Turn left on the pavement and follow Hearthstone Drive to Braemere Road (mile 9.8). Turn right on Braemere Road and zoom down to Curling Drive. Turn right on Curling Drive and return to Highlands School (mile 9.9).

Variation: Turn left at the Corrals saddle junction and take Scott's Trail (short but steep uphill) to Eighth Street. Turn right and descend several miles to the Eighth Street parking lot above Hulls Gulch. Descend into Hulls, and drop back into Boise on the Hulls Gulch or Crestline trail.

4

Hulls Gulch–Sidewinder– Crestline Loop

Location:	Boise foothills.
Distance:	6.6 miles, one-way.
Time:	1 hour.
Tread:	6.6 miles of singletrack.
Aerobic level:	Strenuous on uphill sections of Hulls Gulch and Sidewinder trails.
Technical difficulty:	2+ to 3+.
Highlights:	Premium singletrack in the core of the Boise foothills trail system and a challenging descent on Trail 4.
Hazards:	Ruts, rocks, and poison ivy.

Hulls Gulch–Sidewinder–Crestline loop

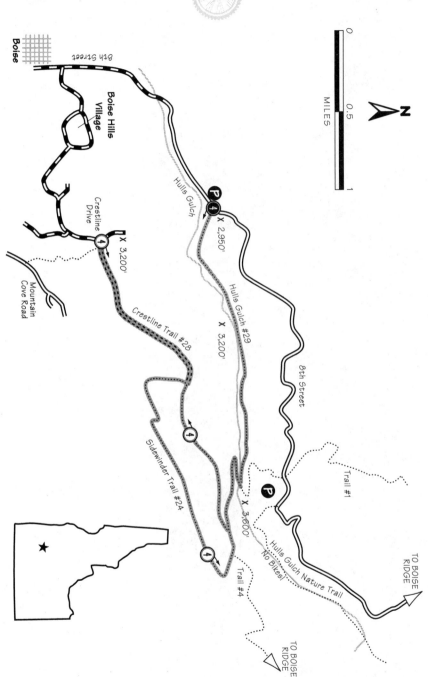

Boise

8th Street

Boise Hills Village

Hulls Gulch

P 4 X 2,950'

Crestline Drive

4 X 3,200'

Mountain Cove Road

Crestline Trail #28

Hulls Gulch #29

X 3,200'

8th Street

4

Sidewinder Trail #24

P

X 3,500'

Trail #1

4

Trail #4

Hulls Gulch Nature Trail
(No Bikes)

TO BOISE RIDGE

TO BOISE RIDGE

MILES
0   0.5   1

N

31

The Sidewinder singletrack contours around the grassy Boise foothills like a snake that insists on a smooth and scenic course.

Land status:	Private land and BLM. Trail easements provided by benevolent landowners.
Maps:	USGS Boise North; Ridge-to-Rivers Trail System map.

Access: This ride begins at the junction of Eighth Street and the lower Hulls Gulch Trail. Either ride or drive north on Eighth Street to a point where the road turns to dirt. Watch for a trailhead sign for Trail 29 and a vehicle pullout and parking area 0.6 mile after the pavement ends. Mileage for the ride starts here.

Notes on the trail: This is a nifty singletrack loop that combines some of the best singletrack riding in the Boise foothills. It's also a climber's special because you'll climb 3 miles on the Hulls Gulch singletrack, get a short rest on the way to Sidewinder, and then climb Sidewinder for 1.4 miles before beginning a fast descent down a short section of Trail 4 to finish out on Crestline, a cruiser also known as the Freeway.

A word of caution: The Hulls Gulch Trail is probably the most popular trail in the Boise Front. That means you should expect to encounter many walkers, joggers, dogs, and downhill mountain bikers, so be prepared to yield to other trail users. In the event of an encounter with a downhill rider, local rules state that uphill riders have the right-of-way. In areas where visibility is poor, whistle or sing, or make some kind of noise to forewarn people that you're coming. Beware of the poison ivy drooping into the trail tread.

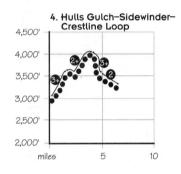

4. Hulls Gulch–Sidewinder–Crestline Loop

THE RIDE

0.0 Lift your bike over the bar at the Hulls Gulch Trailhead and head up Trail 29. The wide singletrack is uphill all the way.

0.5 Cross the creek (ridable), climb a short steep pitch, and cross the creek again (ridable).

1.4 Encounter steep rock drop. Find a line and try to ride it.

1.5 Steep rock drop. Not ridable unless you're a world champion BMX trick rider.

2.0 Arrive at Hulls Gulch-Crestline junction. Turn right, cross the creek, and ride a gentle downhill grade on the Crestline Trail to the marked junction with Sidewinder Trail 24 on the left.

2.5 Sidewinder junction. Head up the winding singletrack built by SWIMBA volunteers in 1996. The trail will get progressively steeper as you climb toward a saddle.

3.5 May be time to drop into the small ring for the steepest section of Sidewinder.

3.9 Arrive at saddle junction with Trail 4 and Sidewinder. Take a breather and enjoy the broad view of the foothills. Then, turn left on Trail 4, a steep and technical descent back to Crestline. The trail is dished out and v-rutted down the middle in places, so pick your line carefully.

4.4 Return to Crestline. Turn left to descend Crestline.

6.6 Arrive at Crestline trailhead. To return to Boise, turn left on the pavement (Crestline Drive). The road intersects Eighth Street at the bottom of the hill. Head home, or ride back to the Hulls Gulch junction to fetch your rig.

Variation 1: Instead of dropping down Crestline after riding the Sidewinder loop, return to the Hulls Gulch–Crestline junction, and ride down Hulls Gulch to Eighth Street.

Variation 2: When you reach the Crestline junction at the end of the ride, turn left on a connector trail that drops into Military Reserve Park. Cross the dirt road (Mountain Cove Road) and explore Military Reserve, which has a number of short singletrack and doubletrack trails in the 2-square-mile park.

Mores Mountain Loop

Location:	19.3 miles north of Boise.
Distance:	4.3-mile loop.
Time:	1 hour.
Tread:	1.5 miles of singletrack, 2.8 miles of doubletrack and gravel roads.
Aerobic level:	Easy to moderate.
Technical difficulty:	1 to 2. Mores Mountain singletrack has a number of dips and slippery spots that will challenge beginning riders. The rest of the loop is not technically demanding.
Highlights:	Huge views of the Boise National Forest and the Sawtooth Range off to the east; cool singletrack riding on the shoulder of Mores Mountain.
Hazards:	Keep your speed in check on the Mores Mountain singletrack.
Land status:	Boise National Forest.
Maps:	USGS Shafer Butte.

Access: From downtown Boise, take Harrison Boulevard north to the traffic light at the junction of Hill Road and Bogus Basin Road. Proceed north on Bogus Basin Road 16 miles to the ski area. Continue on the dirt road another 3.3 miles to a signed junction for the Shafer Butte Picnic Area. Turn right and head another mile to the paved parking area for the picnic area. The site has restrooms and water in the summer.

Mores Mountain Loop

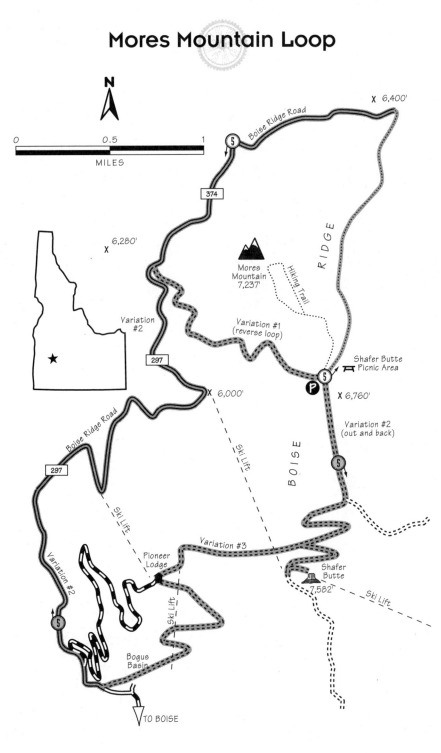

Are we there yet? Ellie Rodgers summits Shafer Butte near the top of Bogus Basin Ski Area. Mores Mountain lies directly to the north.

Notes on the trail: The Mores Mountain Loop is a premium singletrack ride for families and novice mountain bikers. Riders will descend the Mores Mountain singletrack, which features a number of up-and-down features known as whoop-de-doos. Then

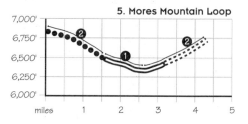

the route follows the Boise Ridge Road on a moderate to flat grade for a bit before climbing back on the unimproved forest road to the picnic area. After finishing this loop, stronger riders may want to try one or both of the variations listed below.

THE RIDE

0.0 Ride out of the parking area to the trailhead for the Mores Mountain Interpretive Trail (the log-lined hiking trail is not open to mountain biking). Look for a singletrack trail that immediately peels off to the right of the interpretive trail. Ride this trail into the trees and follow it along the shoulder of Mores Mountain. Stop for a moment along the trail and enjoy the colorful wildflowers, granite spires, and scenic vistas.

1.5 Singletrack ends and dumps out on the Boise Ridge Road. Turn left and ride the ridge road back to the Shafer Butte Picnic Area junction.

3.1 Arrive at picnic area junction. Turn left and ride uphill to the picnic area. This is the most strenuous portion of the ride.

4.3 Arrive at the picnic area.

Variation 1: Reverse the loop.

Variation 2: Ride to the top of Bogus Basin ski area from the picnic area. This alternative begins on a doubletrack road that heads out of the picnic area parking lot in the south end of the site. Follow the doubletrack as it climbs at a progressively steep pitch to a switchback junction. Bear right and follow the doubletrack as it switchbacks up the north side of Shafer Butte. It's 3 miles to the top of Shafer Butte (elev. 7,582 feet). Return the way you came.

Variation 3: Ride to the top of Bogus Basin from the picnic area. Descend two switchbacks to the Pioneer Lodge traverse (signed), turn left, and ride toward the Pioneer Lodge. Turn left at the chairlift above the lodge and tennis courts and follow the doubletrack dirt road as it switchbacks down to the lower lodge. Turn right on the dirt road in front of the lodge and follow it back to the picnic area. This loop is about 9 miles long.

Oregon Trail–Bonneville Point–Greenbelt Loop

Location:	Surprise Valley in east Boise.
Distance:	15-mile loop.
Time:	3 hours.
Tread:	1 mile of paved road, 3 miles of Greenbelt pathway, 11 miles of doubletrack.
Aerobic level:	Mostly moderate climbing to Oregon Trail Monument; strenuous from the monument to Bonneville Point.
Technical difficulty:	2 to 2+ on doubletrack tread.
Highlights:	Historic recreation ride along the Old Oregon Trail; nice views of the Boise Valley from Bonneville Point.
Hazards:	Nothing in particular.
Land status:	Mixture of BLM, Bureau of Reclamation, and private land.
Maps:	USGS Lucky Peak.

Oregon Trail–Bonneville Point–Greenbelt Loop

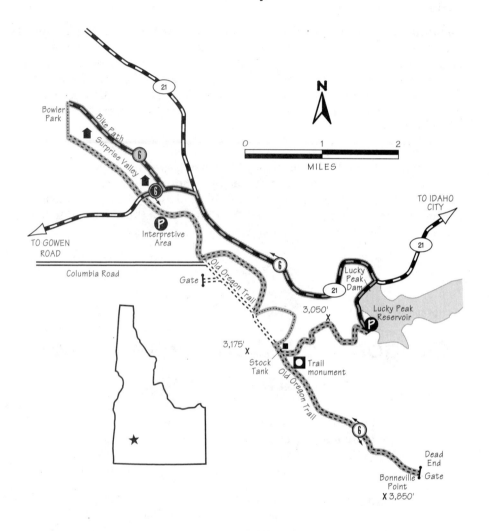

Bowler Park

Bike Path

Surprise Valley

TO GOWEN ROAD

Interpretive Area

Columbia Road

Gate

Old Oregon Trail

3,050' X

3,175' X

Stock Tank

Trail monument

Old Oregon Trail

N

0   1   2
MILES

TO IDAHO CITY

Lucky Peak Dam

Lucky Peak Reservoir

Dead End Gate

Bonneville Point
X 3,850'

Riders should follow the cliffside doubletrack along the Old Oregon Trail to avoid fences and private property.

Access: From Boise, ride or drive to the east side of town on Warm Springs Avenue and Idaho Highway 21 or the Greenbelt. Continue east to the junction with the ID 21 connector to Gowen Road and Interstate 84. Turn right and go up the hill less than a mile to a left-hand turnoff for the Oregon Trail trailhead parking area and kiosk. The ride starts here.

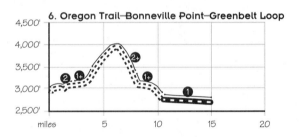

Notes on the trail: The Oregon Trail–Bonneville Point–Greenbelt Loop ride features a historical tour of the countryside that approximately 300,000 emigrants passed through on wagon trains as they crossed southern Idaho to "greener pastures" in Oregon between 1840 and 1860. The cottonwood-lined Boise River was a refreshing sight to pioneers after a very hot and taxing trip across the dry Snake River Plain. Although much of the Boise Valley is settled today, the ride to Bonneville Point passes through the same sagebrush flat that pioneers crossed as they made their way to the river. Some of the old wagon ruts are still visible in the basalt cliffs between the upper bench and the second bench on the south side of the river. The ride out to Bonneville Point features several steep pitches to reach the upper bench, and then it's mostly rolling and flat to a concrete cylinder monument at a four-way junction. Then the doubletrack climbs in earnest to Bonneville Point, the steepest continuous climb of the ride. On the way back, the route takes you over to Lucky Peak Dam and follows the Greenbelt back toward town.

THE RIDE

0.0 Head out of the parking lot, heading east on a doubletrack tread under some powerlines. After a short distance, follow the doubletrack to the top of the upper bench.

0.6 Reach the upper bench. Bear left immediately and follow the jeep trail closest to the rim to avoid running into fences.

1.0 Bear left again at a dirt road circle, drop into a gully, and climb back to the rim again. This is the most scenic route, and it avoids posted private property.

1.6 Doubletrack runs into an unposted barbed-wire fence. Lift your bike over the fence and continue heading east.

2.6 Bear right and follow the doubletrack to a rusted stock tank.

3.1 Arrive at the stock tank. Look around for the cylinder-shaped concrete monument. Turn left at this three-way junction and climb the doubletrack up the ridgeline to Bonneville Point. You'll see a series of monuments along the way.

4.4 Ignore jeep road on left.

5.1 Bear right for the most gradual grade to Bonneville Point, which is now visible (lots of radio towers).

5.9 Arrive at Bonneville Point interpretive and picnic area. Read the signs to learn more about Oregon Trail history. Turn around and head back to the stock tank/monument junction.

8.7 Turn right at the stock tank/monument junction and follow the doubletrack road at the base of the hills over to Lucky Peak Reservoir.

10.1 Pass through gate (please close it behind you). Now the doubletrack descends at a steeper gradient toward Lydle Gulch.

10.4 Turn left at a junction in the gulch and follow the doubletrack to the paved road on the top of Lucky Peak Dam. Head over to ID 21 and follow the highway down to Discovery State Park.

11.4 Arrive at the park and pick up the Boise River Greenbelt. Ride back to the ID 21 connector to Gowen Road and I-84, turn left, and return to the interpretive area parking lot.

15.0 Arrive at the parking area.

Variation: It's possible to explore the Old Oregon Trail on a much shorter ride by going across the highway and visiting the Oregon Trail Reserve, a city-owned open space park. There is a nifty doubletrack that follows the upper rim of the reserve for a mile or so to a dead end. You can drop down a singletrack trail above a water tank at this point and take a gravel path through the Surprise Valley development back to the parking area. This is a 2.5-mile loop.

Swan Falls Petroglyph Tour

Location:	Snake River Birds of Prey National Conservation Area, Swan Falls Dam, 19 miles south of Kuna on Swan Falls Road.
Distance:	12.2 miles, out and back.
Time:	1.5 hours to 3 hours.
Tread:	0.8 miles of singletrack; 11.4 miles of doubletrack.
Aerobic level:	Easy to moderate.
Technical difficulty:	1+ to 2.
Highlights:	View extensive petroglyphs on large boulders at Wees Bar; catch a glimpse of a golden eagle, prairie falcon, or red-tailed hawk soaring above the Snake River, or white chicks in cliffside nests. The Snake River Birds of Prey National Conservation Area is home to more than 200 pairs of nesting birds of prey, the largest such population in North America.
Hazards:	Large heaps of tumbleweeds blocking trail; hikers and equestrians.
Land status:	Snake River Birds of Prey National Conservation Area, managed by the BLM.
Maps:	BLM Murphy; USGS Initial Point, Sinker Butte.

Access: Take exit 44 from Interstate 84 and head south to Kuna on Ada County Road 69. As you enter Kuna, turn left at the well-signed turn for Swan Falls Dam and the Snake River Birds of Prey National Conservation Area. Head south 19 miles to the Swan Falls Dam. Public parking is provided by the restrooms, adjacent to the dam. The ride starts here.

Notes on the trail: The Swan Falls area is an excellent place to ride in the spring and fall, when the weather is cool. In meager snow years, I have ridden in this area on Christmas Day. The canyon is home to North America's largest nesting population of birds of prey, so in the springtime the vertical-walled canyon is full of golden eagles, red-tailed hawks, prairie falcons, and many other raptors. It's possible to ride on both sides of the Snake River downstream from Swan Falls Dam, but the best riding is on the south side, where very few people travel.

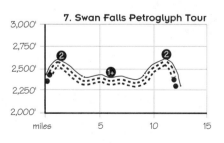

Swan Falls Petroglyph Tour

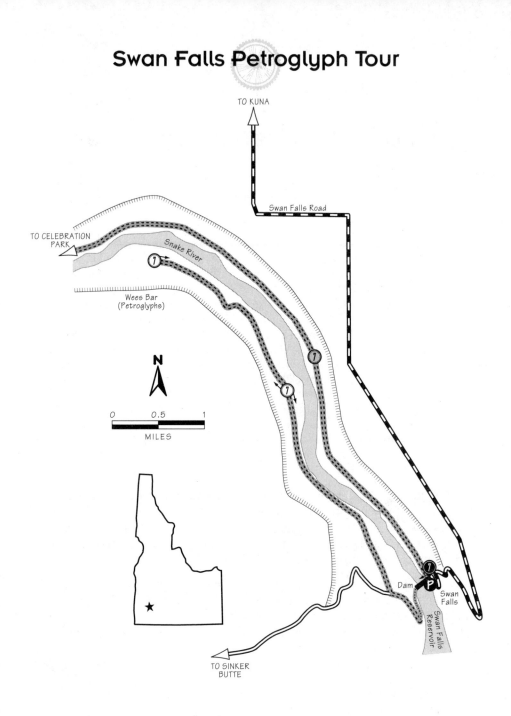

TO KUNA

Swan Falls Road

TO CELEBRATION PARK

Snake River

Wees Bar (Petroglyphs)

N

0   0.5   1

MILES

Dam

Swan Falls

P

Swan Falls Reservoir

TO SINKER BUTTE

At Wees Bar, it's time to hunt for Native American inscriptions, known as petroglyphs, on large boulders.

THE RIDE

0.0 Ride or walk your bike across the crest of the dam to the south bank.

0.2 Turn left in the gravel parking area next to the dam, and head upriver on a sandy singletrack.

0.6 Take a hard right at the junction with a doubletrack climbing up the hillside. It's a short but steep hill.

0.9 Turn right on the major doubletrack road.

1.1 Turn right again on a doubletrack heading downhill to the bench above the Snake River.

3.2 Trail enters old homestead on a broad bench above the river.

4.5 Bear left at junction to climb around small butte.

4.8 Proceed through narrow slot in gate and continue heading west.

6.1 Trail becomes braided and fizzles out by Wees Bar. Now it's time for a petroglyph hunt: Look around for Indian inscriptions on rocks. Turn around and return the way you came.

Variation: Instead of crossing Swan Falls Dam to ride to Wees Bar, follow the gravel road heading downstream (west) along the Snake River to Halverson Lake (8.3 miles) or Celebration Park (10 miles). The road is mostly level and sandy as it proceeds along the Snake River, and it gets a lot of use by 4WD vehicles, horseback riders, ATVs, and mountain bikes.

8

Silver City Scenic Loop

Location:	Historic mining town of Silver City in Owyhee County
Distance:	6.6-mile loop.
Time:	1.5 hours.
Tread:	2.5 miles of singletrack, 2.3 miles of doubletrack, 1.8 miles of gravel road.
Aerobic level:	Moderately strenuous on climb up Presby Creek.
Technical difficulty:	2. Nothing too technical on this ride.
Highlights:	Scenic rock outcroppings in Avondale Basin; cool singletrack riding in historic mining town.
Hazards:	Watch out for livestock.
Land status:	BLM.
Maps:	USGS Silver City, Delamar Mountain; BLM Murphy general map.

Access: From downtown Nampa, take Idaho Highway 45 south toward Melba. Continue south across the Snake River to Idaho Highway 78. Turn left and head for Murphy, the tiny county seat for Owyhee County. The signed turnoff for Silver City is 4 miles ahead on the right. Follow the dirt road for about 18 miles, over New York Summit, to a two-way junction (marked by a public outhouse) before you arrive in Silver City. Turn right and follow the road about 1.3 miles to a primitive camping area next to Jordan Creek. Park. The ride starts here.

Notes on the trail: The Silver City Scenic Loop features a relatively short but fun ride among the rocks, juniper, and aspen in the high desert. You'll ride several miles of fairly steep singletrack to a summit and descend then on a grassy doubletrack back to the Jordan Creek Road. Be sure to stop at the Silver City Hotel on your way back for a meal and refreshments. Silver City is a great place to camp and explore.

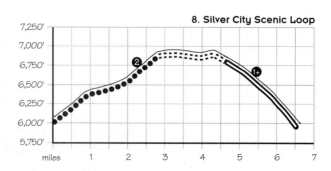

Silver City Scenic Loop

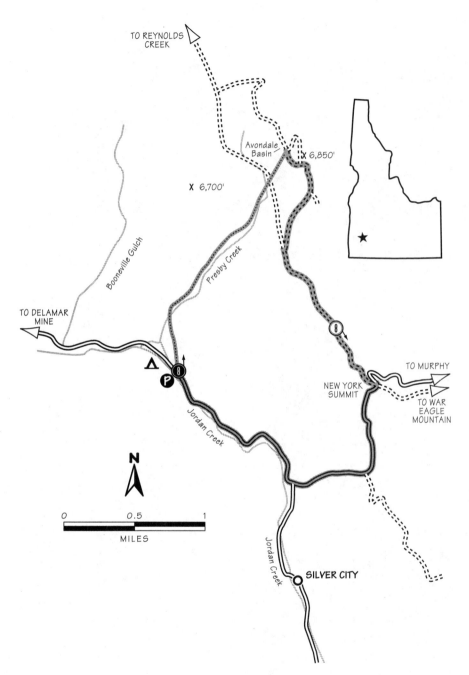

TO REYNOLDS CREEK

Avondale Basin

X 6,850'

X 6,700'

Booneville Gulch

Presby Creek

TO DELAMAR MINE

8

Jordan Creek

TO MURPHY

NEW YORK SUMMIT

TO WAR EAGLE MOUNTAIN

N

0   0.5   1
MILES

Jordan Creek

SILVER CITY

Tyler Allyn, 9, and his dad, Mike, ride by one of many rock towers along Presby Creek near Silver City.

0.0 Hook up with the singletrack on the north side of Jordan Creek, next to the primitive camping area. The trail climbs into a draw called Presby Creek and winds through juniper trees and rock spires.

1.8 The trail levels out at a meadow and broken-down corral. Proceed behind the corral and go left on a primitive doubletrack that climbs to a saddle.

1.9 Trail dissolves into singletrack and climbs at a steep, small-ring pitch.

2.8 Reach the saddle junction adjacent to rocky towers ringing Avondale Basin. Doubletrack roads head off to the north, east, and west, if you're interested in exploring the area further. Turn right on the doubletrack road heading east for New York Summit. Follow the skyline trail and enjoy the views.

4.8 Doubletrack merges with main gravel road at New York Summit. Turn right and head back to your rig.

5.3 Turn right at outhouse junction on Jordan Creek Road.

6.6 Arrive at the camping area/trailhead.

Wilson Creek Mini-Moab Loop

Location:	30 miles south of Nampa.
Distance:	15.6-mile loop.
Time:	3 to 4 hours.
Tread:	6.3 miles of dirt road, 7.7 miles of primitive doubletrack, 1.6 miles of singletrack.
Aerobic level:	Moderate to strenuous climbing on the way to Wilson Butte, and a number of super-steep climbs on the way "down" toward Reynolds Creek.
Technical difficulty:	2 on Wilson Creek Road; 3 to 4 on the second half of the ride.
Highlights:	Technically challenging riding will test the best on the descent from Wilson Butte toward Reynolds Creek. Great views of the front side of the Owyhee Mountains. Possibility of seeing wild horses.
Hazards:	Divots, sandy gouges, and loose rocks create many opportunities for crashing.
Land status:	BLM Boise District.
Maps:	USGS Wilson Peak, Soldier Cap; BLM Murphy map.

Access: From Nampa, take Idaho Highway 45 south toward Melba. Cross the Snake River and turn right at the Idaho Highway 78 junction, heading for Marsing. After 3 miles, turn left on Wilson Creek Road (a signed road).

Wilson Creek Mini-Moab Loop

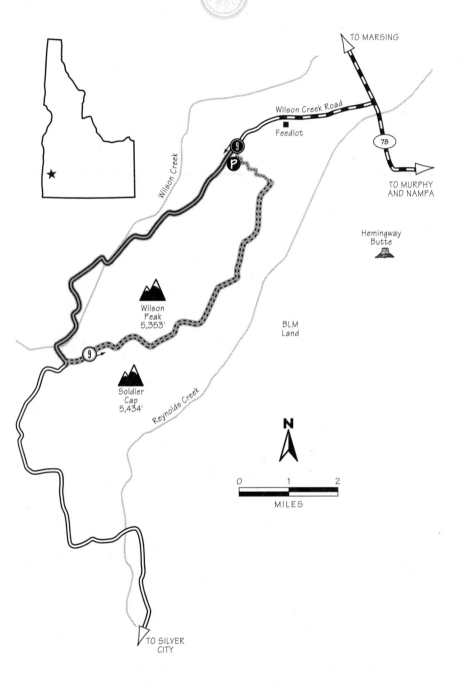

Head up the road 3.7 miles, past a feedlot, to a dirt pullout on the left. Park. The ride starts and ends here.

Notes on the trail: The Wilson Creek Mini-Moab Loop was quite a find. Advanced mountain bikers should consider this ride as an essential and fun tune-up for Moab in the springtime. The uphill portion of the ride is scenic but nothing more than a dirt-road grind. Things get more interesting after you approach the giant hulk of Wilson Peak on a steeper, more primitive doubletrack road and pass through a number of stunted rock spires, known as hoodoos. The downhill portion of the ride features just about any kind of technical obstacle imaginable, at times forcing riders to get into the butt-polish position on steep descents. Look forward to a few heartbreak steep climbs after equally steep descents. Many rocky sections will make anyone without a front shock wish they had one. Hard-tails may take a licking, too. The ride mellows at the end with a nifty singletrack sagebrush cruise back to the start.

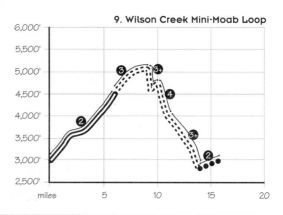

9. Wilson Creek Mini-Moab Loop

THE RIDE

0.0 Head up the Wilson Creek dirt road. It's washboard-prone in places, and it rises at a fairly steep pitch at the outset.

2.0 Road levels out and descends for a nice break.

3.3 Ignore road on left. Bear right, cross the creek, and climb.

3.5 Bear left and stay on main road.

4.5 Ignore primitive jeep trail on right.

6.5 Turn left onto a primitive doubletrack road and head for the Wilson Peak southside saddle. Several steep pitches are ahead.

8.3 Bear left at junction.

8.9 Crest the southside saddle. It's a short trip to the top of Wilson Peak if you wish to go there. Time to break out the lunch fixings or energy bars. On a clear day, the Snake River and the Owyhee Front are visible. As you descend on the first mile, stay left and avoid right-hand spur roads. The trail drops for a bit, and then climbs at a super-steep pitch.

10.0 Reach top of hill. Spectacular views of the redrock rhyolite Reynolds Creek canyon open up to the east.

10.2 Encounter a three-way junction. Take the middle route, a steep drop-off. Time to maneuver behind the seat and keep a good clench on the brakes. Try to stay out of the ruts.

13.0 Descend onto a rocky flat offering more views of Reynolds Creek. Got to take a break to give the aching arms and legs a rest from the rocky climbs and descents.

14.1 After you've made all the big drops, you're riding in sand and watching for a left-hand turn on a doubletrack. It's the second left in the flat sandy hollow. The doubletrack dissolves into singletrack and heads across the sagebrush.

15.2 Bear right, cross the dry gulch, and keep heading west toward your rig, which may be visible now.

15.6 Arrive at your rig. Self-support camping is legal here if you wish.

The Stick in the Sky

Location:	13 miles southwest of Marsing.
Distance:	17-mile loop.
Time:	3 hours.
Tread:	14.7 miles of doubletrack, 2.3 miles of pavement
Aerobic level:	Gonzo heart-racing steep strenuous climb for 5 miles to the Stick in the Sky.
Technical difficulty:	3 to 3+.
Highlights:	Riders who like to punish themselves will find this ride to be delightful. Cool views of Owyhee Mountains from the Stick in the Sky. Raging downhill on the Wildcat Ridge.
Hazards:	Ruts and rocks on the doubletrack downhill will try to eat your front wheel. Jumping obstacles is key on the descent.
Land status:	BLM.
Maps:	USGS Jump Creek Canyon, Opaline Gulch; BLM map.

Access: From Nampa, take Idaho Highway 55 south to Marsing. Drive through downtown Marsing, and then turn left on U.S. Highway 95 heading south for Jordan Valley. The unsigned trailhead turnoff is 7.5 miles south of the ID 55–US 95 junction, just a couple miles after US 95 begins to climb into the Owyhee Mountains. Park next to the highway because you'll be climbing back to this spot at the end of the ride.

Notes on the trail: This ride is truly a climber's special. After several miles of climbing, riders will see a lone radar tower off in the distance, which is the summit of the ride. Hence, my comrades and I decided to call the ride the Stick in the Sky. Another nice benefit about the Stick is that it's really close to the Treasure Valley: it's an easy day trip to bag this ride

The Stick in the Sky

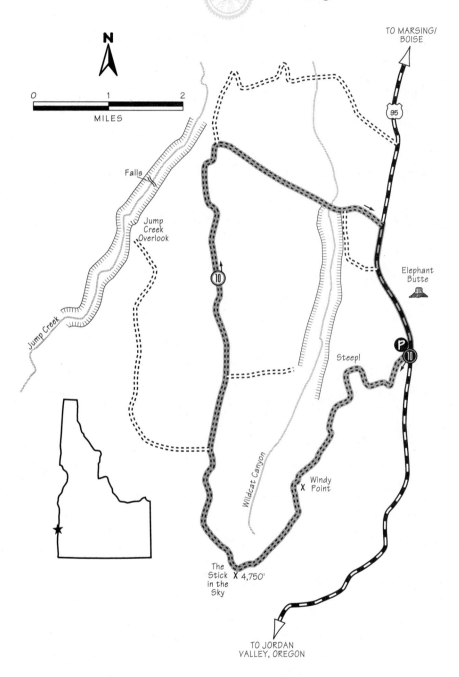

N

0   1   2

MILES

TO MARSING/
BOISE

95

Falls

Jump
Creek
Overlook

10

Jump Creek

Elephant
Butte

Steep!

Wildcat Canyon

P 10

Windy
X Point

The
Stick X 4,750'
in the
Sky

TO JORDAN
VALLEY, OREGON

in an afternoon and still be home for supper on time. All of the climbing is worthwhile, however, because the downhill doubletrack is a straight shot down a broad sagebrush ridge, making it seem as though you can really let 'er rip. Many divots, rocks, and man-sized ruts will try to eat you on the way down, however, so be aware that obstacles are ahead. I got pitched twice on one ride— once by a large rut and a second time by a major tire blowout (even with slime), creating much humor for my riding partners.

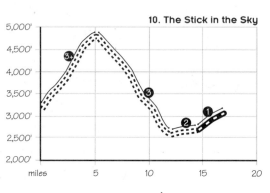

T H E R I D E

0.0 Head out on the doubletrack road next to a fenced wellhead called Alkali Springs.

0.2 Bear right at two-way junction, cross the creek, and climb a granny-gear steep rocky pitch. Unfortunately, you start out at an anaerobic rate and stay there at the redline level for the first 1.8 miles.

1.8 Cross a saddle next to a livestock pond. Take a breather.

2.6 Ignore junction on left, bear right, and climb. The doubletrack meanders through the grass and sagebrush here. Stay with the trail and it will become more defined in 50 yards.

4.7 Breathtaking overlook of the interior Owyhee Mountains, just below the final climb to the Stick.

5.1 Reach summit next to radio tower. The doubletrack road heading off to the right is your downhill route back to the valley. Take a moment to rest and then head down the doubletrack, going dead north.

7.2 Junction on left to Jump Creek canyon, a deep chasm and a neat hiking area. Note for future reference.

11.6 Doubletrack drops into the valley floor. Turn right at this junction and follow a doubletrack that runs east, paralleling a set of powerlines. The road beelines for U.S. 95, passing over a small set of hills. Notice the hidden Wildcat Creek canyon on your way out. The canyon is a great desert hike.

14.7 Reach the highway. Turn right and climb back to your rig.

17.0 Arrive at the parking area.

Variation: Reverse the loop.

Grave Creek–Cottonwood Creek Loop

Location:	30 miles south of Jordan Valley, Oregon.
Distance:	15.7-mile loop.
Time:	2 to 3 hours.
Tread:	7.8 miles of gravel road, 7.9 miles of doubletrack.
Aerobic level:	Moderate to easy.
Technical difficulty:	1 on gravel road; 2 on doubletrack sections.
Highlights:	Rolling moderate trail, excellent for intermediate riders, deep in the Owyhee Mountains.
Hazards:	Rattlesnakes in midsummer.
Land status:	BLM.
Maps:	USGS Fairylawn; BLM Jordan Valley map.

Access: Take U.S. Highway 95 south to Jordan Valley, Oregon. Turn left on the BLM road heading for the DeLamar Mine and Juniper Mountain in downtown Jordan Valley. You're heading for the North Fork of the Owyhee River BLM campground on the road to Juniper Mountain, about 26 miles southeast of Jordan Valley. Follow your BLM map to the campground. Park. The ride starts here.

Notes on the trail: The Grave Creek–Cottonwood Creek Loop is a long way from the Treasure Valley, so it's best to bring your camping gear and spend the night in the BLM campground. But this is a rare loop ride that features rolling, moderate terrain in piñon pine and juniper country in the high desert. It's possible to shorten the ride by shuttling a vehicle to the point where the Grave Creek Trail intersects the Mud Flat Road, or by taking the shorter of the two loops (see variation).

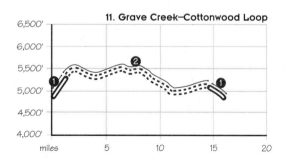

53

Grave Creek–Cottonwood Creek Loop

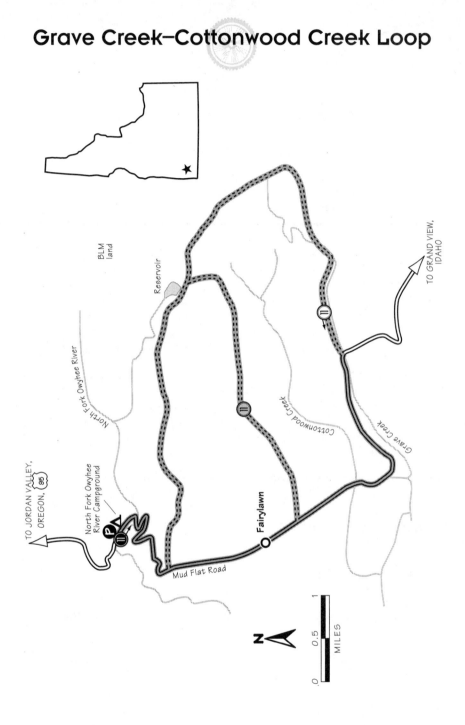

BLM land

Reservoir

North Fork Owyhee River

TO JORDAN VALLEY, OREGON, (95)

North Fork Owyhee River Campground

Mud Flat Road

Fairylawn

Cottonwood Creek

Grave Creek

TO GRAND VIEW, IDAHO

N

0   0.5   1
MILES

0.0 Turn right (south) out of the campground, cross the North Fork Owyhee on a bridge and climb the dirt road switchbacks to the crest of the hill.

1.3 Cross a cattle guard and turn left on an unmarked primitive doubletrack road. Enjoy the up and down rolling terrain. Out here it's so quiet that you will feel total solitude.

1.8 Bear left at two-way junction. The trail climbs a bit for the next 0.6 mile.

2.4 Trail levels out again.

4.5 Encounter a small reservoir. Ride around the outside edge of the pond and you'll come to a signed two-way junction on the other side. Turn right to take the short loop back to Mud Flat Road and the campground. Go left for the long loop.

5.4 Ride by another small reservoir.

6.4 Uphill section crests a small summit. Trail takes nifty meandering course through juniper trees.

7.1 Cross upper Cottonwood Creek.

8.0 Come to another small reservoir and cross another branch of upper Cottonwood Creek. Follow the doubletrack under the gateway to the reservoir.

8.5 Reach summit of ride at the top of Grave Creek. It's all downhill to the Mud Flat Road.

9.2 Arrive at Mud Flat Road. Turn right and spin back on the dirt road to the campground.

15.7 Return to campground.

Variation: To ride the short loop, follow the description above to the first reservoir (mile 4.5). Turn right and follow the trail toward a small stock pond (mile 5.3). The doubletrack fizzles by the stock pond. Follow a cow trail up the drainage to a point where the doubletrack is visible again (mile 5.5). Nice meadow and shady lunch spot at mile 6. At mile 7.1, doubletrack gets rocky and leads to a high point with great views of South Mountain and surrounding countryside. Now it's all downhill to the Mud Flat Road (mile 8.1). Go through a barbed-wire gate and turn right on the Mud Flat Road to return to the campground (mile 10.5).

Piney Forests, Rivers, and Lakes

The Boise and Payette national forests present a stark contrast to the desert Southwest environment. From the forested edge of the Boise Front and fanning out to the north, east, and west, pine and fir forests cloak the mountains near Idaho City, Garden Valley, Banks, Lowman, Weiser, and McCall. It's a decidedly wetter environment, with long winters and deep snow at high elevations. The riding season is more typical of the rest of Idaho in this region, usually extending from late May to early October.

Mountain bike trails in this area provide a cooler, shady experience on a mix of dirt roads, jeep trails, and singletrack. In some cases, the trails offer scenic vistas of tranquil Payette Lake, the boiling whitewater of the Payette River, or high mountain pools such as Loon Lake and Bull Trout Lake. Many rides course along small creeks in deep woods, offering an opportunity to see a wide variety of wildlife.

Both national forests provide extensive camping opportunities at developed and primitive sites. A number of hot springs in the region are worth visiting, especially Burgdorf Hot Springs north of McCall; Kirkham, Pine Flats, and Bonneville near Lowman; and the family-friendly Warm Springs Pool in Idaho City. Other activities include boating, floating, and fishing on the Boise, Payette, and Weiser rivers and on a variety of reservoirs. Brundage Mountain ski area is open every weekend during the summer, and it hosts a number of musical artists on Saturday and Sunday evenings.

Idaho City–Charcoal Gulch Loop

Location: Idaho City, a charming historic mining town.

Distance: 6.3-mile loop.

Time: 1 to 2 hours.

Tread: 4.3 miles of 2WD gravel road, 1.5 miles of singletrack, 0.5 mile of doubletrack.

Aerobic level: Moderate. The most strenuous part of the ride is the uphill portion from Idaho City on a 2WD gravel road to an initial summit, about 1,000 vertical feet above town. The rest of the ride is mostly downhill or flat.

Technical difficulty: 3. The Charcoal Gulch singletrack can be technically difficult for novice riders due to a number of divots, cracks, and crevices in the trail.

Highlights: Fun and fast singletrack descent in Charcoal Gulch. Scenic views of piney forests surrounding Idaho City.

Hazards: Watch out for vehicles on the Centerville road from Idaho City to the summit of this ride, and keep your speed under control in Charcoal Gulch so you can yield to horseback riders or hikers.

Land status: Boise National Forest.

Maps: USGS Idaho City.

Access: From Boise, take Idaho Highway 21 to Idaho City. Turn left on Montgomery Street and then take the third left-hand turn and follow the dirt road to the Idaho City Airport. The ride starts here.

Notes on the trail: The Idaho City–Charcoal Gulch Loop provides an introduction to mountain biking in this historic gold-mining area. It's a good loop for beginning and intermediate riders because it features a variety of

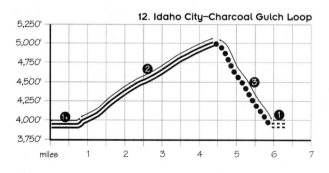

12. Idaho City–Charcoal Gulch Loop

Idaho City–Charcoal Gulch Loop

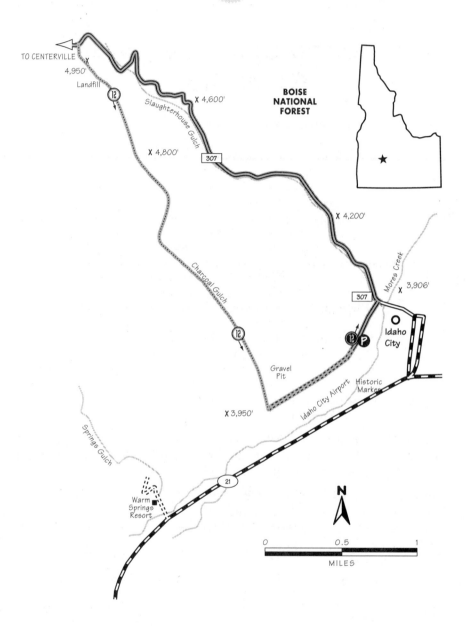

TO CENTERVILLE
4,950'
Landfill
X 4,600'
Slaughterhouse Gulch
X 4,800'
307
BOISE NATIONAL FOREST
X 4,200'
Charcoal Gulch
Mores Creek
X 3,906'
307
Idaho City
P
Gravel Pit
Idaho City Airport
Historic Marker
X 3,950'
Springs Gulch
21
Warm Springs Resort

N

0   0.5   1
MILES

Creek crossings can be wet and fun in the spring on the Charcoal Gulch singletrack in Idaho City. PHOTO BY LEO HENNESSY

riding surfaces and technical challenges in Charcoal Gulch. The uphill portion of this ride can be eliminated with a vehicle shuttle to the top.

THE RIDE

0.0 Head back to the main street of Idaho City, turn left and follow the street to the Idaho City school. Turn left and follow the signs for the road to Centerville, Forest Road 307. As you leave the outskirts of Idaho City, the road begins to climb at a steady but reasonable grade.

4.3 Riders will reach a summit. Watch for a sign for the Idaho City Landfill on the left. Turn left on the road, and then peel off to the left immediately on the left embankment of the road into the trees. You'll see a blue diamond marking nailed to a ponderosa pine tree, marking the trail. (This is a ski trail in the winter.)

4.6 Watch out for cracks and crevices in the trail tread on your way down Charcoal Gulch.

5.8 At a T-intersection at the bottom of the gulch, turn left on a doubletrack and head for the Idaho City Airport.

6.3 Arrive at the trailhead and your vehicle. Take a moment after the ride to check out a few sights, shops, and eateries in town.

Pine Creek–Bannock Creek Loop

Location:	Idaho City.
Distance:	10.2-mile loop.
Time:	1 hour.
Tread:	6.1 miles of gravel road, 4.1 miles of doubletrack.
Aerobic level:	Moderate.
Technical difficulty:	1+ to 2 on West Fork Bannock Creek downhill.
Highlights:	Smooth dirt road ride with moderate hill-climbs for family-oriented riders seeking that kind of experience. Dads and moms can consider towing a baby trailer on this ride.
Hazards:	None.
Land status:	Boise National Forest/Idaho Department of Lands.
Maps:	USGS Idaho City.

Access: Take Idaho Highway 21 to Idaho City. Drive through town and head for Mores Creek Summit. About a mile northeast of town, watch for a signed turnoff for Pine Creek Road (Forest Road 304). Drive to a junction with FR 304 and FR 203, the Bannock Creek Road. Park in a dirt pullout area. The ride starts here.

Notes on the trail: Here's an excellent loop ride for intermediate riders, kids, and families who want to take a day trip in the Idaho City area on their mountain bikes. There are lots of places to camp in the area, too, so consider staying overnight or for the weekend. The whole loop route follows dirt roads that receive a fair amount of traffic—the Pine Creek road in particular—so watch out for vehicles, ATVs, and motorcycles speeding down the road. Experienced riders may want to peel off on several singletrack trails that course down the West Fork Bannock grade, leaving the main doubletrack at several intervals, only to rejoin the road again farther down.

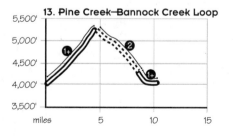

13. Pine Creek–Bannock Creek Loop

Pine Creek–Bannock Creek Loop

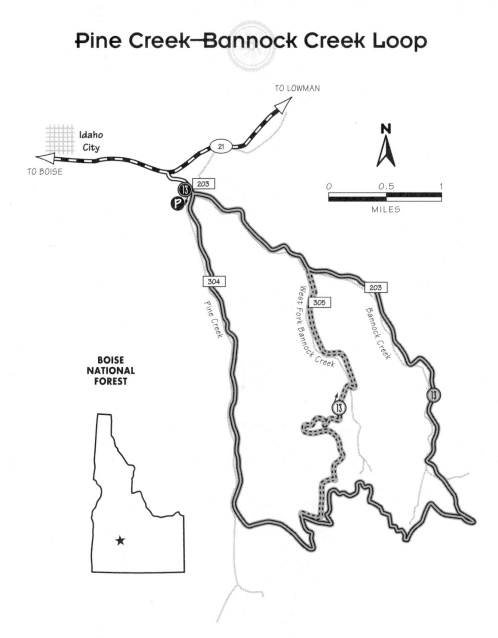

TO LOWMAN

Idaho City

21

TO BOISE

N

0   0.5   1

MILES

13 203

P

304

203

Pine Creek

West Fork Bannock Creek

305

Bannock Creek

13

13

BOISE
NATIONAL
FOREST

★

0.0 Head up the Pine Creek Road (FR 304). It's a gradual climb for about 4.5 miles.

3.0 Road gradient gets a little steeper toward the top of the Pine Creek drainage.

4.5 Reach signed junction of Pine Creek Road, West Fork Bannock Road, and Bannock Creek Road. Turn left on the West Fork Bannock Road doubletrack (FR 305). The road goes up and down for a bit and then descends in earnest. Watch for singletrack trails taking off from the road, providing an alternative way to descend the draw.

8.6 West Fork Bannock road merges with Bannock Creek Road (FR 203). Go left and ride back to your vehicle. The first half-mile of the road below the junction was heavily damaged by flooding in 1997. Follow the singletrack through the rough washouts and you'll get through. The Forest Service plans to improve the trail.

10.2 Arrive at your rig.

Variation: Instead of turning left on the West Fork Bannock Road (FR 305), you could lengthen the ride by about 3 miles by following FR 304 over to the Bannock Creek Road (FR 203).

14

Pilot Peak–Bear Run Raging Downhill

Location:	Start: 60 miles northeast of Boise; Finish: Idaho City, a charming historic mining town.
Distance:	20.8 miles, one-way.
Time:	3 to 4 hours.
Tread:	20 miles of 2WD and 4WD gravel road, 0.8 mile of pavement.
Aerobic level:	Moderate to strenuous. The first one-third of the ride involves a rigorous and steady 1,500-foot climb, but even if intermediate riders have to walk some of it, the all-downhill 14-mile descent on Bear Run Road makes it all worthwhile.
Technical difficulty:	2+. The 4WD dirt road coming down Bear Run Road contains a number of ruts, but otherwise the surface is smooth and sandy.
Highlights:	Raging downhill on Bear Run Road, scenic forest vistas, and high potential to see wildlife.
Hazards:	Watch out for snow at the top of this ride in June.

Pilot Peak—Bear Run Raging Downhill

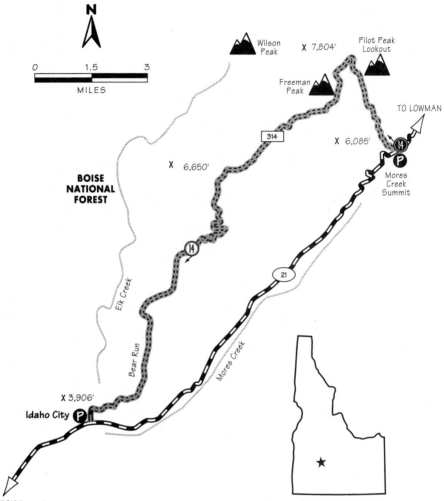

N

0   1.5   3
MILES

Wilson Peak

X 7,804'

Pilot Peak Lookout

Freeman Peak

TO LOWMAN

314

X 6,085'

X 6,650'

14

Mores Creek Summit

BOISE NATIONAL FOREST

Elk Creek

Bear Run

21

Mores Creek

X 3,906'

Idaho City

TO BOISE

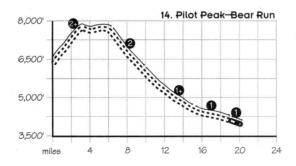

14. Pilot Peak—Bear Run

8,000'

6,500'

5,000'

3,500'

miles   4   8   12   16   20   24

If you lose the trail tread to snow, you can follow the snowmobile signs to stay with the route.

Land status: Boise National Forest.

Maps: USGS Pilot Peak, Idaho City; Boise National Forest general map.

Access: From Boise, take Idaho Highway 21 to Idaho City. Drop a vehicle in the visitor center parking lot. Continue on ID 21 northeast to Mores Creek Summit, an even 60 miles from Boise. Park in the large gravel parking lot. There is a modern outhouse here.

Notes on the trail: The Pilot Peak–Bear Run Raging Downhill is a local favorite for downhill speed-demons. But you've got to earn your keep, first. It's a steady, continuous climb for 3.3 miles and 1,400 vertical feet to the Pilot Peak saddle and several more miles of ridgetop climbing until you bail off the backside of Freeman Peak and cruise 14 miles downhill on a fairly smooth and winding 4WD road. The road surface can be slippery, and it contains people-eating ruts in places. The ride ends in Idaho City, a quaint historic gold mining town that has a number of excellent restaurants and bars as well as a hot springs resort.

THE RIDE

0.0 Head up the Pilot Peak access road, directly across the highway from the Mores Creek Summit parking area. Conserve energy: the grade is fairly continuous for the next 3 miles.

3.2 Reach a three-way junction at a saddle. Stay on the main road that goes straight and then bends to the right. A hard right-hand turn here would take you to the Pilot Peak Lookout (7,804 feet).

3.4 Turn left at junction with Bear Run Road to Idaho City. The turn is marked by a snowmobile sign for Bear Run–Idaho City.

3.9 Bear left at junction and follow orange snowmobile signs and arrows for Bear Run Road on the ridgetop.

6.0 Road begins to descend into Elk Creek and Bear Run areas. There will be numerous minor roads peeling off to the left and right. Stay on the main road and follow orange snowmobile markers.

10.6 The road forks. Stay left.

17.0 Bear Run Road drops into the first of several private subdivisions. Please stay on the main road.

20.0 At Bear Run junction with Main Street in Idaho City, turn left to return to the visitor center.

20.8 Visitor center parking lot.

Variation 1: Starting from Mores Creek Summit, ride out and back to Pilot Peak Lookout. It's about 8 miles, round-trip. Follow directions above to the Pilot Peak saddle and take the hard right-hand turn at the saddle to climb to the lookout.

Variation 2: Ride up to Sunset Peak Lookout, starting from the Mores Creek Summit parking lot. It's 4.7 miles to the lookout, for a total of 9.4 miles. The elevation gain from Mores Creek Summit to Sunset Peak is slightly less than climbing to Pilot Peak, but FR 480 features more undulating terrain than the continuous uphill climb on the Pilot Peak side.

Ride to Sunset Lookout

Location:	13 miles northeast of Idaho City.
Distance:	9.4 miles, out and back.
Time:	1.5 hours.
Tread:	9.4 miles of doubletrack.
Aerobic level:	Strenuous to moderately strenuous on the 4.7-mile climb to the lookout.
Technical difficulty:	2 to 2+.
Highlights:	Awesome 360-degree views of the upper North Fork Boise River country and the Sawtooth Range from the top of the lookout.
Hazards:	None.
Land status:	Boise National Forest.
Maps:	USGS Sunset Mountain.

Access: From Idaho City, head northeast on Idaho Highway 21 to a large parking lot at Mores Creek Summit. Park. The ride starts here.

Notes on the trail: The ride to Sunset Lookout features a challenging uphill climb to the manned lookout on top of Sunset Mountain, but the view and the fun downhill cruise are worth the effort. Intermediate riders should be able to tackle this ride, even if they have to stop and rest along the way. In addition, more gradual sections of road follow the steepest sections, giving riders a breather.

THE RIDE

0.0 Head out of the parking area and spin up the unimproved jeep road to Sunset Lookout. The first half-mile of the ride rises at a 20 percent in-your-face grade, but the slope will ease up a bit very soon. (The road never gets any steeper than that.)

0.7 Ignore minor road peeling off to the right.

1.2 Lookout comes into view around a bend in the road. Ignore minor roads on the right ahead.

Ride to Sunset Lookout

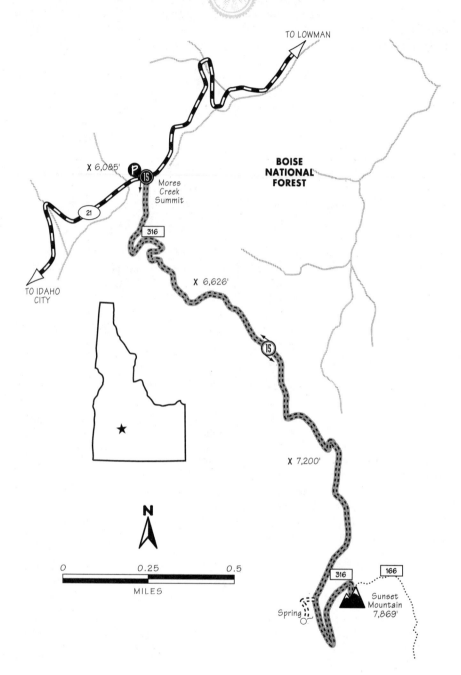

TO LOWMAN

X 6,085'

P 15

Mores
Creek
Summit

21

316

BOISE
NATIONAL
FOREST

X 6,626'

15

TO IDAHO
CITY

★

X 7,200'

N

0   0.25   0.5

MILES

316   166

Spring

Sunset
Mountain
7,869'

The author scales the road to Sunset Mountain Lookout with his son, Quinn, in tow in the baby trailer.

2.4 Steep pitch again for a half-mile.

3.0 Reach saddle. Consider taking a breather before the final push to the top.

4.7 Crest the summit of the lookout. Ask the Forest Service fire lookout for assistance in identifying landmarks, or orient your Boise National Forest map to the compass and see if you can find Pilot Peak to the north, Steel Mountain to the south, and the Sawtooths to the east. Return the way you came.

9.4 Arrive back in the Mores Creek Summit parking lot. This is the same place from which the Pilot Peak–Bear Run Raging Downhill starts (see Ride 14 for details).

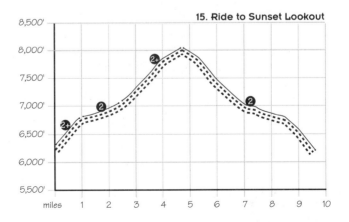

16

Thorn Butte–Cottonwood Creek Loop

Location:	37 miles northeast of Boise.
Distance:	21.3 to 23.7-mile loop.
Time:	4 to 6 hours.
Tread:	12.9 miles of 4WD dirt road, 8.4 miles of singletrack.
Aerobic level:	Strenuous. The climb to Thorn Butte is continuous and taxing; the ride down Cottonwood Creek is arduous because of heavy brush and many stream crossings; and the ride back to your rig features a second, continuous uphill for 4 miles.
Technical difficulty:	1+ to 3. Many technical maneuvers on the Cottonwood singletrack push this ride into the level 3 category. The 4WD road to Thorn Butte is relatively smooth but sandy and rutted in places.
Highlights:	Humongous and impressive views of the surrounding countryside on the climb to Thorn Butte make this a beautiful outing. The singletrack descent down Cottonwood Creek is fun and challenging (I biffed three times!).
Hazards:	Junglebrush—that is, stinging nettles, waist-high ferns, and thimbleberry leaves—in Cottonwood Creek. Hazardous rocky creek crossings.
Land status:	Boise National Forest.
Maps:	USGS Arrowrock Reservoir; Boise National Forest general map.

Access: Since a winter storm in 1997 caused massive mudslides along the Cottonwood Creek Road, it's no longer possible to access this ride from Idaho Highway 21. Alas, a 1.5-hour drive along Arrowrock Reservoir is the only way in. From Boise, take ID 21 east about 16 miles to the Spring Shores marina turnoff by the Mores Creek bridge. Turn right and follow Forest Road 268 about 15 miles to Cottonwood Creek Road, Forest Road 377. Turn left and follow the road about 6 miles (past the Cottonwood Creek trailhead) to a three-way junction at a saddle. Here, an unmarked dirt road peels off to the right, the main access road for Thorn Butte Lookout. Park in a dirt pullout. The ride starts here.

Notes on the trail: The Thorn Butte–Cottonwood Creek ride is a local favorite for advanced and expert riders. Since the Cottonwood Creek Road

Thorn Butte–Cottonwood Creek Loop

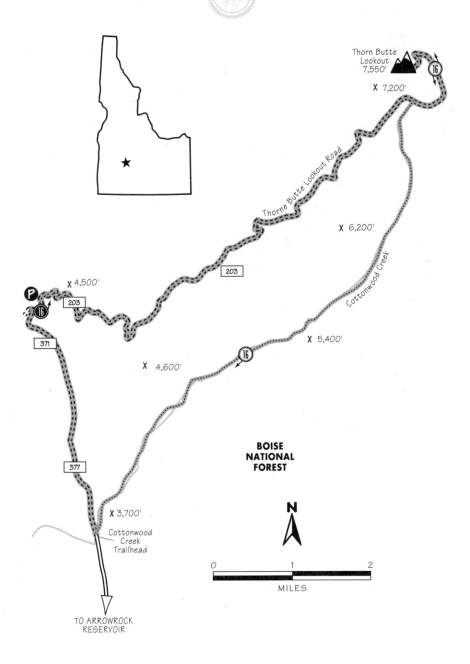

Thorn Butte
Lookout
7,550'

X 7,200'

Thorne Butte Lookout Road

16

X 6,200'

Cottonwood Creek

203

X 4,500'

P

203

16

371

X 5,400'

X 4,600'

16

377

BOISE
NATIONAL
FOREST

N

X 3,700'

Cottonwood
Creek
Trailhead

0   1   2

MILES

TO ARROWROCK
RESERVOIR

Kurt Holzer enjoys a rare straightaway amid ponderosa pine trees in Cottonwood Creek.

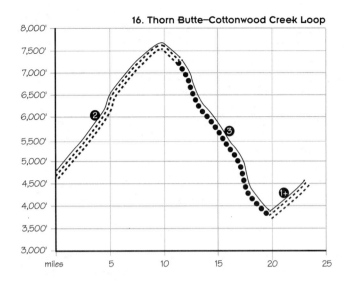

16. Thorn Butte–Cottonwood Creek Loop

was closed from the ID 21 side in the winter of 1997, public use of the Cottonwood Trail has diminished markedly. Hence, solitude is almost guaranteed on this loop ride. A blazing wildfire charred many of the old-growth ponderosa pine trees in Cottonwood Creek and the surrounding mountains, but the regrowth over the last two years has added lush new vegetation and color to the area. Look forward to big expansive views on the way up the Thorn Butte 4WD road—the vistas just keep getting bigger and better as you climb toward the 7,550-foot summit. Then, prepare for a brushy descent with multiple hike-a-bike creek crossings on a sandy singletrack down Cottonwood Creek canyon. Be sure to pack a lunch for this ride and allow lots of time to enjoy the day. An optional 1.7-mile climb (one-way) to Thorn Butte Lookout is well worth the effort.

THE RIDE

0.0 Get into a comfortable spinning gear and head up the smooth dirt road. I found it comfortable to ride much of the uphill in the middle ring, until the pitch gets quite steep later on.

0.4 Ignore right-hand spur, stay left, and drop momentarily before climbing again.

1.5 Big views begin to open up to the east and west.

1.9 Note narrow singletrack peeling off to the right. A potential side trip.

3.2 Ignore minor logging road on left. Same goes for minor roads coming in from the left at mile 3.5 and mile 4.2.

4.4 Grade gets steeper and road becomes more rocky and rutted.

6.1 Ignore trail on right.

6.8 4WD road levels out and Thorn Butte Lookout comes into view.

7.5 Ignore doubletrack on right and stay on main road.

8.0 Come to Cottonwood Creek junction on right. The singletrack is marked by a sign indicating the trail is open to horses, hiking, and mountain bikes. Take a break here or forge on to the lookout for a better view (3.4 miles up and back).

9.7 Arrive at top of Thorn Butte Lookout.

11.4 Return to Cottonwood Creek Trailhead. Head down the trail through a grassy meadow dotted with purple lupine in season.

12.0 The trail traverses a bog and several minor creek crossings. There are too many creek crossings ahead (more than 20) to mention each one individually. Slow down and take a good look at the crossings before attempting to ride them—most of them are too hazardous to cross on your bike, even at low water.

18.0 The trail becomes very eroded in the middle as you make a final descent to the trailhead. Exercise caution and stay out of the narrow rut in the center of the trail.

19.8 Arrive at the trailhead. Please register in the box. Now it's time to spin up the road for almost 4 miles back to your rig.

23.7 Reach the saddle junction, and your vehicle. If you want to eliminate the 4-mile climb at the end of the ride, leave an extra vehicle at the Cottonwood Creek trailhead on your way in, or start the ride at the Cottonwood Creek trailhead.

Skyline Loop

Location:	20 miles north of Idaho City.
Distance:	5.5-mile loop.
Time:	1 hour or less.
Tread:	5.5 miles of doubletrack dirt road.
Aerobic level:	Moderately strenuous climbing for 2 miles of the 3-mile climb to Skyline yurt, followed by a fast all-downhill descent back to the start.
Technical difficulty:	2. Road ruts, water dips, and uneven doubletrack tread provide a few technical challenges in the beginning. Otherwise, trail surface is mostly smooth.
Highlights:	Fairly short loop ride to the brand new Skyline yurt. Try to coordinate your ride with a yurt rental (see appendix).
Hazards:	Large ruts on dirt road.
Land status:	Boise National Forest.
Maps:	USGS Big Owl Creek. The Idaho Department of Parks and Recreation has a detailed map of summer and winter trails in the area.

Skyline Loop

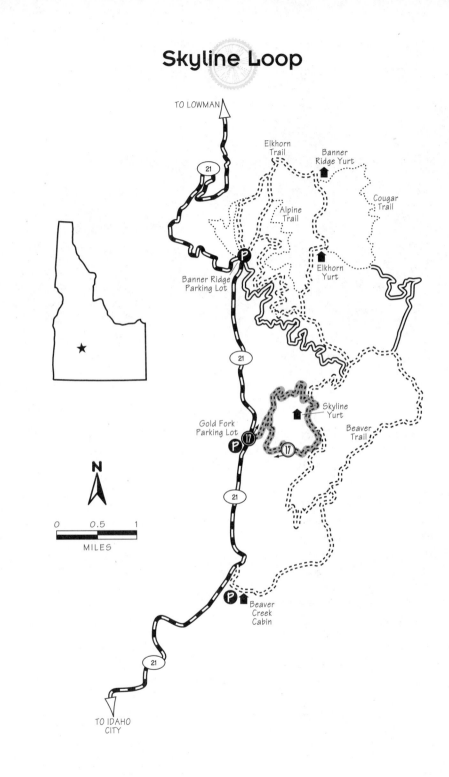

TO LOWMAN

21

Elkhorn
Trail

Banner
Ridge Yurt

Cougar
Trail

Alpine
Trail

Banner Ridge
Parking Lot

Elkhorn
Yurt

21

Skyline
Yurt

Gold Fork
Parking Lot

17

Beaver
Trail

17

21

N

0   0.5   1

MILES

Beaver
Creek
Cabin

21

TO IDAHO
CITY

Leo Hennessy takes a moment to soak in the view on the deck of the Skyline yurt in the Boise National Forest. Volunteers with Nordic Voice and SWIMBA helped build Skyline and two other yurts in a popular park-and-ski area that boasts 50 miles of summertime trails.

Access: Take Idaho Highway 21 northeast from Boise to Idaho City; continue on ID 21 about 20 miles past the historic mining town to the signed Gold Fork parking area. Park. The ride starts here.

Notes on the trail: This is a relatively short loop ride, passing by the Skyline yurt at the top of the loop and then descending back to the Gold Fork parking lot on a different doubletrack. You'll never retrace your tracks. The ride follows a continuous uphill grade on the way to the yurt. Even if novice or intermediate riders have trouble riding the uphill grade, it's worth walking because it's not very far. It's possible to enjoy this loop as a day trip, or you can try to rent the Skyline yurt for a night or the weekend ($60 per night for a group of six) by calling the Idaho Department of Parks and Recreation (see appendix). All of the trail junctions are signed along the route; if in doubt, follow the blue diamonds on the trees.

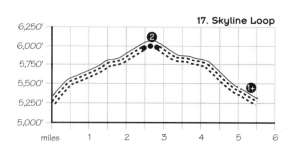

0.0 Head out of the Gold Fork parking area (no parking sticker is required in the summer), cross the highway, and head up the dirt doubletrack road. You are now on the Skyline Trail.

0.5 Encounter loop junction on the right. You'll return to this point on the way out.

1.2 Bear right at the T-junction.

2.3 Pass by Ralph's Trail on the left. This trail is part of the vast network of park-and-ski trails in the area. Ralph's Trail connects to the Elkhorn Trail and the yurts near Elkhorn and Banner Ridge. Keep climbing for the Skyline yurt.

2.7 Reach the road summit and encounter a yellow "Wolf Crossing" sign. Turn right and take the singletrack to the yurt. It's less than one-tenth of a mile. There is a picnic table under the trees at the top. Turn around and go back to the "Wolf Crossing" sign. Bear right and take the doubletrack road back to the highway.

3.1 Pass junction with Summit Trail. Go straight.

5.0 Doubletrack ends and merges with Skyline Trail. Bear left on the mail road.

5.5 Loop ends at the highway.

Elkhorn–Alpine Loop

Location:	22 miles north of Idaho City.
Distance:	7.5-mile loop.
Time:	45 minutes to 1 hour.
Tread:	5 miles of doubletrack, 2.5 miles of singletrack.
Aerobic level:	Strenuous at the start, giving way to delightful, very moderate up-and-down terrain.
Technical difficulty:	2 +. Road ruts, water dips, and uneven doubletrack tread provide a few technical challenges. Trail surface is mostly smooth.
Highlights:	Riding in the piney forests of Banner Ridge provides big views of Steel Mountain, the Sawtooths, and Sunset and Pilot peaks to the west. When the weather gets hot in Boise, the partially shaded trails on Banner Ridge provide a pleasantly cool riding environment. This ride also works as a yurt-to-yurt trip.
Hazards:	Large ruts on dirt road.
Land status:	Boise National Forest.
Maps:	USGS Lowman, Big Owl Creek. The Idaho Department of Parks and Recreation has a detailed map of summer and winter trails in the area.

Elkhorn–Alpine Loop

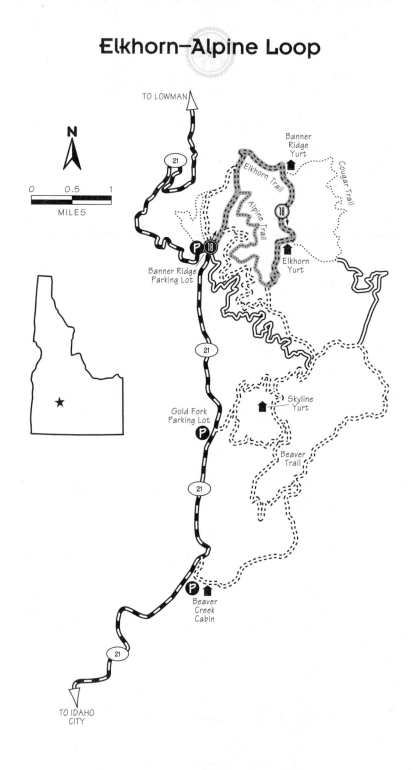

N

0   0.5   1
MILES

TO LOWMAN

21

Banner
Ridge
Yurt

Elkhorn Trail

Cougar Trail

Alpine Trail

18

P 18

Banner Ridge
Parking Lot

Elkhorn
Yurt

21

Gold Fork
Parking Lot

P

Skyline
Yurt

Beaver
Trail

21

P

Beaver
Creek
Cabin

21

TO IDAHO
CITY

Access: Take Idaho Highway 21 northeast from Boise to Idaho City; continue on ID 21 about 22 miles past the historic mining town to the signed Banner Ridge parking area.

Notes on the trail: Elkhorn-Alpine loop is just one of many mountain bike loops in the extensive network of roads and trails in the Banner Ridge/ Beaver Creek/Gold Fork park-and-ski area. The ride provides connections from the trailhead to the Banner Ridge yurt to the Elkhorn yurt, and then it loops back to the main road on the delightful elk-trail-like singletrack on the Alpine Trail. It's possible to enjoy this loop as a day trip, or you can rent one or both of the yurts for the weekend and do a yurt-to-yurt tour; call the Idaho Department of Parks and Recreation for information (see appendix).

All of the trail junctions are signed along the route; if in doubt, follow the blue diamonds on the trees. The Alpine portion of this loop was built by volunteers associated with Nordic Voice and the SWIMBA, under the direction of state parks trail coordinator Leo Hennessy and Ralph McAdams of Nordic Voice.

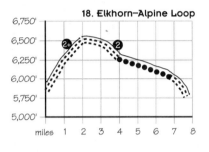

18. Elkhorn–Alpine Loop

THE RIDE

0.0 Head out of the Banner Ridge parking area (no sticker is required in the summer) and head up the main dirt road. You are now on the Elkhorn Trail.

0.3 The road begins a steep climb, gaining 600 vertical feet over the next 1.5 miles to Banner Ridge. Watch for the best lines for negotiating ruts and water dips on the edges of the road.

0.6 Alpine Trail comes in from the right. This is where you will emerge upon completing the loop.

0.9 Ignore junction with Banner Trail on the left and continue climbing on the Elkhorn trail.

2.0 Elkhorn Trail peels off of the main dirt road to the right onto a primitive grassy doubletrack just prior to arriving at the Banner Ridge yurt. If you're heading for the Banner yurt, continue on the dirt road for about 100 yards and watch for a singletrack marked with yellow diamond tree markers on the left. This trail leads to the Banner yurt, which is about 0.1 mile off the main road.

2.6 Bear right on trail marked with blue diamonds.

2.9 Bear left on trail marked with blue diamonds.

3.0 Junction with Cougar Trail, a possible variation. Stay to the right and you'll pass by the Elkhorn yurt in less than one-tenth of a mile. The grand view of Steel Mountain to the south and the headwaters of the North Fork Boise River country spill out the front door of the Elkhorn yurt.

3.6 Junction with Alpine Trail. Turn right on the faint doubletrack trail, which dissolves into singletrack. Watch for black bears and elk. This portion of the ride is mostly level with a few short climbs and longer downhill sections.

6.4 Arrive back at the main road and Elkhorn Trail. Turn left to return to the parking lot on ID 21 or turn right to climb back to the Banner Ridge yurt.

7.5 Arrive at the highway.

Variation: At the Banner Ridge yurt, instead of going right on the Elkhorn Trail, take a side trip on the Cougar Trail. The self-enclosed loop is about 4 miles long. The Cougar Trail features more technical difficulty than the Elkhorn-Alpine trail, and some of it is singletrack tread.

Beaver Creek Cabin Gravity Ride

Location:	22 miles north of Idaho City.
Distance:	11.3 miles, one-way.
Time:	2 to 3 hours, depending on downhill speed.
Tread:	8.3 miles of doubletrack, 3 miles of gravel road.
Aerobic level:	Strenuous at the start, moderate in the middle, and then it's all downhill for 7 miles.
Technical difficulty:	1+ to 2+. Road ruts, water dips, and uneven doubletrack tread provide a few technical challenges in the beginning. Otherwise, trail surface is mostly smooth.
Highlights:	Big gravity descent from the Banner Ridge area to the Beaver Creek cabin. Try to coordinate the rental of the Banner Ridge yurt and the Beaver Creek cabin and turn this into a sweet yurt-to-yurt ride.
Hazards:	Large ruts on dirt road.
Land status:	Boise National Forest.
Maps:	USGS Lowman, Big Owl Creek. The Idaho Department of Parks and Recreation has a detailed map of summer and winter trails in the area.

Access: Take Idaho Highway 21 northeast from Boise to Idaho City; continue on ID 21 about 22 miles past the historic mining town to the signed Banner Ridge parking area just before Beaver Creek Summit. Shuttle: Drop a vehicle at the Beaver Creek cabin to avoid riding on the highway about 5 miles (uphill) back to the Banner Ridge parking lot.

Notes on the trail: This ride provides the longest possible gravity ride from the Banner Ridge area to the Beaver Creek cabin, a vertical drop of 1,400 feet over about 7 miles. Because the route follows a wide—and sometimes heavily

Beaver Creek Cabin Gravity Ride

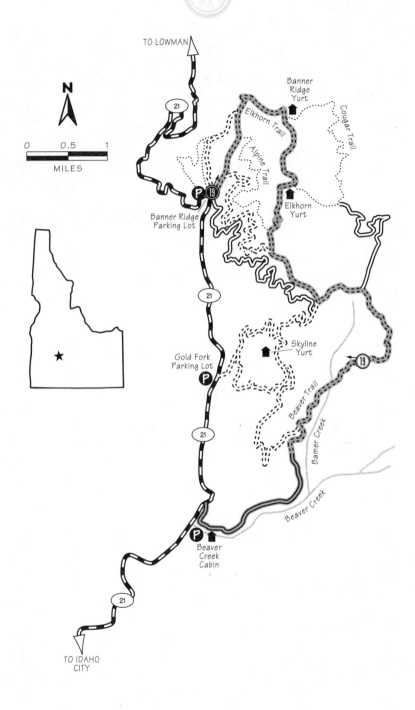

TO LOWMAN

N

0   0.5   1
MILES

21

Banner
Ridge
Yurt

Elkhorn Trail

Cougar Trail

Alpine Trail

P 19

Banner Ridge
Parking Lot

Elkhorn
Yurt

21

Skyline
Yurt

Gold Fork
Parking Lot

P

19

21

Beaver Trail

Bamer Creek

21

Beaver Creek

P

Beaver
Creek
Cabin

21

TO IDAHO
CITY

Leo Hennessy rides along the crest of Banner Ridge, overlooking the Lowman area and the Boise National Forest.

rutted—2WD forest road for most of the way, this ride is recommended for beginners and intermediate riders. Even if the first 1.5 miles of the ride require some walking for novice riders, the lengthy gravity descent is worth the effort. It's possible to enjoy this loop as a day trip, or you can try to rent one or both of the yurts for the weekend and do a yurt-to-yurt tour. You may have some difficulty scheduling because the Beaver Creek cabin is rented by the Idaho City Ranger District and the Banner Ridge yurt is rented by the Idaho Department of Parks and Recreation. Make your reservations early (see appendix). All of the trail junctions are signed along the route; if in doubt, follow the blue diamonds on the trees.

THE RIDE

0.0 Head out of the Banner Ridge parking area (no sticker is required in the summer) and head up the main dirt road. You are now on the Elkhorn Trail.

0.3 The road begins a steep climb, gaining 600 vertical feet over the next 1.5 miles to Banner Ridge. Watch for the best lines for negotiating ruts and water dips on the edges of the road.

0.6 Ignore junction with Alpine Loop on the right and with the Banner Trail on the left in 0.3 more mile.

2.0 The road levels out on top of Banner Ridge. Follow the Elkhorn Trail to the right as it peels off of the main dirt road onto a primitive grassy doubletrack just prior to arriving at the Banner Ridge yurt. If you're heading for the Banner

yurt, continue on the dirt road for about 100 yards and watch for a
marked with yellow diamond tree markers on the left. This trail le
Banner yurt, which is about one-tenth of a mile off the main road.

2.6 Bear right on trail marked with blue diamonds.

2.9 Bear left on trail marked with blue diamonds.

3.0 Junction with Cougar Trail, a possible variation. Stay to the right on the Elkhorn
Trail. You'll pass by the Elkhorn yurt in less than one-tenth of a mile. Enjoy
the grand view of Steel Mountain to the south and the headwaters of the
North Fork Boise River country to the east.

4.0 Junction with Alpine Trail. Bend to the left on the Elkhorn Trail.

4.2 Junction with the Beaver Trail. This is the beginning of the continuous and
lengthy gravity descent on dirt roads back to the Beaver Creek cabin. Follow
the blue blazes at unsigned junctions.

5.1 Two-way junction with Ralph's Trail, which provides access to the Skyline
yurt, the Skyline Loop Trail, and the Gold Fork parking area on ID 21. Turn
left at this T-junction to follow the Beaver Trail.

5.7 Junction with Wayout Trail on left. Bend to the right to stay on the Beaver Trail.

8.3 Pass through gate. Should be open during the summer and closed during the
fall hunting season (after September 15).

8.7 Junction with Summit Trail on right, the last link to the Skyline yurt and loop.
Stay to the left on the Beaver Trail.

9.7 Bear right at unsigned road junction. Follow blue blazes on Beaver Trail.

11.3 Arrive at Beaver Creek cabin, next to the beautiful meadows of Beaver Creek.
As you will see, there are ample camping areas near the cabin, if you weren't
able to rent it.

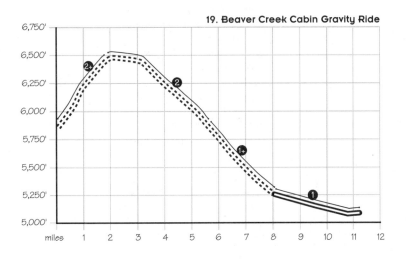

19. Beaver Creek Cabin Gravity Ride

20

m Springs Plunge

Location:	35 miles east of Lowman.
Distance:	15 miles, one-way.
Time:	2.5 to 4 hours.
Tread:	15 miles of singletrack.
Aerobic level:	Moderate to strenuous. Most of this ride is downhill, starting at an elevation of 6,950 feet and ending at 4,625 feet. But don't be fooled by the numbers. A narrow granite canyon toward the bottom of the ride forces the trail uphill at a very steep and strenuous pace.
Technical difficulty:	3 + . Portions of the singletrack along Dead Man Creek are very technical, eroded, loose, and rocky with mobile death cookies. The Warm Springs Trail contains many rocks and tree roots.
Highlights:	Gravity ride on challenging singletrack in pristine forest setting. Big bonus: The ride finishes at Bonneville Hot Springs, a clean and beautiful undeveloped hot springs pool. There is a day use fee at the springs in the summer season.
Hazards:	Beware that you don't fly off the trail into aptly named Dead Man Creek in the first steep downhill section. Watch for equestrians, hikers, and motorcyclists.
Land status:	Boise National Forest.
Maps:	USGS Bull Trout Point, Eight Mile.

Access: Take Idaho Highway 21 east of Lowman or west of Stanley to the signed turnoff for Bonneville Campground. Leave a vehicle here (or plan to hitchhike to pick up your rig). Drive east about 16 miles to the signed turnoff for Bull Trout Lake. Follow the dirt road 1.7 miles to the Warm Springs Trailhead parking area. Park. The ride starts here. There is a parking fee in the Bonneville Campground area; if you park in an undeveloped parking area outside of the campground, there is no fee.

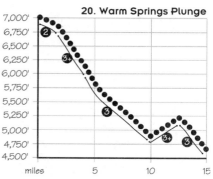

20. Warm Springs Plunge

Warm Springs Plunge

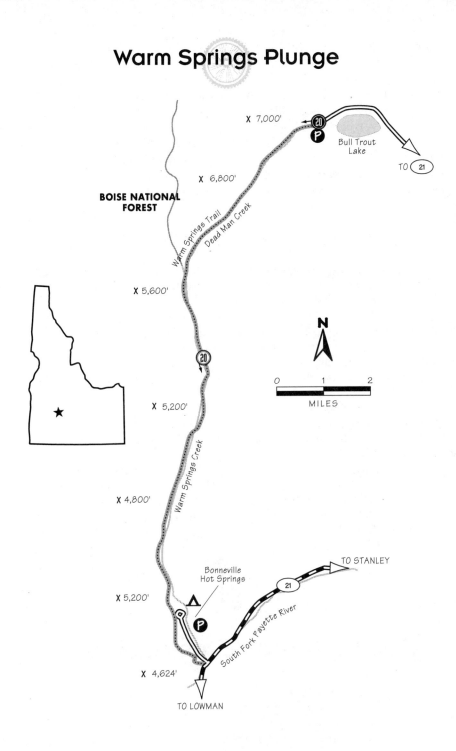

X 7,000'

20
P
Bull Trout Lake

TO **21**

X 6,800'

BOISE NATIONAL FOREST

Warm Springs Trail

Dead Man Creek

X 5,600'

N

0   1   2
MILES

20

X 5,200'

Warm Springs Creek

X 4,800'

TO STANLEY

Bonneville Hot Springs

21

X 5,200'

P

South Fork Payette River

X 4,624'

TO LOWMAN

Notes on the trail: Local mountain bikers love this ride because of the gravity pitch, technical singletrack, and hot springs dividend at the end. I know of several folks who rode this trail three weekends in a row after first discovering it, so it's a keeper. As mentioned above, the most important things to remember about this trail are to exercise caution during a scary 3-mile, 1,200-vertical-foot descent along Dead Man Creek. It's better to walk questionable sections than cartwheel down a scree slope. After you drop into Warm Springs Creek, it's a very pleasant but bumpy ride. You will encounter several washout sections of the trail near the bottom. Remember to save some energy for a steep uphill near the end.

THE RIDE

0.0 Head out of the parking lot and pick up the Warm Springs Trail, marked by a trail registration box. Don't be confused with several other trails that start here for other destinations. In the first half-mile, ignore spur trails heading over to Bull Trout Lake and stay on the main trail.

0.5 Initial climb begins for a small summit overlooking Dead Man Creek. Here comes the steep part! Use caution on steep sidehill.

4.0 Trail junction with Warm Springs Creek. Bend to the left and ride down the creek. The creek bottom opens up into a broad rocky plain under tall old-growth trees.

7.1 Trail crosses the creek on wooden bridge.

8.9 Trail washout by side draw. You'll have to hike over it.

12.5 Here comes the climb. Gear down into your little ring and try to clean a steep section for the next mile.

14.5 Junction with Link Creek Trail. Stay to the left to drop down a grassy slope by a backcountry airstrip. It'll take you to ID 21 at the entrance to the campground.

15.0 Go left to skirt a Forest Service guard station and drop into the campground parking lot. Time to soak in the hot springs. Then go back and fetch your rig on Bull Trout Lake Road.

Packer John–Zimmer Shuttle

Location:	Smith's Ferry.
Distance:	26.8 miles, one-way.
Time:	3.5 to 5 hours, depending on riding speed.
Tread:	4 miles of dirt road, 22.8 miles of doubletrack.

Packer John–Zimmer Shuttle

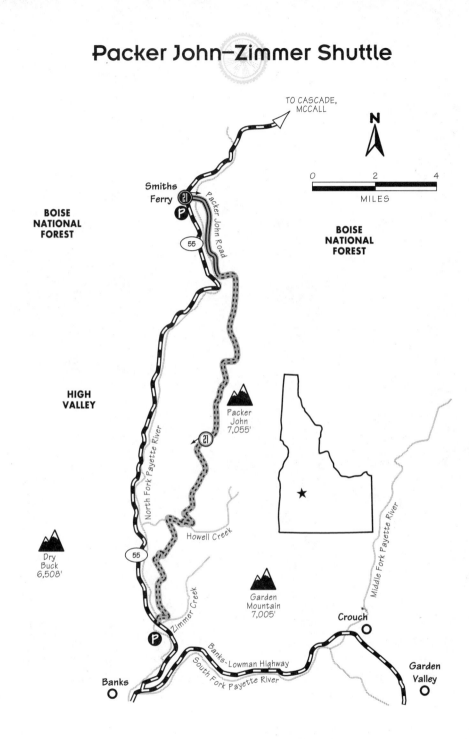

TO CASCADE, MCCALL

N

0   2   4
MILES

BOISE NATIONAL FOREST

Smiths Ferry

21

P

55

Packer John Road

BOISE NATIONAL FOREST

HIGH VALLEY

Packer John 7,055'

21

North Fork Payette River

Howell Creek

Dry Buck 6,508'

55

Garden Mountain 7,005'

Middle Fork Payette River

Crouch

Garden Valley

Zimmer Creek

P

Banks

Banks-Lowman Highway

South Fork Payette River

Two women enjoy a brisk descent down the Zimmer Creek Trail, which features a number of whoop-de-doos for optional air. PHOTO BY STEVE JONES

Aerobic level:	Moderate to strenuous on continuous 8-mile climb to the top of Packer John Mountain. Be sure to conserve energy.
Technical difficulty:	2+. Downhill sections of the doubletrack road from the top of Packer John Mountain to Howell Creek are gnarly in places, with multiple hazards such as large divots, rocks, and man-sized crevices.
Highlights:	Big views of the piney Boise National Forest off the top of Packer John; whooping fun descent on the Zimmer doubletrack, which offers multiple opportunities for big air off of rolling dips.
Hazards:	Don't get too carried away on downhill sections: doubletrack roads contain many man-eating ruts.
Land status:	Idaho Department of Lands, Boise Cascade, Boise National Forest.
Maps:	USGS Smith's Ferry, Packer John Mountain, Banks; Boise National Forest.

Access: Drive to Smith's Ferry on Idaho Highway 55, about 60 miles north of Boise. Park at the Cougar Mountain Lodge, where the ride begins. Shuttle: Leave a vehicle at the bottom of the Zimmer doubletrack road, about 3 miles north of Banks. The Zimmer trailhead is marked by a vehicle pullout and a rusty-colored locked gate (to keep vehicles out).

Notes on the trail: The Packer John–Zimmer Shuttle is a day-long advanced ride that promises an excellent workout on the uphill climb to Packer John Mountain (2,500 vertical feet of gain) and oodles of fun on two major descents—one from the top of Packer John to Howell Creek, and another from Howell down Zimmer Road. The total vertical drop from the top of Packer

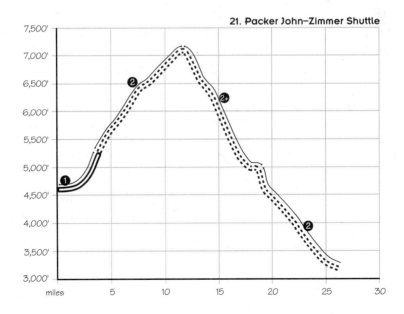

21. Packer John–Zimmer Shuttle

John is just an eyelash under 4,000 vertical feet. Be sure to spin comfortable gears on the uphill portion of the ride because it's 12.8 miles of continuous climbing to the top of Packer John. Stay in control on the downhill sections—it's very tempting to really let it rip on the smooth sections only to run into triple-rutted sections of doubletrack road at high speed, creating nerve-wracking situations that could pitch you, Superman-style, over the handlebars. I got pitched at over 30 m.p.h. on one occasion and fortunately did not break anything major.

THE RIDE

0.0 Head out on the gravel road leading east from Cougar Mountain Lodge. Cross the North Fork of the Payette River and enjoy the pastoral vistas in the verdant valley around Smith's Ferry. Watch for ospreys flying above, hunting for fresh trout in the North Fork.

0.7 Go straight on Packer John Road at the junction with Smith's Ferry Road. For the next 3.5 miles the road is mostly flat with a slight uphill gradient.

2.6 Ignore the dirt roads that peel off to the left here and at mile 2.8.

4.0 The single-lane gravel road begins to climb at a steeper pace. Spin in easy gears and conserve energy because this pitch is almost continuous now to the top, with a few breaks.

5.6 Bear left at a two-way junction. The gated road on the right is a highline doubletrack that parallels the North Fork of the Payette River and dumps out on the Zimmer Road.

7.4 Bear right at road junction.

8.0 Bear right at signed road junction. A left-hand turn here would send you toward Scriver Creek and the Middle Fork of the Payette River.

10.8 The road flattens out for a bit before climbing in earnest for the top of Packer John.

12.4 Junction with road to dismantled lookout tower. Stay right to ride over the three-hump summit of Packer John.

14.2 Reach the top of the third knob. Enjoy the fetching, 360-degree view of the North Fork Payette River watershed. To the north is Smith's Ferry, Round Valley, and Granite Mountain near McCall. Scott Mountain and Peace Rock are the high points to the east. High Valley and Tripod Mountain are the high points to the west. Looking south, you can see the undulating folds of the lower Payette River country flowing toward the river.

14.6 Head south on the doubletrack road (more primitive than the road leading to the top). Watch out for rocks, divots, and large crevices on the descent.

15.2 Ignore road peeling off to the left.

19.0 Road climbs a short section before descending into Howell Creek.

19.7 Pass by three-way junction at Howell Creek. You must climb a very short section here to link up with the Zimmer doubletrack road.

19.9 Arrive at unsigned Zimmer doubletrack junction. The right-hand turn is marked by a large burnt log on the right side of the road. It's all downhill from here, folks, for the next 7 miles. Wa-hoo! Ignore minor logging roads peeling off to the right and stay on the main doubletrack road.

26.4 Zimmer Road junction with eroded singletrack. Turn right and cruise down to the Zimmer Trailhead.

26.8 Arrive at Zimmer Trailhead. Cross the highway to a camping area by Otter's Slide Rapids if you wish to take a refreshing swim. The Banks store has food and refreshments.

Scriver-Sixmile Shuttle

Location:	7 miles north of Crouch (Garden Valley area).
Distance:	19 miles, one way (32.5 without shuttle).
Time:	4 hours.
Tread:	10 miles of gravel road, 9 miles of doubletrack.
Aerobic level:	Moderately strenuous climb up the Scriver Creek Road due to continuous 10-mile uphill grind.
Technical difficulty:	1+ to 2.
Highlights:	Excellent workout on the Scriver Creek uphill grade and a raging descent down Sixmile Creek back to the Middle Fork of the Payette River. Scenic secluded setting the whole way.
Hazards:	Watch out for slippery white sand on the Sixmile descent.
Land status:	Boise National Forest.
Maps:	USGS Pyle Creek, Sixmile Point; Boise National Forest.

Access: Drive to Banks on Idaho 55. Turn east on the paved road to Garden Valley following the South Fork of the Payette River. Turn left off the Garden Valley road and head for Crouch. Pass through the little 'burb with a grocery store and several small restaurants and head up Middle Fork Payette River Road 698 about 6 miles to the Scriver Creek road on the left. Proceed up the Scriver Creek Road about 2 miles (past the summer cabins) and park in a dirt pullout. The ride starts here. Shuttle: Unless you've got a strong rider with you who's willing to ride 13 miles down the washboard-prone Middle Fork Road to fetch your vehicle, it's best to drop a rig at the Sixmile junction, Forest Road 670 (a bridge crosses the river here). A campsite is next to the bridge.

Notes on the trail: The Scriver-Sixmile Shuttle is a nice ride for those who like to ride on dirt roads (sorry, no singletrack on this one). Very few people travel up the Scriver Creek road, so you feel as though you've got your own private Idaho on the climbing portion of the ride (your dogs will like that, too). Many wildflowers dot the sides of the road along the climb, including

Scriver-Sixmile Shuttle

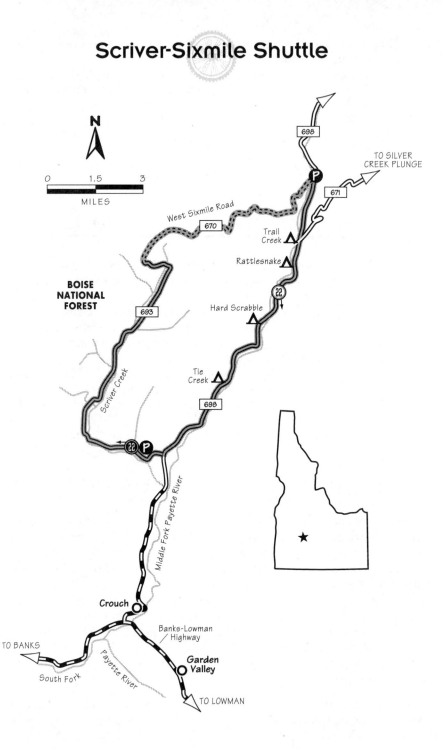

N

0   1.5   3
MILES

West Sixmile Road

670

698

671

TO SILVER
CREEK PLUNGE

P

Trail
Creek

Rattlesnake

BOISE
NATIONAL
FOREST

693

22

Hard Scrabble

Scriver Creek

Tie
Creek

698

22 P

Middle Fork Payette River

Crouch

Banks-Lowman
Highway

TO BANKS

South Fork

Payette River

Garden
Valley

TO LOWMAN

★

scarlet gilia, Indian paintbrush, syringa, and showy daisies, among others. Try to ride the loop in June to see and smell the flowers. The descent on the Sixmile doubletrack offers even more solitude, as well as some cool views of granite spires poking up out of the pine and fir forest. The ride ends at the Sixmile bridge, where fishing and camping abound. It's also possible to canoe the flat-water portion of the Middle Fork from Tie Creek Campground to Crouch. Note: Because the Scriver Creek road is mostly smooth and accommodating to 2WD vehicles, it's possible to provide vehicle support for people who might need a rest or a ride on the uphill grade.

THE RIDE

0.0 Head up the Scriver Creek road.

1.2 Ignore junction on left to Terrace Lakes.

2.8 Ignore junction on left.

4.4 Ditto.

5.0 Ignore logging road on right.

5.9 The road makes a hairpin turn to the right to cross the creek and begin a long climb along the mountainside.

9.8 Junction with Bear Wallow Trail. Ignore it.

10.0 You made the summit. Sixmile doubletrack takes off to the right here (the turn is signed). It's 9 miles and a 2,200-foot vertical drop down to the Middle Fork. As you look to the east, it's obvious that you are way above the bottom of the canyon. There are no junctions to worry about on the way down, just stay on the main road and cruise.

19.0 Cross a wooden bridge over the Middle Fork and arrive at the Middle Fork dirt road. Now it's time to soak your feet in the river and cool off! Drive your shuttle to fetch the rig or send a hard-core rider back to retrieve it.

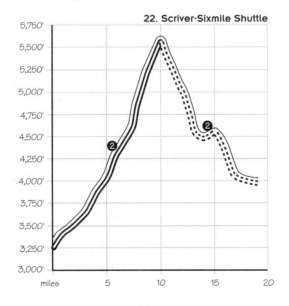

22. Scriver-Sixmile Shuttle

Deadwood–Julie Creek Loop

Location:	65 miles northeast of Boise.
Distance:	24.5-mile loop.
Time:	4 to 6 hours.
Tread:	17.5 miles of singletrack; 7 miles of 4WD gravel road.
Aerobic level:	Gonzo-strenuous. The first half of the ride is so strenuous that even hard-core experts will curse the steep grade. It's 12 miles and 3,200 vertical feet of gain to the high point of the ride.
Technical difficulty:	3+ to 4. The singletrack on the Deadwood Ridge is beautiful and buffed. It's very technical and rocky on the Julie Creek singletrack on the way down.
Highlights:	Fetching views of the Deadwood River canyon and giant pumpkin (ponderosa) pines; raging descent down Julie Creek.
Hazards:	Beware that your rims don't catch fire from squealing pigs braking action coming down Julie Creek. Also, watch out for motorcyclists and horseback riders.
Land status:	Boise National Forest.
Maps:	USGS Pine Flat, Miller Mountain, Scott Creek; Boise National Forest map.

Access: From Boise, drive north on Idaho Highway 55 for 34 miles to Banks. Turn right and drive up the South Fork of the Payette for 30 miles to the Deadwood Campground, a fee campground with an outhouse but no water. Park. The ride starts here.

Notes on the trail: This ride is a climber's special for experts only. Anyone who can't ride for three hours continuously uphill in granny gear should not attempt this ride. However, it's a rewarding loop for the hard-cores, one that requires lots of pizza and beer for ample recovery. Overall, it's a 12-mile, 3,200 vertical foot climb on Deadwood Ridge to the Julie Creek turn-off, and then a very steep and fast descent on the Julie Creek singletrack, 2,500 vertical feet over 5 miles. Then it's a blitz down the Deadwood River road for 7 miles back to the campground.

Deadwood–Julie Creek Loop

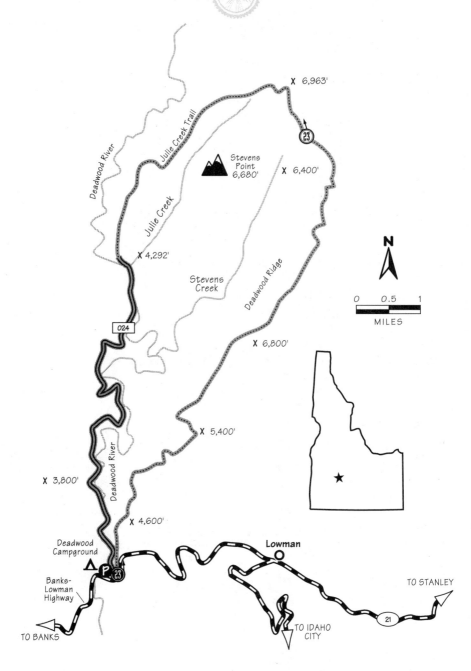

X 6,963'

23

Stevens
Point
6,680'

X 6,400'

Julie Creek Trail

Deadwood River

Julie Creek

X 4,292'

Stevens
Creek

Deadwood Ridge

024

X 6,800'

N

0   0.5   1

MILES

Deadwood River

X 5,400'

X 3,800'

X 4,600'

Deadwood
Campground

Lowman

Banks-
Lowman
Highway

23

TO BANKS

TO IDAHO
CITY

21

TO STANLEY

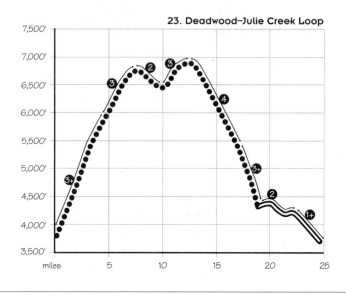

23. Deadwood–Julie Creek Loop

THE RIDE

0.0 Head into the back end of the campground and pick up the Deadwood Ridge Trailhead, marked by a trailhead registration box. Get into granny gear and gut it out. You may have to hike-a-bike a bit early on.

0.5 Trail gradient moderates slightly—enough that the trail is ridable most of the time.

3.0 View of Deadwood River canyon emerges as you climb in and out of ponderosa pine and Douglas-fir forest.

7.0 Trail reaches an initial high point and descends for 2.5 miles on the west slope of the ridge for a refreshing change of pace.

9.5 Trail crosses creek on bridge. Get ready for more climbing.

11.3 Ignore junction with trail to Stevens Point.

12.0 Watch closely for signed junction with Julie Creek Trail on the left. Some people have missed this turn. At the junction, take a break and munch. Then head down the Julie Creek Trail. It's a steep descent with v-trenching, rocks, and ruts. Your rims will turn into squealing pigs on this descent.

17.5 Reach the Julie Creek Trailhead at the end of the Deadwood River road. Turn left and cruise down the road back for 7 miles to the campground and highway.

24.5 Return to the campground. Congratulations. Take a moment to cool off in the Deadwood River.

Weiser River Rail-Trail

Location:	Cambridge.
Distance:	14.3 miles, out and back.
Time:	1 to 2.5 hours.
Tread:	14.3 miles of doubletrack rail-trail.
Aerobic level:	Moderate.
Technical difficulty:	1 + . Mostly smooth doubletrack with a few sections of rough, bottomless, large-diameter gravel.
Highlights:	Excellent family-oriented trail; nice views of the cottonwood-lined Weiser River.
Hazards:	Loose gravel. Angry landowners.
Land status:	Public rail-trail corridor adjoining private land. Trail managed by the nonprofit Friends of the Weiser River Trail.
Maps:	Best map available is from Friends of Weiser River Trail.

Access: Take Interstate 84 to the Weiser/U.S. Highway 95 exit. Head north on US 95 to Cambridge, about 25 miles north of Weiser. To shorten the ride, a shuttle vehicle could be placed at the Shoepeg bridge, 5 miles south of Cambridge.

Drive through the town of Cambridge to a sharp right-hand turn where US 95 continues on to Council. Watch for the railroad signs about 100 feet after the sharp turn and park on the right (south) side of the road.

Notes on the trail: The Weiser River Rail-Trail is in its formative stages, with only 7 miles (one-way) of the 83-mile rail-trail corridor open as of the summer of 1998. However, as landowner conflicts and lawsuits get resolved, the entire 83-mile route, from New Meadows to Weiser, will be open for public use sometime in the future. Novice riders and families will enjoy the rail-trail because the tread is mostly flat, with a slight downhill grade, from Cambridge to Shoepeg Bridge. My wife and I logged this trail with our infant son in tow in the baby trailer. The tread is smooth enough for baby trailers and Trail-A-Bikes.

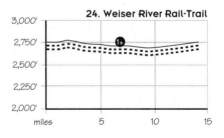

Weiser River Rail-Trail

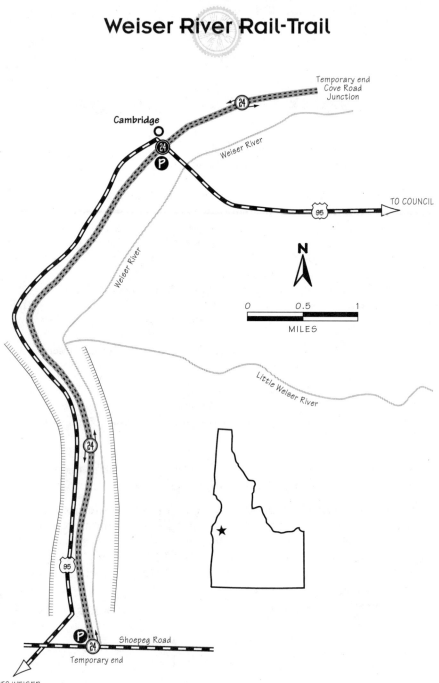

Temporary end
Cove Road
Junction

Cambridge

Weiser River

Weiser River

TO COUNCIL

N

0   0.5   1

MILES

Weiser River

Little Weiser River

Shoepeg Road

Temporary end

TO WEISER

Carol Bearce and her husband, Paul, and Chris Malloy cruise along the Weiser River Rail-Trail, south of Cascade.

THE RIDE

0.0 Ride north out of the parking area and head for Cove Road. This is an option for riders who want to make the most of the ride. The trail is open about 2.2 miles north of Cambridge to a temporary end of the trail just north of Cove Road.

0.2 Cross a wooden bridge.

2.2 Reach the temporary end of the trail. Turn around and head back to Cambridge.

4.4 Arrive back in Cambridge. Continue south on the rail-trail.

4.9 Pass through green gate.

5.3 Cross bridge.

6.3 Arrive at Silver Junction, a spot with a portable restroom in the summertime.

7.5 Enter cottonwood-lined canyon of Weiser River. Watch out for areas of loose gravel.

9.4 Arrive at Shoepeg Bridge. This is the temporary end of the trail. If you have kids, you may want to plant a vehicle here, or send one person back to fetch the rig while the rest of the family hangs out at the bridge or turn around and pedal back to Cambridge.

14.3 Arrive back in Cambridge.

Parlor of Pain Loop

Location:	22 miles north of Weiser.
Distance:	19.5-mile loop.
Time:	4 hours.
Tread:	14 miles of doubletrack, 5.5 miles of singletrack.
Aerobic level:	Strenuous climb on 5.5-mile singletrack section, for which the ride was named; otherwise, the rest of the climbs are in the moderate category.
Technical difficulty:	1+ to 2 on doubletrack sections; 3 to 3+ on singletrack.
Highlights:	Beautiful round-the-world loop ride, with challenging singletrack climb and very cool contour trail on high ridgetops of Sturgill Mountain. Raging descent on the Mann Creek road.
Hazards:	None.
Land status:	Payette National Forest (west side).
Maps:	USGS Sturgill Peak.

Access: Take U.S. Highway 95 to Weiser. Head north on US 95 about 11 miles to a signed left-hand turn for Mann Creek Reservoir. Go left and follow the road into the Mann Creek drainage. Turn right at the Fourth of July junction and follow Forest Road 009 for 1 mile to a junction with a doubletrack road on the right. Park off to the side of the road. The ride starts here.

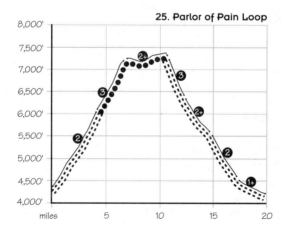

Parlor of Pain Loop

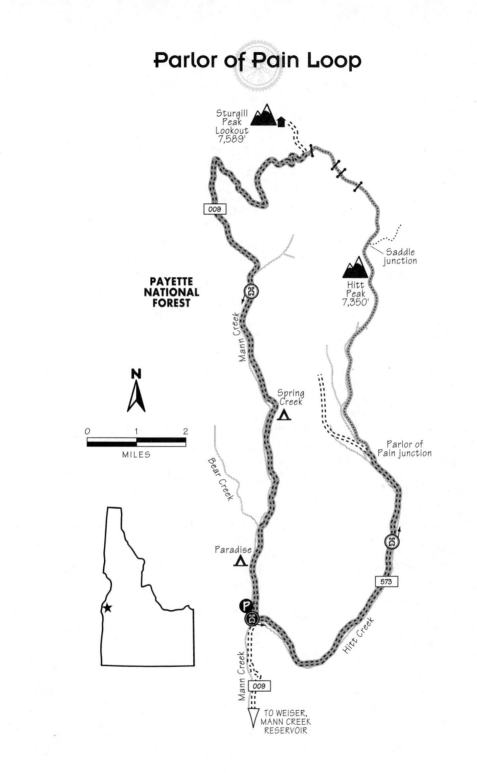

Sturgill
Peak
Lookout
7,589'

Saddle
junction

Hitt
Peak
7,350'

PAYETTE
NATIONAL
FOREST

009

Mann Creek

Spring
Creek

Parlor of
Pain junction

N

0   1   2
MILES

Bear Creek

Paradise

573

P

Hitt Creek

Mann Creek

009

TO WEISER,
MANN CREEK
RESERVOIR

Notes on the trail: This is a nifty loop ride close to the towns of Fruitland, Payette, and New Plymouth, Idaho, and Ontario, Oregon. It's also close enough to Nampa, Caldwell, and Boise that it's a worthwhile day trip to check out a new trail and some new scenery. Riders from the Making Tracks bike shop in Ontario scouted this ride and named it. Thanks, dudes! There are lots of camping opportunities in the Mann Creek area, as you'll see on the downhill portion of the ride, and the fishing on Mann Creek Reservoir can be good for rainbow trout.

THE RIDE

0.0 Head up the primitive doubletrack road along side Hitt Creek. It's a moderate middle-ring climb for a ways before you reach the singletrack steep stuff.

3.7 Ignore minor road on right.

4.0 Ditto.

4.5 Come to singletrack junction. Turn right and head up the wide-track trail, which also is used as an ATV trail. A steep pitch comes right at you at the start, but it never gets any steeper than that.

6.3 Rocky creek crossing (hike-a-bike).

6.6 Ignore spur trail on right and keep climbing in granny gear.

7.0 Crest the top of the ridge. Enjoy the fetching views of Cuddy Mountain to the north. Hells Canyon, the nation's deepest gorge, isn't too far from here as the crow flies. Bear left on the ATV trail and head for the next saddle.

7.9 Saddle junction. Ignore trail peeling off to the right and go straight.

8.1 Pass through barbed-wire gate (please close it behind you).

8.8 Pass through barbed-wire gate (please close it behind you).

9.1 Pass through barbed-wire gate (please close it behind you).

9.4 Bear left at two-way junction and continue climbing for the high saddle near Sturgill Peak and Lookout.

10.0 Saddle junction. Pass through barbed-wire gate to a T-intersection with a doubletrack road. Turn right and follow the road for 100 yards to the main Mann Creek road. Here you can either turn left and begin the long descent back to the rig or turn right and take a 1 mile side trip to the lookout for the best view. Turn left and begin the descent. The road is rocky and somewhat technical in the first couple miles.

13.5 Junction with road on right. Bear left and go down. The road gets progressively smoother as you descend. You'll pass three Forest Service campgrounds on the way down.

19.5 Arrive at your rig.

Crown Point Rail-Trail

Location:	Cascade Reservoir.
Distance:	5.5 miles, out and back.
Time:	45 minutes and up.
Tread:	5.5 miles of smooth rail-trail.
Aerobic level:	Easy.
Technical difficulty:	Easy.
Highlights:	Scenic riding on the shore of Cascade Reservoir near campground, fishing, and picnic sites.
Hazards:	None.
Land status:	U.S. Bureau of Reclamation.
Maps:	USGS Cascade.

Access: From the city of Cascade, take Idaho Highway 55 to the north end of town. Turn left on Lake Way and follow signs for the Crown Point Recreation Area. At the entrance for Crown Point Campground, look for a blue gate and the Crown Point Rail-Trail to your right. This is the trailhead. Park off to the side of the road. There is another parking area on the right side of the road before the campground.

Notes on the trail: This is an excellent family ride. The trail is short and smooth—ideal for pulling baby trailers. Several lakeside beach areas make excellent spots for having a picnic. Watch for waterfowl and bald eagles along the ride. The only disappointing aspect to this trail is that it ends too soon. For kids with a short attention span, however, it's probably the ideal distance.

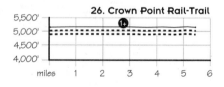

THE RIDE

0.0 Go around the gate and head up the trail.

0.9 Rail-trail narrows and gets kind of rough for a moment.

1.2 Pass by a beach.

1.4 Surface is wide and smooth again.

2.2 Pass by another beach. There is a singletrack leading down to the water's edge.

2.7 Reach the end of the trail by a wooden gate, marking the beginning of private property. Turn around and retrace your tracks.

5.5 Arrive at the trailhead.

Crown Point Rail-Trail

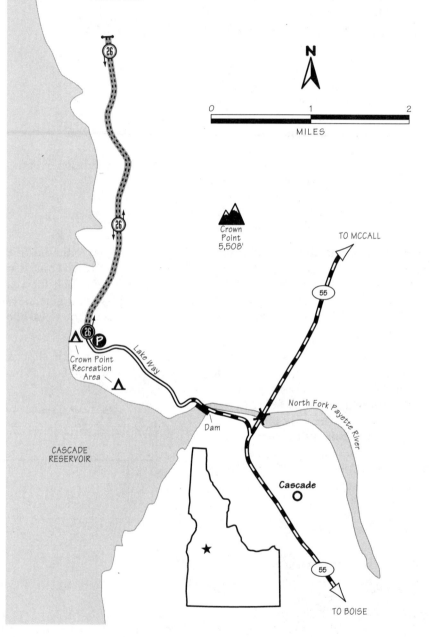

PRIVATE LAND

N

0   1   2

MILES

26

26

Crown
Point
5,508'

TO MCCALL

55

26

P

Crown Point
Recreation
Area

Lake Way

Dam

North Fork Payette River

CASCADE
RESERVOIR

Cascade
O

55

TO BOISE

Tyler Allyn and his brother, Stuart, 6, scoot along the Crown Point Rail-Trail, a perfect family ride, near Cascade.

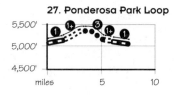

Ponderosa Park Loop

Location:	McCall.
Distance:	7.5-mile loop.
Time:	1.5 hours.
Tread:	2.5 miles of pavement, 2.5 miles of doubletrack, 2.5 miles of singletrack.
Aerobic level:	Easy to moderate. The final climb to Osprey Point is a bit strenuous, but it's short. Much of the riding on this loop is nearly level.
Technical difficulty:	1+ on dirt road sections to 3 on technical portions of the singletrack (many tree roots cross the trail).
Highlights:	Scenic ride with multiple tread in old-growth ponderosa pine forest.
Hazards:	Watch out for tree roots on the singletrack, and please yield to other folks on the trail (hikers and runners).
Land status:	Ponderosa State Park, Idaho Department of Parks and Recreation.
Maps:	USGS McCall. The state park has free trail brochures and maps posted at trailhead signs.

Access: From downtown McCall, follow brown signs to Ponderosa State Park along the east side of the lakeshore drive to the park. If you bicycle to the park, there is no entrance fee. If you drive, there's a fee to park in the state park.

Notes on the trail: Ponderosa State Park has a number of nifty scenic trails in the finger-like peninsula bordered by beautiful Payette Lake. The 840-acre park is conveniently located just a couple miles from downtown McCall. Park personnel do an excellent job of maintaining trails. Mountain bikers are welcome here. About 140 developed campsites are scattered throughout the southern end of the park. If you wish to camp here, be sure to make reservations very early in the summer (see appendix). The campground is often booked by July for the whole summer.

Be sure to stay off trails designated for hikers only and be courteous to hikers encountered on the trail. If you bring your dogs, they must be leashed while you travel on the paved road next to campsites.

27. Ponderosa Park Loop

5,500'
5,000'
4,500'
miles   5   10

Ponderosa Park Loop

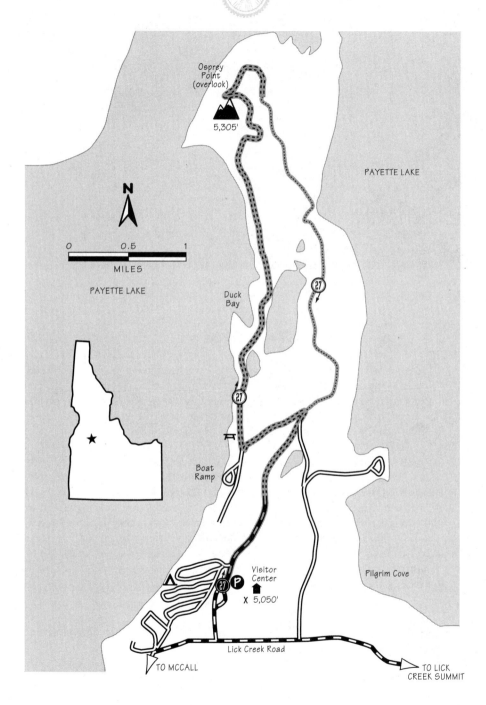

PAYETTE LAKE

Osprey
Point
(overlook)

5,305'

N

0   0.5   1

MILES

PAYETTE LAKE

Duck
Bay

Boat
Ramp

Pilgrim Cove

Visitor
Center

X 5,050'

Lick Creek Road

TO MCCALL

TO LICK
CREEK SUMMIT

Osprey Point, the high point in Ponderosa State Park, affords a rooftop view of Payette Lake, near McCall.

THE RIDE

0.0 From the park headquarters and visitor center, head north on the paved road toward Osprey Point.

1.5 Paved road turns to dirt near the singletrack junction on the right (this is where you end up on the way back). Bear left and ride along the west side of the park under giant ponderosa pine trees.

2.5 Pass junction with doubletrack trail.

3.0 Climb dirt road to Osprey Point overlook. Take a left on the trail at the top to check out sparkling Payette Lake. Go back to the dirt road and turn left, following the circular one-way loop around the point.

3.5 Singletrack junction on left. Now the real fun begins. Follow the singletrack as it winds through the dense forest on the east side of the park. Views of Payette Lake are visible on your left. Stop to take a dip if you wish.

6.0 Singletrack drops back to dirt road in between two huge ponderosas. Go left to return to the park exit.

7.5 Arrive at the park visitor center.

Variation 1: Reverse the loop.

Variation 2: Try out the Fox Trail, a fun rolling doubletrack gravel road. See park brochure for details.

Brundage Mountain Elk Trail Loop

Location:	8 miles west of McCall.
Distance:	8.2-mile loop if you take the jeep trail; 5 miles, one-way, if you ride the chairlift.
Time:	2 hours.
Tread:	3.2 miles of dirt road; 5 miles of singletrack.
Aerobic level:	It's a continuous uphill climb on the dirt road to the top of Brundage, but if you spin in easy gears, it's a moderate grade. Then it's all downhill.
Technical difficulty:	2.
Highlights:	Beautiful trails in scenic setting. Riding down a very smooth, serpentlike singletrack on Elk Trail.
Hazards:	Watch out for elk in the trees.
Land status:	Payette National Forest.
Maps:	USGS Brundage Mountain.

Access: Take Idaho Highway 55 from McCall about 4 miles to Goose Lake Road, turn right, and follow the road about 4 miles to Brundage Mountain ski area on the right.

Notes on the trail: Brundage Mountain ski area offers some of the finest singletrack riding in the McCall area. That's why Ron Dillon has held the Idaho State Championships for his Wild Rockies race series at Brundage for a number of years. And there's another bonus—a high-speed quad chair lift takes riders up the mountain every weekend all summer long, from Memorial Day to Labor Day. On many weekend evenings,the resort hosts live music in a grass amphitheater at the base area. In case you can't get to Brundage on a weekend, or if you prefer to climb to the top of the mountain to get a workout, this ride description shows you the best route to the top and the best way down: Elk Trail, a smooth singletrack that winds through the deep woods of Brundage Mountain. All told, Brundage has about 15 miles of singletrack to explore, most of it was designed with mountain biking in mind. Camping is available nearby in the Payette National Forest. McCall has many options for lodging and eating.

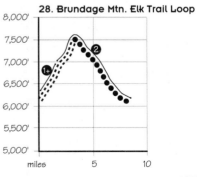

28. Brundage Mtn. Elk Trail Loop

Brundage Mountain Elk Trail Loop

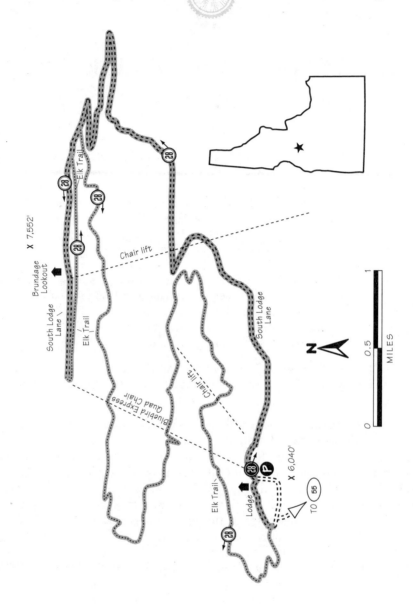

Roger Phillips crosses under a chair lift at Brundage Mountain ski area in a rare moment when Elk Trail is not slithering through heavy timber. PHOTO BY SHELLEY PHILLIPS

0.0 Ride the chair lift to the top or pick up a jeep trail on the right side of the quad lift called South Lodge Lane. This jeep trail is the best route to the top.

1.3 Jeep road passes under the Centennial Triple chair lift. Continue climbing.

2.9 Reach an initial summit. Bear left and continue to climb to the top of Brundage Mountain.

3.2 Reach the top of Brundage. Follow signs for Elk Trail from the top of the quad chair. It's 5 miles of very cool singletrack to the bottom of the ski area.

8.2 Reach the bottom. Try another trail, or do Elk Trail again.

Variation: Take ID 55 to Forest Road 451, Bear Basin Road, about 1 mile west of McCall. Turn right and ride the dirt road 8 miles to the top of the ski area at Brundage Lookout (8 miles). Then take Elk Trail down the mountain to the base of the ski area. To finish the ride, either ride the gravel road to the top and retrace your tread on Bear Basin Road back to McCall, or ride the pavement back to town. Or you could have someone pick you up at the ski area.

Ruby Meadows–Loon Lake Loop

Location:	28 miles north of McCall.
Distance:	25-mile loop.
Time:	3.5 to 6 hours.
Tread:	4.6 miles of doubletrack, 11.4 miles of singletrack, 9 miles of gravel road.
Aerobic level:	Moderately strenuous. The first half of the ride is fairly moderate in terms of climbing and aerobic demand, but the second half is more demanding and physically taxing.
Technical difficulty:	2+. The Willow Basket singletrack contains many tight corners and tree roots, but otherwise the trail is quite buffed.
Highlights:	Gorgeous setting in shady forest and tallgrass meadows adorned with colorful wildflowers. High likelihood of seeing wildlife in the Loon Lake area or Ruby Meadows. This is one of the most beautiful loop rides in the state.

Ruby Meadows–Loon Lake Loop

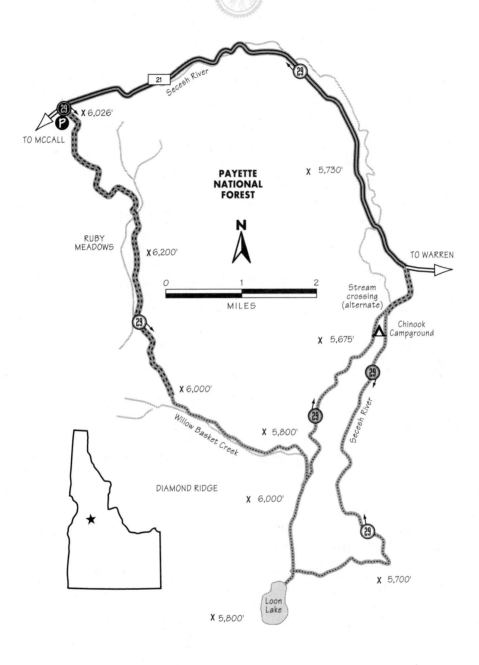

TO MCCALL

X 6,026'

21 Secesh River

29

PAYETTE
NATIONAL
FOREST

X 5,730'

N

RUBY
MEADOWS

X 6,200'

0   1   2

MILES

TO WARREN

Stream
crossing
(alternate)

Chinook
Campground

X 5,675'

29

X 6,000'

Willow Basket Creek

Secesh River

X 5,800'

29

DIAMOND RIDGE

X 6,000'

29

★

X 5,700'

Loon
Lake

X 5,800'

Hazards:	Mosquitos. As you herd back to your rig, watch out for vehicles on the Forest Service road from Chinook Campground to Ruby Meadows Trailhead.
Land status:	Payette National Forest.
Maps:	Burgdorf SE and SW, Victor Peak, Loon Lake.

Access: In McCall, travel to the west edge of town to Warren Wagon Road (just west of Shore Lodge), turn right. Go north about 28 miles, past Secesh Summit, to a signed turnoff for the Ruby Meadows trail on the right. Turn right and park in a suitable roadside pullout. The ride starts here. Alternative access: Take Warren Wagon Road 9 miles past Ruby Meadows to the Chinook Campground and park. This is the starting point for the Loon Lake short loop, which requires fording the Secesh River.

Notes on the trail: This is another Idaho classic, one of my personal favorites. It's a beautiful loop ride on singletrack trail through a lovely alpine forest and spongy meadows to Loon Lake and the Secesh River. Let's face it: It's a rare thing to be able to ride on a wilderness-quality trail to a high mountain lake and see animals like moose, deer, and elk. My wife and I saw a great horned owl on our first trip through the area. On the way back, cyclists will follow the Secesh River singletrack to Chinook Campground and ride a slightly uphill 2WD dirt road back to Ruby Meadows. Bring a lunch, and, if you like to catch trout, a fishing rod. This is a long ride that deserves a nice easy pace to soak in the scenery. Don't forget your bug juice—mosquitos can be nasty in late June and July.

THE RIDE

0.0 Head up the doubletrack road and ride past a gate. The trail features a few steep pitches early on as it winds through a lodgepole forest.

2.1 Deep creek crossing in the Ruby Meadows area. Stay on the main road ahead and ignore minor roads branching off on the right.

4.6 The doubletrack road dissolves into singletrack when it meets the Loon Lake/ Willow Basket Creek Trail; go left. It's 6 miles to the lake. The singletrack trail descends along Willow Basket Creek through small grassy meadows and a subalpine fir–lodgepole pine forest. Be ready for tight switchback turns, boggy spots that may require walking, and big tree roots.

8.3 Junction with the Victor Creek Trail and Trail 081 leading to Chinook Campground. Go straight on the Willow Basket Trail, cross the bridge, and head for Loon Lake, 1.5 miles ahead.

9.6 Arrive at four-way meadow junction with Loon Creek Trail. Turn right and head for Loon Lake.

9.8 Arrive at Loon Lake. This is an excellent lunch spot. Enjoy the setting and take a stroll around the lake if you have time. Cool off and take a swim. Listen for the gigglelike call of the loon. Then retrace your steps back to the Loon Creek meadow junction.

10.0 Turn right in the meadow and follow the trail on a flat for a short way. Then it descends at a fairly steep pitch to the Secesh River, a major tributary of the South Fork of the Salmon River.

12.0 Cross the white bridge at the Secesh, turn left, and head for Chinook Campground, 4 miles ahead. It's a slight uphill grade to the campground.

16.0 Arrive at the campground. Follow the dirt access road to a T-intersection with the main road to Warren. Turn left and follow the washboard-prone 2WD dirt road 9 miles back to your rig. Before starting the ride, you could shuttle an extra vehicle to the campground to avoid riding the dirt road back to your rig. Or send a hard-core rider to fetch the vehicle and the rest of the group can soak their toes in the Secesh River.

25.0 Pull into Ruby Meadows trailhead area. Burgdorf Hot Springs is less than 2 miles away if you're inclined to enjoy a soak.

Variation: Drive to Chinook Campground and do a short loop between the campground and Loon Lake. Take Trail 081 on the way to the lake and Trail 080 on the way back. Both trails begin at Chinook Campground, but the short loop requires crossing the Secesh River, a deep stream that cannot be crossed at high water (be careful).

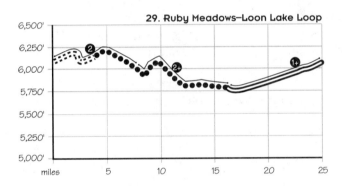

South Hills, Sawtooths, and Sun Valley

In south-central Idaho, all the mountain bike trails can be found in places starting with the letter S—the Soldier Mountains, the Smoky Mountains, the South Hills, Sun Valley, the Sawtooth National Forest, the Sawtooth Mountains, and Stanley. It's coincidental, perhaps, that other S-words describe the quality of trails in the region—sweet, silky-smooth singletrack.

Impressive, hulking mountains with clusters of aspens in the draws make for scenic riding. Most rides start at higher elevations, reducing the amount of vertical gain required. A few of them, such as at Galena Lodge, feature very moderate terrain good for kids and the family.

Nearly all of the rides in this region, even those at low elevation, are not accessible until late May or early July, depending on snowpack. The South Hills, south of Twin Falls, are free of snow first. Here riders can sample oodles of singletrack in an unsung area.

For a low-key uncrowded experience, head for the Soldier Mountains north of Fairfield, a windswept farm and ranch town in southern Idaho's Camas Prairie. In the Sun Valley area, the rides are extensive and legendary. The same goes for the Sawtooth Valley and Stanley areas, where the weather is cool and clear in midsummer.

You'll find tons of camping areas throughout the Sawtooth National Forest, and be sure to check out the hot springs near Ketchum and Stanley. Fly-fishing is good on the Wood River after peak runoff. Try hiking or backpacking in the Sawtooth Wilderness or the White Cloud Mountains, white-water boating on the Salmon River, or canoeing Alturas Lake, Stanley Lake, and Pettit Lake.

Sun Valley has everything you'd expect: luxurious accommodations, golf, shopping and fine dining, and even Olympic figure skaters on ice.

In the Twin Falls area, check out the Snake River canyon, Hagerman Fossil Beds National Monument, and a number of hot springs pools in the Hagerman-Buhl area. A scenic drive on U.S. Highway 30 by Thousand Springs is worth the trip.

Big Smoky Hot Springs Cruise

Location:	25 miles north of Fairfield.
Distance:	6 miles, out and back.
Time:	30 minutes to the hot springs, 30 minutes back.
Tread:	6 miles of singletrack.
Aerobic level:	Moderate.
Technical difficulty:	2. The Big Smoky singletrack is pretty wide and buffed, but it still has a number of technical features such as rocks, tree roots, and divots.
Highlights:	Easy ride to soakable hot springs. Take a towel.
Hazards:	Blind corners on the trail. Please watch out for other folks on the trail.
Land status:	Sawtooth National Forest, Fairfield Ranger District.
Maps:	USGS Paradise Peak.

Access: Take U.S. Highway 20 to Fairfield, the southern gateway to the Soldier Mountains. Turn north on Main Street and follow signs for Big Smoky Creek. It's about 22 miles of dirt road over Couch Summit to the Big Smoky/South Fork Boise junction. Turn right at the Big Smoky junction and proceed a mile or so to a parking lot at the Big Smoky Trailhead. The ride starts here.

Notes on the trail: This is a casual ride on a slightly uphill singletrack to Skillern Hot Springs, a soakable spring with a temperature of about 101 degrees. Be sure to take a towel—maybe some wine and cheese—and enjoy the day. (Swimsuits are optional, depending on the wishes of the soakers present.) Ambitious riders looking for more of a workout should continue up the Big Smoky trail for more than 10 miles of progressively steep and gnarly riding to the headwaters of the creek.

THE RIDE

0.0 Head up the Big Smoky Trail. The singletrack follows an open sagebrush sidehill in the first mile or so.

1.0 Cross Barlow Creek, a side stream (ridable).

1.8 Cross Poison Creek, a side stream (ridable).

3.0 Cross Skillern Creek and then watch for the rock-lined pools of the hot springs on the right, between the trail and Big Smoky Creek. You can't miss them: watch for rising steam. Retrace your tracks to the trailhead.

6.0 Arrive at Big Smoky parking lot.

Big Smoky Hot Springs Cruise

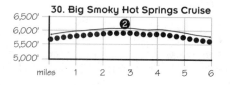

Canyon
Campground

Big Smoky Creek

30 — Skillern
Hot Springs

Big Smoky
Guard Station

085

TO FEATHERVILLE

227

Lick Creek

464

227

TO FAIRFIELD
20

N

0   1   2

MILES

30. Big Smoky Hot Springs Cruise

6,500'
6,000'
5,500'
5,000'

miles   1   2   3   4   5   6

31

Couch Summit–Miller Creek Shuttle

Location:	15 miles north of Fairfield.
Distance:	20.1 miles.
Time:	4 hours.
Tread:	18 miles of doubletrack, 2.1 miles of singletrack.
Aerobic level:	This ride is surprisingly strenuous during the contoured climb to Miller Creek. The initial doubletrack descent is not taxing, but the singletrack descent is highly technical and deeply rutted, requiring some walking.
Technical difficulty:	2 to 4.
Highlights:	Skyline Road from Couch Summit provides broad views of the Soldier and Smoky mountains.
Hazards:	None.
Land status:	Sawtooth National Forest, Fairfield Ranger District.
Maps:	USGS Boardman Creek.

Access: Take U.S. Highway 20 to Fairfield, the southern gateway to the Soldier Mountains. Turn north on Main Street and follow signs for Big Smoky Creek. It's 15 miles to Couch Summit, the starting point for this ride. Shuttle: Even expert riders will want to plant a vehicle at the bottom of Miller Creek. To get there, drop from Couch Summit to the Big Smoky Creek/South Fork Boise junction. Turn left toward Featherville. After the road crosses Big Smoky Creek at 0.3 mile, turn left on a dirt road and park at the bottom of Miller Creek. This is where the ride ends.

Notes on the trail: The Couch Summit–Miller Creek Shuttle provides riders with a grand view of the backside of the Soldier Mountains and the headwaters of the Boise River's South Fork, and the Smoky Mountains. The road takes off from Couch Summit and twists and turns at skyline level toward the west for 13 miles. Then it's a banzai down the Miller Creek doubletrack before confronting a narrow singletrack for the final descent into the valley. In places, the singletrack is deeply gouged and technical. Because of the length of the ride, be sure to pack plenty of water and food.

Couch Summit–Miller Creek Shuttle

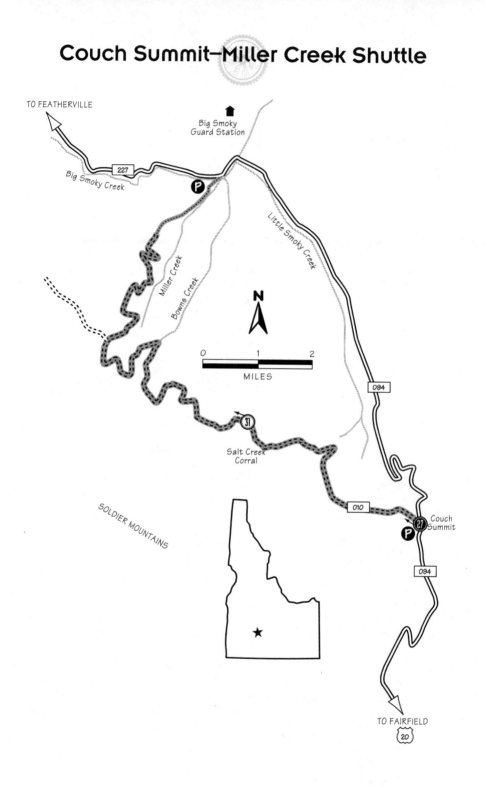

TO FEATHERVILLE

Big Smoky
Guard Station

227

Big Smoky Creek

Little Smoky Creek

Miller Creek

Bowns Creek

N

0 1 2
MILES

094

31

Salt Creek
Corral

SOLDIER MOUNTAINS

010

Couch
Summit
27

094

★

TO FAIRFIELD
20

0.0 Head west from Couch Summit for the Salt Creek Corrals. You're on Forest Road 010. It's a steady but subtle uphill grade.

3.3 Ignore old mining road on right.

5.0 Arrive at the corrals. Stay on FR 010 heading west.

9.3 Pass junction with the West Fork of Salt Creek.

12.1 Junction on right with Bowns Creek. Stay on FR 010.

13.1 Singletrack and doubletrack peel right into Miller Creek. Turn right on the doubletrack road—it's in better condition.

14.3 Encounter a junction on right and a gate on the left. Pass through the gate (please close behind you) and continue riding downhill.

17.6 Come to junction in logging area. Go right and continue downhill.

18.2 Step over big tree across the trail. Then bear left on the singletrack and descend to the valley. At some times, the trail is perfectly ridable. At others, it's cut deep and is too narrow to use your pedals. You may have to hike by these sections.

19.7 Cross a stream (ridable).

19.8 Emerge into a primitive campground. Follow the road across Bowns Creek (ridable).

20.1 Arrive at your rig.

Variation: Views from FR 010 are so spectacular that some riders may want to park at Couch Summit and do an out-and-back ride on the road for whatever distance is comfortable.

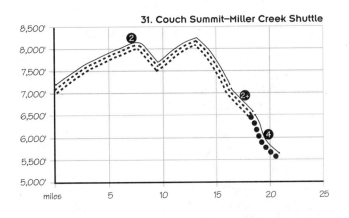

31. Couch Summit–Miller Creek Shuttle

Third Fork–Heart Attack Loop

Location:	30 miles southeast of Twin Falls.
Distance:	13.7-mile loop.
Time:	2 to 4 hours.
Tread:	13.7 miles of singletrack.
Aerobic level:	Moderate to strenuous. Steepness factor increases as you get closer to the summit. Strong intermediate riders may want to try this ride and walk the steeper uphill and downhill sections.
Technical difficulty:	2 to 3+. The Third Fork singletrack is very buffed and sweet, but the trail down Heart Attack is very technical in places, with rock drops, steep sections with death cookies, rough stream crossings, and tree roots.
Highlights:	Primo singletrack ride through shady and fragrant aspen groves. Nice views of the South Hills finger ridges at the summit.
Hazards:	Watch out for and yield to equestrians, motorcyclists, and hikers.
Land status:	Sawtooth National Forest, south half.
Maps:	USGS Rams Horn Ridge, Trapper Peak, Pike Mountain. Sawtooth National Forest, south half.

Access: Take Interstate 84 to the Twin Falls city center exit. Head south for Twin Falls and enjoy a stunning view of the Snake River canyon as you pass over the highway bridge. The road turns into Blue Lakes Boulevard. Drive through a number of stoplights to the East Five Points intersection and head east on U.S. Highway 30. Follow the highway as it passes through the small town of Kimberly. About 9 miles from Twin Falls, turn right (south) on County Road G3. Follow CR G3 into Rock Creek Canyon; it's 20 miles to the junction with the Third Fork trailhead. The ride starts here.

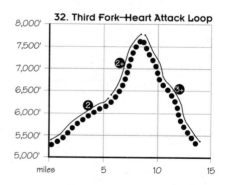

32. Third Fork–Heart Attack Loop

Third Fork—Heart Attack Loop

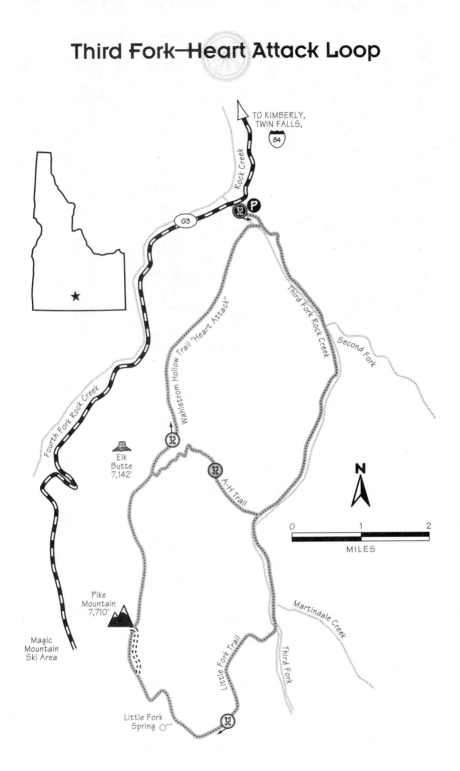

TO KIMBERLY, TWIN FALLS, 84

Rock Creek

G3

P

32

Third Fork Rock Creek

Second Fork

Wahlstrom Hollow Trail "Heart Attack"

Fourth Fork Rock Creek

Elk Butte 7,142'

32

32

A-H Trail

N

0   1   2
MILES

Pike Mountain 7,710'

Magic Mountain Ski Area

Martindale Creek

Little Fork Trail

Third Fork

Little Fork Spring

32

Chip Dillman climbs through an aspen grove on a sweet singletrack in the South Hills.

Notes on the trail: The Third Fork–Heart Attack Loop will acquaint riders with a general overview of the vast network of singletrack trails in the South Hills. Many trails peel off from the Third Fork trail, creating many options. The ride up the Third Fork Trail is very scenic, next to a perennial stream (with wild trout). Meadows give way to shady aspen groves on the climb up the Little Fork of Rock Creek. The view opens up on a high ridgetop summit at 7,800 feet. It's a raging, fun downhill ride on the trail locals call Heart Attack, which, fortunately, they named for the experience of riding up the trail. Novice riders, however, might just come close to the state of stunned disbelief if they try to ride down the butt-wiper descents.

THE RIDE

0.0 Pick up the Third Fork trail in the south end of the parking lot and take off. Be ready for a couple short, granny-gear technical sections in the first half-mile.

1.2 Cross two side creeks in the next half-mile.

1.7 Pass Second Fork junction, Trail 236. Bear right on the Third Fork trail.

2.5 Cross wooden bridge.

3.0 Following a steep pitch in the trail, notice the abundance of phallic spires in this portion of the Third Fork canyon.

4.4 Junction with A-H Trail, a possible variation (see below). Go straight on the Third Fork Trail.

5.5 Junction with Martindale Creek singletrack. Go straight.

5.8 Turn right on the Little Fork Trail. You're climbing in earnest now to the top.

6.2 Two stream crossings (ridable).

6.3 Junction with Trail Creek Canyon Trail 241.

7.6 First switchback by a spring box for cattle. The water may not be safe to drink for humans.

8.1 Reach top of saddle at a junction with the Pike Mountain Trail. Take a moment to rest. To reach the summit of this ride, you can either turn right on the jeep trail and follow the ridge or bear left on the singletrack and follow it through the sagebrush along a series of wooden poles marking the route.

8.5 Crest the summit. Time for some food and drink. Climb the doubletrack to the top of Elk Butte for the broadest view. Follow Trail 239 into the trees and get ready for a fun descent.

10.0 Junction with A-H Trail, a possible shortcut. Go left and climb a hill.

10.1 Bear left on the Wahlstrom Hollow Trail, also known as Heart Attack.

11.5 Stream crossing, difficult to ride.

12.7 Stream crossing, difficult to ride.

13.3 Cross bridge and rejoin the Third Fork Trail. Turn left and head back to the trailhead.

13.7 Return to the parking area.

Variation 1: Ride up the A-H Trail to the summit and reverse the loop from the ridgetop, coming down Little Fork to the Third Fork and zoom back from there.

Variation 2: Want to try conquering Heart Attack? Reverse the loop. You'll be doing some hiking.

South Hills Singletrack Nirvana

Location:	30 miles southeast of Twin Falls.
Distance:	26.8-mile loop.
Time:	5 to 8 hours.
Tread:	22.5 miles of singletrack, 4.3 miles of paved road.
Aerobic level:	Strenuous. Two strenuous uphill pulls, combined with several technical downhills, and the overall length of the ride make this a full-on strenuous ride.
Technical difficulty:	2+ to 3. Nearly all of the singletracks on this ride are very buffed and sweet. Be ready for a number of rocky sections, tree roots, and creek crossings.
Highlights:	Awesome singletrack for nearly 27 continuous miles through shady and fragrant aspen groves. Big vistas of the South Hills finger ridges at two different and distinct summits.

South Hills Singletrack Nirvana

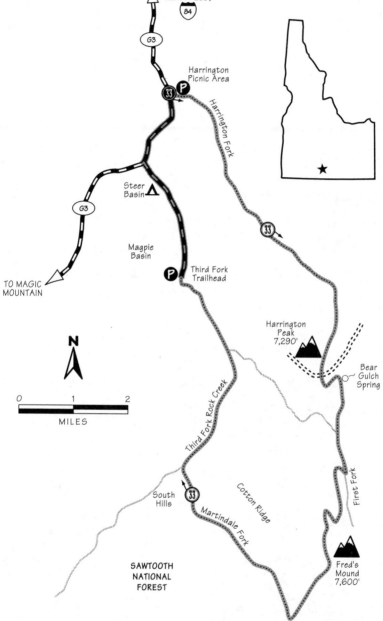

TO KIMBERLY, TWIN FALLS, 84

G3

Harrington Picnic Area

P 33

Harrington Fork

33

Steer Basin

G3

Magpie Basin

TO MAGIC MOUNTAIN

P Third Fork Trailhead

Harrington Peak 7,290'

Bear Gulch Spring

N

Third Fork Rock Creek

First Fork

Cotton Ridge

0   1   2
MILES

South Hills

33

Martindale Fork

SAWTOOTH NATIONAL FOREST

Fred's Mound 7,600'

Ross Blanchard takes a welcome breather near Fred's Mound on a day-long singletrack ride in the South Hills.

Hazards:	Watch out for and yield to equestrians, motorcyclists, and hikers.
Land status:	Sawtooth National Forest, south half.
Maps:	USGS Grand View Peak, Rams Horn Ridge, Trapper Peak; Sawtooth National Forest, south half.

Access: Take Interstate 84 to the Twin Falls city center exit. Head south for Twin Falls and enjoy a stunning view of the Snake River canyon as you pass over the highway bridge. The road turns into Blue Lakes Boulevard. Drive through a number of stoplights to the East Five Points intersection and head east on U.S. Highway 30. Follow the highway as it passes through the small town of Kimberly. About 9 miles from Twin Falls, turn right (south) on County Road G3. Follow CR G3 into Rock Creek Canyon; it's 17 miles to the CR G3 junction with the Harrington Fork Trail. The ride starts here.

Notes on the trail: For strong riders who lust for long continuous singletrack rides, this one is a humdinger. This tour of the South Hills country provides a beautiful cruise up Harrington Fork for 7 miles to a summit, a raging downhill past Bear Gulch Spring, and another big pull up the First Fork singletrack to a summit on the shoulder of Fred's Mound. Then you can look forward to an incredibly fun and long descent down the Martindale Creek singletrack and the Third Fork singletrack. The double pull will test advanced riders who haven't developed solid endurance levels for a 6-hour tour, but hey, even if you have to walk a little, the downhill sections and the scenery are worth the effort. Note: If you're already pooped at the top of the Harrington Fork climb, be sure to bail out by going down the First Fork Trail back to the Third Fork Trail. Otherwise, you'll be likely to bonk on the second climb. Also, carry a full lunch and a bunch of energy bars for this ride. There's lots of water next to the trail if you want to take a filter.

0.0 Head out of the Harrington Fork picnic area parking lot, cross a wooden bridge, and head up the canyon. Spin a comfortable gear to conserve energy.

1.0 First major stream crossing (ridable).

1.4 Second crossing, a bit technical but ridable.

2.1 Third crossing (narrow and deep).

2.4 Fourth crossing (very technical).

3.7 Cross cattle guard and wooden pasture fence at a tributary junction.

4.9 Fifth crossing (ridable).

5.2 Sixth crossing (ridable).

5.7 Cross a side creek in a gorgeous grassy meadow.

6.5 Spring on right, possible refill spot.

6.9 Very close to the summit, the singletrack crosses a jeep road and winds through the woods to the top. Stay with the singletrack.

7.1 Cross a jeep road again and cross a narrow cattle guard. Now you're looking out into the First and Second Forks of Rock Creek, and Fred's Mound is off in the distance to the south. You're about to lose a bunch of elevation and then you'll climb to Fred's Mound. Follow the singletrack through an old clearcut of small-diameter stumps and bend left toward Bear Gulch Spring.

8.1 Arrive at Bear Gulch Spring, a possible refill spot.

8.3 Cross side draw and angle for the First Fork of Rock Creek.

9.0 Junction with First Fork. This is a possible bail-out spot. Go left to continue the ride and climb up First Fork. Go right and bail out to the Third Fork Trail if you're wiped.

10.2 First Fork singletrack crosses the creek on a doubletrack tread and climbs in earnest for Fred's Mound. You're entering a shady section in the woods now. Ignore little trails peeling off the main trail from motorcycles playing around in the area.

11.5 Emerge in a beautiful high mountain meadow on the shoulder of Fred's Mound. Ignore jeep trail and stay on singletrack heading dead south. This is a possible lunch spot.

12.1 Junction with two jeep trails. One of them leads to Second Fork. Go straight to stay on the main route.

12.8 Cross cattle guard and pass by an old corral.

13.7 Reach a signed junction with the Martindale Creek singletrack. The climbing is over, and the downhill fun begins again! This is another possible lunch and refueling spot. The Martindale Trail is a narrow sweet singletrack, at least as buffed and beautiful as Harrington.

14.4 Cross Martindale Creek and cross back; both ridable.

14.6 Two creek crossings in the next half-mile (both ridable).

15.0 Creek crossing (ridable).

17.0 Junction with Third Fork singletrack. Martindale ends. Go right and head down the Third Fork Trail. Beware of blind corners and be prepared to slow down and yield to hikers, equestrians, motorcyclists, and fellow riders.

22.5 Arrive at Third Fork Trailhead. Ride through the parking lot, turn right on the paved road, and cruise downhill to the Harrington Trailhead and parking area.

26.8 Arrive at Harrington Trailhead and your rig. Time to celebrate!

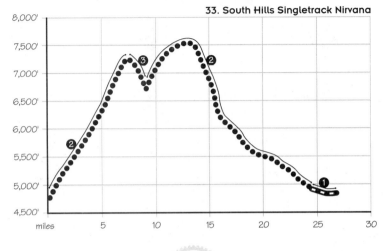

33. South Hills Singletrack Nirvana

Wood River Trail

Location:	Wood River Valley—Bellevue to Hailey to points north of Ketchum, Sun Valley, and Elkhorn.
Distance:	Bellevue to Lake Creek Trailhead, 20.8 miles, one-way; Ketchum–Sun Valley–Elkhorn Loop, 10.8 miles.
Time:	Depends on distance and speed of travel: you make the call. It took me 2 hours.
Tread:	Paved trail.
Aerobic level:	Easy, depending on headwinds.
Technical difficulty:	1.
Highlights:	Beautiful urban trail suitable for all abilities in a picturesque setting.
Hazards:	Please yield to walkers, joggers, and in-line skaters, and follow rules of the trail.
Land status:	Blaine County Recreation District.
Maps:	Blaine County Recreation District map is best.

Access: The Wood River Trail has multiple entry points. The narrative below describes a south-to-north route from Bellevue to the Lake Creek Trailhead and a loop route from Broadway Run, south of Ketchum, to Sun Valley, Elkhorn, and back. Please refer to the map for public parking areas and access points.

Wood River Trail

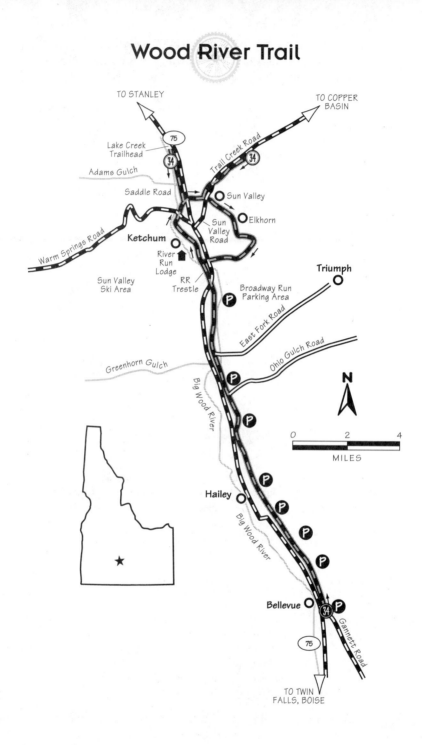

The Wood River Trail system features a number of nifty underpasses, like this one by Elkhorn Road, to avoid riding on busy Idaho Highway 75.

Notes on the trail: Idahoans are blessed to have the Wood River Trail, a well-signed and managed urban trail system in one of the most beautiful settings in the world. Local residents passed a bond measure in 1988 to make the trail development possible. Much of the valley trail was built on the old Union Pacific railroad line, which brought tourists and movie stars to Sun Valley in the early days, beginning in 1938. As part of a trip to Ketchum and Sun Valley, set aside a few hours to tour around the valley on the Wood River Trail with your friends and family; anglers can carry a fly rod and stop to fish. There are many restaurants and galleries to visit in Ketchum and Sun Valley. Hailey has its share of eateries, too. The direct route from Bellevue to Lake Creek is slightly uphill, but during the summer, the prevailing south winds provide a tailwind the whole way. Plant a shuttle rig at the end of your route, or get someone to drop you off. The loop ride features an uphill climb into Sun Valley and Elkhorn, but the toil is worth the breezy downhill back to the Wood River Trail.

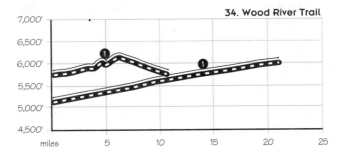

THE RIDE

Bellevue to Lake Creek Trailhead

0.0 Hook up with the southern end of the Wood River Trail in the south end of Bellevue, 16 miles south of Ketchum. Turn right off of Idaho Highway 75 near mile marker 111 on Gannett Road (not signed) and park by the trailhead.

1.5 Alternative entry point and parking at Durg Memorial Pocket Park.

4.2 Enter southern end of Hailey. Parking and trail access are near Blaine County Native Plant Arboretum, across from the airport.

6.0 Parking and trail access on north end of Hailey.

9.7 Parking and trail access at Ohio Gulch Road.

10.7 Trail crosses railroad trestle.

11.1 Parking and trail access at the East Fork Road. The East Fork drains a portion of the Pioneer Mountains. The East Fork Road leads to the historic mining 'burb of Triumph, the birthplace of Olympic skier Picabo Street.

13.9 Parking and trail access at Broadway Run, on the south end of Ketchum. Trail passes through an underpass to cross the highway.

14.4 Junction with Cold Springs Trail from Bald Mountain (Sun Valley ski area).

14.5 Trail crosses railroad trestle.

15.0 Junction with underpass to Lane Ranch and Elkhorn.

15.6 Bear left at two-way junction to bypass the city of Ketchum.

16.0 Junction with River Run access to Bald Mountain. Go straight.

16.7 Paved pathway becomes a streetside bike lane for several blocks in Ketchum. Follow the well-signed pathway to the school and pass through the school grounds to Warm Springs Road.

17.2 Cross Warm Springs Road and then take an immediate right-hand turn on the next street to pick up the paved pathway as it heads for Saddle Road.

17.8 Saddle Road junction (traffic light). This is the pathway access to Sun Valley and Elkhorn. Stay on the left side of ID 75 and continue north to Lake Creek.

19.0 Junction with Adams Gulch Road, access to a plethora of mountain trails in the Sawtooth National Recreation Area. Continue heading north.

19.7 Parking and trail access at Sun Peak picnic area. Nice riverside spot for a picnic.

20.8 Parking and trail access at Lake Creek Trailhead, the northern end of the paved trail.

Ketchum–Sun Valley–Elkhorn Loop

0.0 Start in the Broadway Run Parking Area, south of Ketchum. Ride north out of the parking lot and ride the underpass to the railroad trestle.

1.1 Note Elkhorn Road (traffic light) junction. You will return to the Wood River Trail at this point. Ride north toward Ketchum.

1.7 Bear left at two-way junction to bypass the city of Ketchum.

2.1 Junction with River Run access to Bald Mountain. Go straight.

2.8 Paved pathway becomes a streetside bike lane for several blocks in Ketchum. Follow the well-signed pathway to the school and pass through the school grounds to Warm Springs Road.

3.3 Cross Warm Springs Road and then take an immediate right-hand turn on the next street to pick up the paved pathway as it heads for Saddle Road.

4.0 Saddle Road junction (traffic light). Turn right, cross ID 75, and follow the bike lane on the north side of the street over the hill.

4.6 Junction with Sun Valley Road. Go straight unless you want to turn left and take a side trip to the Sun Valley village.

5.4 Junction with Elkhorn Road. Turn right and climb up a modest hill. Spin easy gears.

6.1 At the top of the hill, bear right and go downhill!

6.6 Enter Elkhorn Village. Follow the main road under the archways and pick up the pathway on the other end of the resort center at mile 6.7. Enjoy a brisk descent and yield to uphill traffic.

9.4 Cruise by Lane Ranch development.

9.7 Follow underpass at Elkhorn traffic light and turn left on the Wood River Trail on the other side of ID 75.

10.8 Arrive at Broadway Run parking area.

Variation: The Wood River Trail also runs along Sun Valley Road, several blocks east of Ketchum. The paved trail follows a moderate uphill gradient to the Sun Valley Lodge and along the lower portion of Trail Creek Road to the Ernest Hemingway Memorial and Trail Creek cabin. It's a worthwhile side trip.

Greenhorn-Mahoney Loop

Location:	6 miles south of Ketchum.
Distance:	12.5-mile loop.
Time:	2 to 3 hours.
Tread:	12.5 miles of sweet, buffed singletrack.
Aerobic level:	Moderate to strenuous. The ride starts in a gentle meadow but it gets increasingly steeper as the trail climbs toward the ridgetop summit.
Technical difficulty:	1+ to 3-. The Greenhorn singletrack is mostly smooth and buffed, but it gets increasingly slippery toward the ridgetop summit. The Mahoney singletrack is rougher with some rock drops, tight switchbacks, and technical sections.
Highlights:	Big vistas of the Smoky, Pioneer, and Boulder mountains. Sweet singletrack in mostly shady forest and mountain meadows.
Hazards:	Loose rock; watch out for and yield to hikers and equestrians.
Land status:	Sawtooth National Forest.
Maps:	USGS Hailey, Mahoney Butte.

Greenhorn-Mahoney Loop

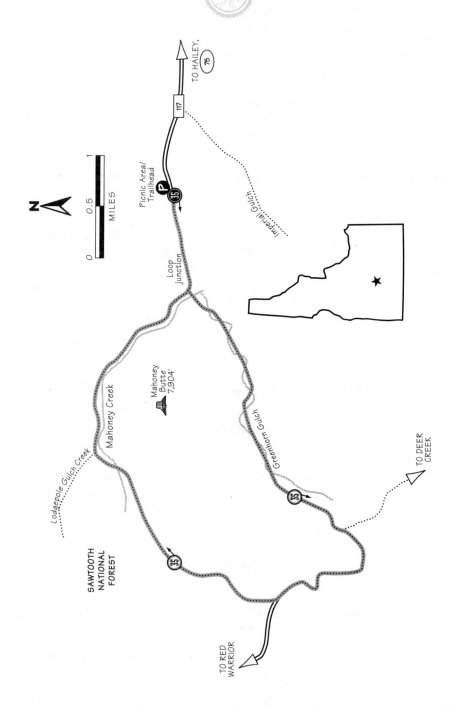

TO HAILEY, 75

117

Picnic Area/ Trailhead

P 35

Loop Junction

N

0   0.5   1
MILES

Mahoney Creek

Mahoney Butte 7,904'

Lodgepole Gulch Creek

Greenhorn Gulch

Imperial Gulch

TO DEER CREEK

35

SAWTOOTH NATIONAL FOREST

35

TO RED WARRIOR

Mark Lisk coasts through a lush meadow along Mahoney Creek, north of Hailey.

Access: From downtown Ketchum, head about 6 miles south on Idaho Highway 75 to the signed turn for Greenhorn Gulch. Turn right (west) and head up the paved and gravel road for 3.8 miles to the trailhead parking area. Watch for hazardous speed dips on the paved road.

Notes on the trail: The Greenhorn-Mahoney Loop is a popular signature singletrack ride in the Wood River valley. After you ride this trail, you'll understand why Ketchum–Sun Valley has a well-deserved reputation for its abundance of sweet singletrack loops. The Greenhorn-Mahoney Loop is very scenic as it crests an 8,000-foot ridge with fetching views of 7,900-foot Mahoney Butte, the Pioneer Range directly to the east, and the Boulder Range off to the north. Because the trail is south of Sun Valley, it doesn't get quite as much use as the rides closer to town, and it also is free of snow sooner than rides farther north in the valley. There are lots of stream crossings on this ride, so expect to get your feet wet.

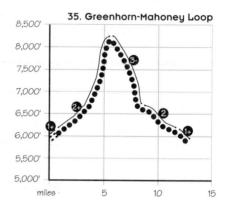

THE RIDE

0.0 Follow the singletrack out of the west side of the parking area and ride up and over a low bench, avoiding a couple of stream crossings.

0.6 Junction with Cow Creek horse trail. Go left on the Greenhorn-Mahoney trail.

0.9 Junction of Greenhorn and Mahoney trails. Go left on the Greenhorn Trail. The tread turns to singletrack here and remains so until you complete the loop.

2.1 Creek crossing (ridable).

2.4 Creek crossing (ridable).

2.6 Creek crossing (ridable).

3.0 Creek crossing (ridable).

3.1 Creek crossing (ridable) marks the beginning of increasingly steeper pitches ahead.

3.7 Two crossings (ridable).

3.9 Creek crossing.

4.3 Series of switchbacks begins.

4.4 Ignore junction with Imperial Gulch Trail 155. Trail drops into Deer Creek valley (see variation).

5.0 Junction with Howard's Trail. Bear right to stay on the Greenhorn-Mahoney trail. Big views of the surrounding countryside open up on the high ridgeline trail.

5.7 The summit. Take a moment to catch your breath and enjoy the views. Get ready for a big and fast descent.

6.1 Junction with Mahoney Creek Trail. Red Warrior Trail continues on the ridge over toward Warm Springs Creek. This is a possible variation. Bear right to descend into Mahoney Creek and complete the loop.

6.8 Rock hop over a series of ledge rocks.

7.4 Two creek crossings (ridable).

7.6 Junction with Lodgepole Gulch Trail. Go right on Mahoney.

8.1 Giant gravel heaps in middle of trail. Carry some speed to avoid bogging down.

9.3 Junction with Lodgepole Gulch. Go right on Mahoney. Drop into your low gear for an abrupt uphill pitch and stream crossing ahead.

10.0 Creek crossing (ridable).

10.4 Short uphill pitch.

10.8 Pass through gate.

11.6 Junction with Greenhorn Gulch Trail. You've completed the loop. As you return to the trailhead, bear left to avoid creek crossings.

12.5 Arrive at trailhead. Wahoo!

Variation 1: At the 4.4-mile mark, turn left and drop into the Imperial Gulch, which loops back to the trailhead, or drop into Deer Creek, another nice singletrack that descends the Deer Creek valley. Both trails are worth checking out after you do the Greenhorn-Mahoney Loop.

Variation 2: After you crest the ridgetop at mile 5.7, it's possible to follow the ridge trail to Red Warrior Creek and drop into Warfield Hot Springs on Warm Springs Road. The Red Warrior Trail is gnarly, with about 20 stream crossings, so this is not a ride for the uninitiated. You also will have to wade across Warm Springs Creek. But a nice hot springs awaits afterward. If you choose to do this lengthy loop, it's best to plant a vehicle on Warm Springs Road to cut down on the mammoth flat ride back to Greenhorn Gulch to pick up your vehicle.

Bald Mountain: Cold Springs Trail

Location:	Ketchum.
Distance:	11.5 miles from the top of the chair lift back to the base area.
Time:	45 minutes and up.
Tread:	8 miles of singletrack, 1.5 miles of doubletrack, 2 miles of paved pathway.
Aerobic level:	Moderate (all downhill).

Bald Mountain: Cold Springs Trail

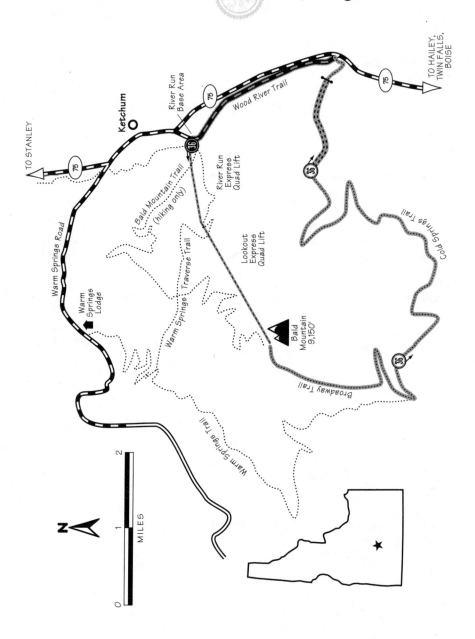

The Cold Springs singletrack at Sun Valley ski area features many nice rounded corners in open terrain on the south side of Bald Mountain.

Technical difficulty:	2. Riders should have some experience riding singletrack trails and know how to use their front brake before attempting this ride.
Highlights:	Glorious singletrack riding on open grassy mountain slopes with awesome views of the Pioneer and Smoky mountains as well as the Wood River valley.
Hazards:	Exercise caution to avoid getting pitched off the steep edges of the trail.
Land status:	Sawtooth National Forest.
Maps:	Sun Valley trail maps are best for this ride.

Access: Ride or drive to the well-signed River Run base area of the Sun Valley ski area, on the south end of Ketchum. Lift tickets are available at the lodge (1998 prices: $14 for one ride; $22 all day). Purchase a ticket and ride the lift.

Notes on the trail: The Sun Valley Company did a beautiful job building the brand new singletrack trails on Bald Mountain. The Cold Springs Trail has a much more open and distinctly different feel than the more woodsy and technical Warm Springs Trail. Local hard-cores ride up the Cold Springs Trail and descend the Warm Springs Trail. After riding down the Cold Springs Trail, you can make the judgment on whether you're interested in gutting out a 3,330-vertical-foot climb to the top of Bald Mountain! New riders should beware of soft dirt on both sides of the well-compacted singletrack, which could cause you to cartwheel off the trail or crash. As you're descending, be sure to use your front brake and feather your back brake to avoid skidding and causing trail damage. Keep most of your weight on the pedals, positioned in a nine o'clock and three o'clock position, for the best stability. The mountaintop restaurant has food and refreshments during the hours of lift operation.

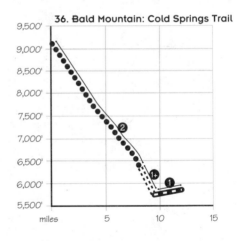

36. Bald Mountain: Cold Springs Trail

THE RIDE

0.0 Soak in the views at the top of Bald Mountain, elevation 9,010 feet, and hook up with the downhill singletrack that carries riders around the back of the mountain to a two-way junction.

1.8 Ignore junction to Seattle Ridge.

2.4 Two-way junction for Cold Springs and Warm Springs trails. Go left on Cold Springs. You can see the trail snake across the grass and sagebrush ahead.

4.5 Overlook rest stop.

5.9 Enter forest cover for a bit. Trail gets steeper.

7.5 Pass Cold Springs lift.

8.0 Singletrack dumps out on doubletrack road. Follow signs to stay on trail.

8.8 Doubletrack intersects with another gravel road. Continue downhill.

9.1 Pass through gate.

9.5 Veer left on singletrack leading to gravel road and then the Wood River paved trail (mile 9.6). Turn left on the paved trail and head back to River Run for your next ride.

11.3 Peel left off the paved trail and ride to the bottom of River Run.

11.5 Arrive at the bottom of River Run.

Bald Mountain: Warm Springs Trail

Location:	Ketchum.
Distance:	14.6 miles from the top of the chair lift back to the base area.
Time:	1 hour and up.
Tread:	11.2 miles of singletrack, 2 miles of paved road, 1.4 miles of paved pathway.
Aerobic level:	Moderate (all downhill).
Technical difficulty:	2 to 2 + . Riders should have some experience riding singletrack trails and know how to use their front brake before attempting this ride.
Highlights:	Very cool singletrack riding through dense forest on Warm Springs (north) side of Bald Mountain.
Hazards:	Exercise caution to avoid getting pitched off the steep edges of the trail and hit a tree.
Land status:	Sawtooth National Forest.
Maps:	Sun Valley has the best trail maps for the ride.

Access: Ride or drive to the well-signed River Run base area of Sun Valley ski area, on the south end of Ketchum. Lift tickets are available at the lodge (1998 prices: $14 for one ride; $22 all day). Purchase a ticket and ride the lift.

Notes on the trail: The Sun Valley Company did a beautiful job building the brand new singletrack trails on Bald Mountain. The Warm Springs Trail is more technical than the Cold Springs Trail because it snakes through a dense lodgepole and fir forest, meaning that a fall off the edge of the trail

Bald Mountain: Warm Springs Trail

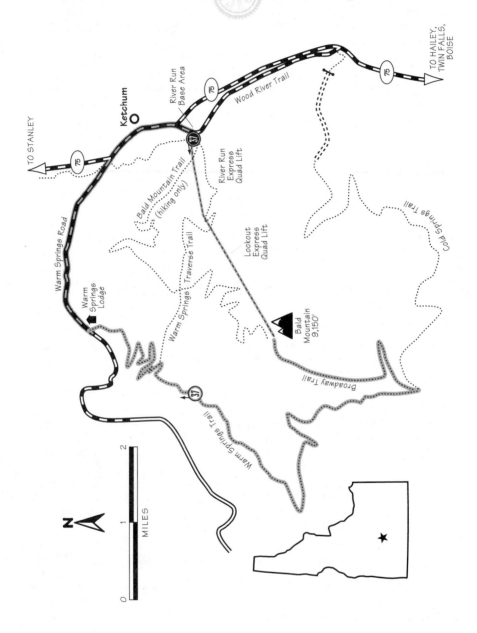

Ketchum

TO STANLEY

TO HAILEY, TWIN FALLS, BOISE

75

75

75

River Run Base Area

Wood River Trail

River Run Express Quad Lift

Bald Mountain Trail (hiking only)

Lookout Express Quad Lift

Warm Springs Road

Warm Springs Lodge

Warm Springs Traverse Trail

37

37

Bald Mountain 9,150'

Broadway Trail

Cold Springs Trail

Warm Springs Trail

N

MILES

0   1   2

The Warm Springs Trail at Sun Valley ski area is wooded and technical on the north side of Baldy.

could have bad consequences. New riders should beware of soft dirt on both sides of the well-compacted singletrack, which could cause you to cartwheel off the trail or crash. As you're descending, be sure to use your front brake and feather your back brake to avoid skidding and causing trail damage. Keep most of your weight on the pedals, positioned in a nine o'clock and three o'clock position, for the best stability. The mountaintop restaurant has food and refreshments during the hours of lift operation.

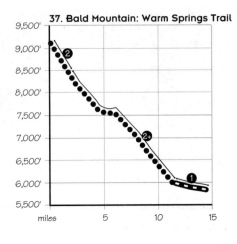

37. Bald Mountain: Warm Springs Trail

THE RIDE

0.0 Hook up with the downhill singletrack that carries riders around the back of the mountain to a well-signed two-way junction.

1.8 Ignore junction to Seattle Ridge.

2.4 Two-way junction for Cold Springs and Warm Springs trails. Go right on the Warm Springs Trail.

4.3 Pass junction with Monarch viewpoint (hiking only).

4.8 Trail climbs for a short distance to mile 5.3.

5.4 Pass Little America Overlook.

8.0 Junction with Warm Springs Traverse Trail. Stronger riders should consider this trail as an alternative route to ride back to River Run on uphill dirt trails. The Traverse Trail is the most challenging trail on Bald Mountain. This junction marks the beginning of a number of fun switchbacks on the final descent to the Warm Springs base area.

11.2 Arrive at Warm Springs lift and lodge. Take the paved road out to Warm Springs Road, turn right, and ride back to River Run.

13.2 Pick up the Wood River Trail in Ketchum and take the paved pathway to River Run.

14.6 Arrive in River Run.

38

Adams Gulch Loop

Location:	2 miles north of Ketchum.
Distance:	7-mile loop.
Time:	1 hour and up.
Tread:	3 miles of doubletrack, 4 miles of singletrack.
Aerobic level:	Moderate climbing at the beginning gives way to strenuous climbing toward the top of the loop cutoff. Then the payoff begins.
Technical difficulty:	2 to 2+ on singletrack.
Highlights:	Premium singletrack riding amid aspen trees and buffed and beautiful Sun Valley people.
Hazards:	Congestion. The Adams Gulch area is the most popular destination for mountain bikers in the Ketchum–Sun Valley area. Please ride at a speed in which you can instantly yield to pedestrians, equestrians, and uphill riders.
Land status:	Sawtooth National Recreation Area.
Maps:	USGS Griffin Butte.

Access: Ride or drive north of Ketchum about 1.5 miles to the well-marked left-hand turn for Adams Gulch Road (accessible from the paved Wood River Trail). Turn left and drive through a subdivision. At a T-intersection, bear left and head for the trailhead, a graveled parking area with a restroom.

Notes on the trail: The Adams Gulch Loop will acquaint riders with the immense possibilities on Sun Valley's buffed singletrack trails. As mentioned above, Adams Gulch is very popular because of the variety of trails in the valley as well as its connections to other trails nearby. After completing this loop ride, riders can try other options in the area. The trail network here is well maintained and well signed, thanks to the hard work of volunteers dedicated to enhancing the Wood River trail system. Inquire at Sun Summit Sports in Ketchum or the Ketchum Ranger District if you'd like to contribute financially or get involved in the next trail work project.

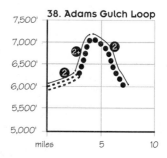

143

Adams Gulch Loop

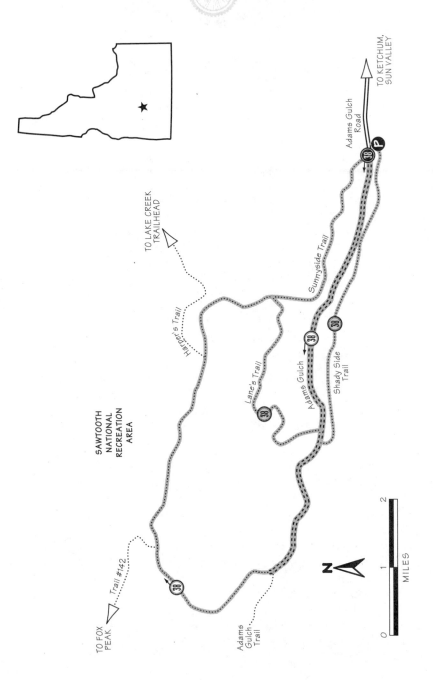

SAWTOOTH
NATIONAL
RECREATION
AREA

TO KETCHUM,
SUN VALLEY

Adams Gulch Road

TO LAKE CREEK
TRAILHEAD

Sunnyside Trail

Harper's Trail

Lane's Trail

Adams Gulch

Shady Side Trail

TO FOX PEAK

Trail #142

Adams Gulch Trail

N

MILES

0   1   2

0.0 Head out of the parking area and ride up the doubletrack road along Adams Gulch. Advanced riders may wish to take the Shady Side singletrack on the left side of the draw.

0.2 Creek crossing (ridable in low water).

1.8 Creek crossing (ridable in low water).

2.5 Two creek crossings (ridable in low water) and junction with Lane's Trail.

3.0 Two-way singletrack junction at end of doubletrack trail. Go right and climb toward the summit of the loop.

3.8 Reach loop summit. Singletrack merges with Lake Creek Trail 142. Here comes the cool downhill section among the aspen trees.

4.8 Junction with Harper's Trail. Bear right to return to Adams Gulch.

6.0 Junction with Lane's Trail on right. Bear left and continue going down.

6.1 Junction with Adams Gulch link. Keep going straight.

6.3 Bear left at fork.

7.0 Arrive in Adams Gulch parking lot.

Variation: Beginning riders may want to shorten the loop going up Adams Gulch to Lane's Trail. Turn right and loop back on Lane's Trail and the Sunnyside Trail to the trailhead. You'll still have to climb up Lane's Trail but it's not as long or steep as the Adams Gulch Loop. This variation is about 6 miles long.

East Fork Baker–Curly's Loop

Location:	14 miles north of Ketchum.
Distance:	12.7-mile loop.
Time:	2 hours.
Tread:	3.1 miles of gravel road, 5.2 miles of doubletrack, 3.3 miles of singletrack, 1 mile of paved road.
Aerobic level:	Moderate. The climb up the East Fork doubletrack road never gets ridiculously steep, and most of it can be ridden in the middle ring. Total vertical rise is 1,525 feet over 8.3 miles.
Technical difficulty:	1+ to 3+. Curly's singletrack features one eroded and trenched-out section that rates 3+. Otherwise, it's a smooth trail.
Highlights:	Spectacular frontal view of the Boulder Mountain range at the summit of the loop ride; gorgeous singletrack descent through the pine trees back to Easley Hot Springs.

East Fork Baker–Curly's Loop

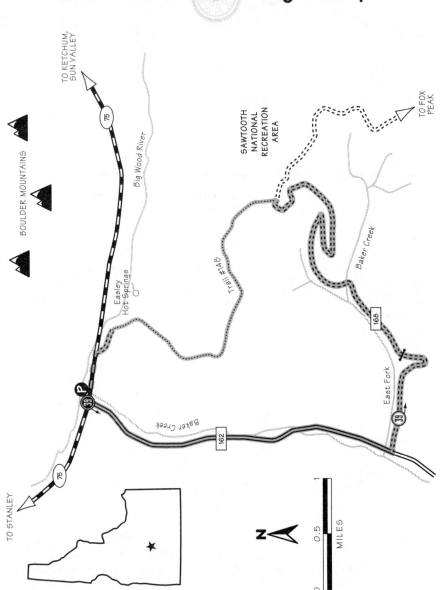

Access: From Ketchum, head north 24 miles on Idaho Highway 75 to a well-signed parking area at the mouth of Baker Creek. There is a restroom here.

Notes on the trail: The East Fork Baker–Curly's Loop is a nifty less-crowded alternative to singletrack riding in the Adams Gulch area. True, you have to climb to the singletrack on gravel and doubletrack roads, but a lot of riders don't mind climbing on doubletracks. The views of the Boulder Mountains from the summit of this loop ride are spectacular. Backcountry skiers who make it a point to visit Tornak yurt in the wintertime will enjoy seeing this area in the summer. For riders who book a night or two at the Coyote yurt (farther up the road, see Ride 40 for details), this is an alternative way out of the Smokies—a must-do ride. Consider camping at least one night along the Baker Creek road. It's a car-camping mecca with a plethora of nice creekside sites (no services).

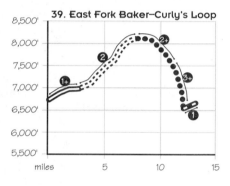

39. East Fork Baker–Curly's Loop

THE RIDE

0.0 Head out of the Baker Creek parking lot, cross ID 75, and head up the Baker Creek gravel road, Forest Road 162.

2.9 Cross the East Fork of Baker Creek on a bridge.

3.1 East Fork doubletrack junction (signed). Turn left and spin up the East Fork road.

4.2 Pass through Forest Service gate (closed August to June).

5.1 Ignore logging road on right. Descend a bit and climb again.

5.7 Ignore logging road on left. Keep climbing on main road.

6.1 The road gets markedly steeper for a short distance and tapers again at mile 6.5.

8.0 Come around a sharp corner and the steep-faced Boulder Mountains come into view. Hello!

8.3 The turn for Curly's comes up on the left in the form of a grassy doubletrack, which dissolves into singletrack immediately. Nordic skiers will recognize this junction. Soak in the view and turn left to cruise into the trees. Here comes the fun part!

10.8 Confront steep eroded section of trail. Correct body position and proper use of brakes are critical here. Following the steep descent the trail winds through tall grass and pine trees—truly gorgeous riding on a curling trail.

11.7 Singletrack dumps out on dirt road by a number of summer cabins. Ride on dirt roads next to highway and then jump on ID 75 and ride a mile back to the Baker Creek parking lot.

12.7 Arrive in parking lot.

East Fork Baker–Coyote Yurt– Adams Gulch Shuttle

Location:	Start: 14 miles north of Ketchum; finish: 1.5 miles north of Ketchum.
Distance:	25 miles, one-way.
Time:	5 hours or more.
Tread:	3.1 miles of dirt road, 11.8 miles of doubletrack, 10.1 miles of singletrack.
Aerobic level:	Moderate to strenuous. Lengthy doubletrack climb to the Coyote yurt will take a bite out of the legs for sure. And the Lake Creek Trail descent into Adams Gulch includes a number of hidden climbs.
Technical difficulty:	2+. Most of the singletrack is nice and buffed, but a number of sections are fairly rocky and technical.
Highlights:	Spectacular frontal view of the Boulder Mountain range and the Smoky Mountains near Fox Peak. Riders can rent the Coyote yurt in the summertime and make this a two- or three-day affair.
Hazards:	Exercise caution on downhill sections of the Lake Creek Trail.
Land status:	Sawtooth National Recreation Area.
Maps:	USGS Easley Hot Springs, Boyle Mountain, Griffin Butte.

Access: From Ketchum, head north 24 miles on Idaho Highway 75 to a well-signed parking area at the mouth of Baker Creek. There is a restroom here. Leave a shuttle vehicle at the Adams Gulch Trailhead.

Notes on the trail: This is a very cool around-the-world loop ride, with an optional stop at the Coyote yurt. Sun Valley Trekking rents the yurt during the summer months for $10 per person (see appendix). Plans call for placing another yurt along the Lake Creek Trail, making for a possible yurt-to-yurt mountain bike tour. It's a long, scenic climb to the Coyote yurt and an arduous descent down the Lake Creek Trail to the Adams Gulch Trailhead. Be sure to carry lots of food and water, and be prepared for changes in

East Fork Baker–Coyote Yurt–Adams Gulch Shuttle

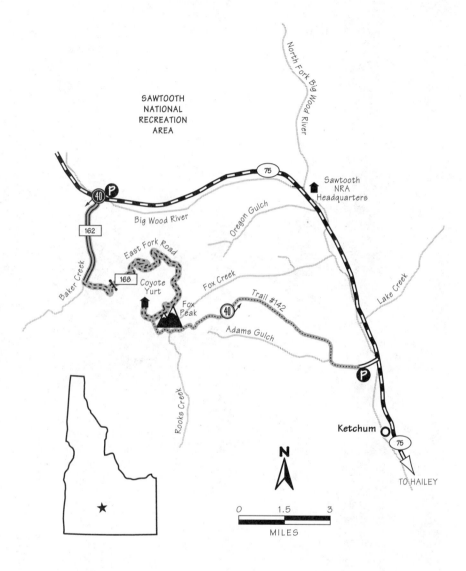

SAWTOOTH
NATIONAL
RECREATION
AREA

North Fork Big Wood River

75

Sawtooth
NRA
Headquarters

Big Wood River

Oregon Gulch

162

Baker Creek

East Fork Road

168

Coyote
Yurt

Fox Creek

Fox
Peak

Trail #142

40

Adams Gulch

Lake Creek

Rooks Creek

Ketchum

75

TO HAILEY

N

0   1.5   3

MILES

Coyote yurt is aptly named for the "yip-yip yeeoo" one is likely to hear at night near Fox Peak in the Smoky Mountains.

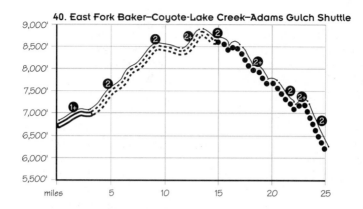

weather. When the gate is open on East Fork Road in midsummer, you can drive a 4WD vehicle with your food and sleeping bags to the Coyote yurt. Venture Outdoors, an outfitter in Hailey, offers guided trips to the Coyote yurt during the summer (see appendix).

THE RIDE

0.0 Head out of the Baker Creek parking lot, cross ID 75, and head up the Baker Creek gravel road, Forest Road 162.

3.1 Turn left at the signed junction for the doubletrack East Fork Road. Conserve energy and spin.

4.2 Pass through Forest Service gate (closed August to June).

5.1 Ignore logging road on right. Descend a bit and climb again.

5.7 Ignore logging road on left. Keep climbing on main road.

6.1 The road gets markedly steeper for a short distance and tapers again at mile 6.5.

8.0 Come around a sharp corner and the steep-faced Boulder Mountains come into view. Hello!

8.3 The turn for Curly's comes up on the left in the form of a grassy doubletrack, which dissolves into singletrack immediately. Nordic skiers will recognize this junction. Soak in the view and turn left to cruise into the trees. Stay on doubletrack.

9.3 Pass by location of Tornak hut on the left. Telemark skiers will be familiar with this site. The road will flatten out shortly and descend toward a trail junction near Fox Peak.

11.4 Singletrack peels left toward the Lake Creek Trail. Continue on the doubletrack road to head for Coyote yurt. Now you're climbing again.

12.4 Bear right at major two-way junction.

13.0 Watch for a grassy doubletrack road on the right. This is the access trail to the Coyote yurt. Drop into granny gear, turn right, cross a little gully, and climb the steep trail to the yurt.

13.5 Arrive at the well-hidden yurt in the trees. Lunchtime! Shuttle in your goods if you're staying here for the night, or take a break.

14.0 Descend back to the doubletrack road. Go left.

14.6 At the major two-way junction, go right.

14.7 Bear left on a doubletrack road.

14.9 Doubletrack dissolves into singletrack. Climb to a saddle.

15.2 Crest saddle and descend to signed junction with Trail 142 (your downhill singletrack) and Rooks Creek. Go left on Trail 142.

15.8 Ignore singletrack on right.

16.5 Crest high summit, followed by steep downhill switchbacks.

16.9 Signed junction with upper Adams Gulch Trail. Go downhill on Trail 142.

18.8 Confront rutted and eroded portion of trail. You may want to hike to avoid crashing.

20.4 Steep uphill on ridge to rocky saddle point. Take a moment to rest. Nice views from here.

21.8 Junction with Adams Gulch loop trail. Go downhill on Trail 142.

22.8 Pass junction with Harper's Trail. This trail goes to the Lake Creek Trailhead.

24.0 Pass junction with Lane's Trail.

24.3 Go left at fork to descend to Adams Gulch Trailhead.

25.0 Arrive in Adams Gulch Trailhead and parking lot. You made it!

41

Galena Lodge Beginner Loop

Location:	22 miles north of Ketchum.
Distance:	4.9-mile loop.
Time:	30 minutes and up.
Tread:	2.9 miles of doubletrack; 2 miles of pavement.
Aerobic level:	Easy.
Technical difficulty:	1+. There are a few rocky and slippery spots on the doubletrack road.
Highlights:	Mostly flat mountain bike riding in the mountains—a rare thing in Idaho.
Hazards:	None.
Land status:	Sawtooth National Recreation Area; Galena Lodge trails are managed by the Blaine County Recreation District.
Maps:	USGS Galena, Horton Peak. Galena Lodge has the best maps for its trail system.

Access: Head north out of Ketchum on Idaho Highway 75 and go 22 miles to the well-signed parking area for Galena Lodge on the right side of the road.

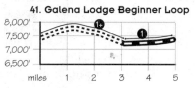

41. Galena Lodge Beginner Loop

Galena Lodge Beginner Loop and
Galena Rip and Tear Loop

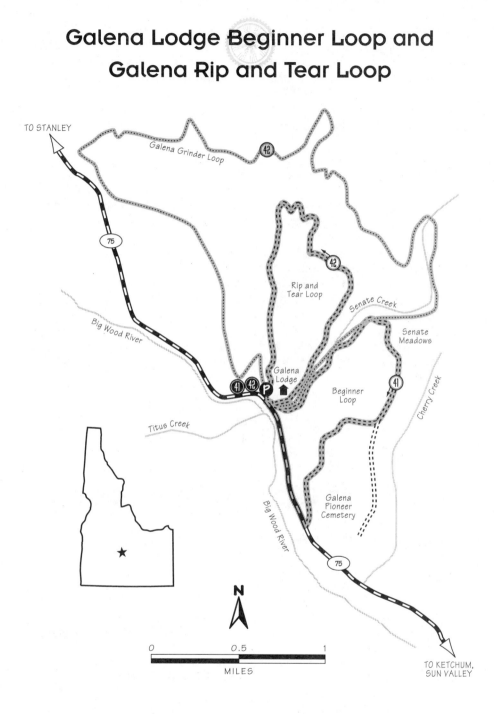

TO STANLEY

Galena Grinder Loop

42

75

42

Rip and
Tear Loop

Senate Creek

Big Wood River

Senate
Meadows

Galena
Lodge

41

41 42

Beginner
Loop

Cherry Creek

P

Titus Creek

Galena
Pioneer
Cemetery

Big Wood River

75

N

0   0.5   1

MILES

TO KETCHUM,
SUN VALLEY

Notes on the trail: The Galena Lodge area is a perfect place for families with children and beginning mountain bikers to get initiated. The loop trail described here follows wide doubletrack roads on a gentle uphill or downhill slope. It's a good warm-up ride before you try something more challenging. There are four major routes at Galena Lodge, so if you're anxious to try something more difficult after finishing this ride, you can do so. Galena Lodge has food and beverage service at certain hours during the day.

THE RIDE

0.0 Head out of the parking area for the signed Galena Lodge Trailhead, next to a wooden post. You're climbing now at a gentle uphill grade.

0.2 Bear left at trail junction.

0.5 Bear left and follow signs for Grinder and Lodge loops.

0.6 Ignore singletrack on left.

1.2 Bear right on doubletrack road. Grinder Trail goes left.

1.5 Doubletrack levels out and goes downhill. Follow trail markers for the Lodge Loop.

2.9 Trail merges with another doubletrack next to fire ring, in sight of ID 75. Drop down to the highway and ride the pavement back to the lodge, or retrace your tracks.

4.9 Arrive at the lodge parking area.

Galena Rip and Tear Loop

<table>
<tr><td rowspan="2">See Map on Page 153</td><td>**Location:**</td><td>22 miles north of Ketchum.</td></tr>
<tr><td>**Distance:**</td><td>3.6-mile loop.</td></tr>
<tr><td></td><td>**Time:**</td><td>30 minutes or less.</td></tr>
<tr><td></td><td>**Tread:**</td><td>3.6 miles of doubletrack.</td></tr>
<tr><td></td><td>**Aerobic level:**</td><td>Moderate except for short steep pitch on switchbacks.</td></tr>
<tr><td></td><td>**Technical difficulty:**</td><td>1+. There are a few rocky and slippery spots on the doubletrack road.</td></tr>
<tr><td></td><td>**Highlights:**</td><td>Scenic but short mountain bike ride—good destination for families with children.</td></tr>
<tr><td></td><td>**Hazards:**</td><td>None.</td></tr>
<tr><td></td><td>**Land status:**</td><td>Sawtooth National Recreation Area; Galena Lodge trails are managed by the Blaine County Recreation District.</td></tr>
<tr><td></td><td>**Maps:**</td><td>USGS Galena, Horton Peak. Galena Lodge has a free trail map.</td></tr>
</table>

Galena Lodge's rolling terrain, north of Sun Valley, is ideally suited for kids learning how to mountain bike.

Access: Head north out of Ketchum on Idaho Highway 75 and go 22 miles to the well-signed parking area for Galena Lodge on the right side of the road.

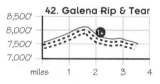

Notes on the trail: The Galena Lodge area is a perfect place for families with children and for beginning mountain bikers to get initiated. The loop trail described here involves more challenging uphill and downhill riding than the Galena Lodge Beginner Loop. This is a good ride to try after the beginner loop. There are four major routes at Galena Lodge, so if you're anxious to try something more difficult after finishing this ride, go for the Grinder. Galena Lodge has food and beverage service at certain hours during the day.

THE RIDE

0.0 Head out of the parking area and ride uphill in Gladiator Meadow. Follow signs for Rip and Tear.

1.1 Cross Gladiator Creek and climb first of several switchbacks. Follow orange diamonds for Rip and Tear. The doubletrack courses through Senate Meadows and heads back to the lodge.

4.5 Arrive back at the parking lot.

Variation: If you survived Rip and Tear, maybe you're ready for the Psycho Trail or the Galena Grinder, the longest and most technical ride here at 10 miles. The Grinder Trail starts with a ride up into Senate Meadows, and then it branches off to the left up Senate Creek. The trail winds up and down as it contours around the headwaters of Gladiator Creek. Follow the signs for the Grinder as it swings back to Galena Lodge. The Grinder Trail is also used as a race course.

Fisher–Williams Loop

Location:	13.5 miles south of Stanley.
Distance:	18-mile loop.
Time:	1.5 to 3 hours, depending on length of lunch break and speed of travel.
Tread:	2.3 miles of paved road, 2 miles of gravel road, 4.8 miles of doubletrack, 8.9 miles of singletrack.
Aerobic level:	Moderate most of the way, with the exception of several short steep climbs.
Technical difficulty:	2 overall. Most of the singletrack is so smooth it would rate 1+, but there are a few rough spots that rate 2+.
Highlights:	Very scenic loop ride in the White Cloud Mountains with nearly 9 miles of very entertaining singletrack—lots of S-curves and fun maneuvering.
Hazards:	Please yield to horseback riders, backpackers, and other cyclists.
Land status:	Sawtooth National Recreation Area.
Maps:	USGS Obsidian, Washington Peak. Sawtooth National Recreation Area map.

Access: From Stanley, take Idaho Highway 75 about 13.5 miles south to the well-marked Williams Creek Trailhead, on the east side of the road. The ride starts here. There is a restroom at the trailhead. A Sawtooth National Recreation Area recreation permit is required for your vehicle. Permits are available at the Mountain Village Hotel in Stanley, the Stanley Ranger District, and several other businesses in town.

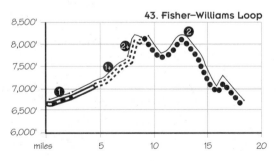

Fisher–Williams Loop

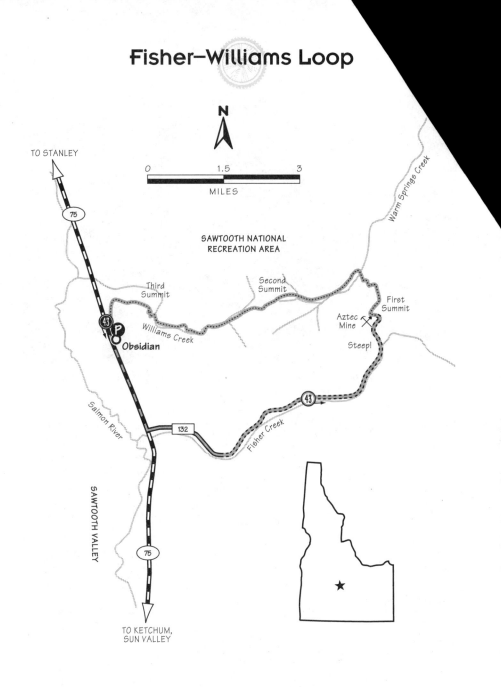

N

0   1.5   3
MILES

TO STANLEY

75

SAWTOOTH NATIONAL
RECREATION AREA

Third
Summit

Second
Summit

First
Summit

Aztec
Mine

43

P

Williams Creek

Obsidian

Steep!

Salmon River

132

43

Fisher Creek

SAWTOOTH VALLEY

75

TO KETCHUM,
SUN VALLEY

Warm Springs Creek

Jenny Hennessy emerges in the Sawtooth Valley on the trail end of the Fisher-Williams Loop, an Idaho classic. PHOTO BY LEO HENNESSY

Notes on the trail: The Fisher-Williams Loop is an Idaho classic. Once we locals discovered this trail in the 1980s, word traveled quickly that it's a must-do type of ride. It became one of the most popular rides in the state, and it remains so today. This reputation is well deserved. The climb up Fisher Creek is secluded and scenic, winding through beaver ponds and aspen trees. A short, abrupt climb to the Aztec Mine is followed by the first of three ripping downhills on incredibly buffed trails. A second moderate climb up the head of Warm Springs Creek is followed by a long continuous descent into Williams Creek. Save energy for a third climb over a sagebrush bluff before the final descent into the Sawtooth Valley. Take a moment to look up as you're descending Williams Creek to soak in views of the Sawtooth Wilderness, directly across the valley.

THE RIDE

0.0 Take ID 75 south from the Williams Creek trailhead to the signed turnoff for the Fisher Creek road on the left.

2.3 Turn left on the Fisher Creek road (Forest Road 132) and head east into the White Clouds on the well-traveled dirt road.

4.5 Tread turns to more primitive doubletrack and climbs at a moderate pace past a series of beaver ponds.

8.0 Fisher Creek doubletrack gets markedly steeper for the next half-mile, culminating in a couple granny-gear steep-faced climbs on a loose gravel surface before the mine summit.

9.1 Crest the summit. A Forest Service registration box is on the right side of the trail. Pass through an open wooden gate and begin the first descent. Wahoo! Watch out for large ruts and obstacles close to the trail.

10.7 At the bottom of the first hill, bear left at a trail junction in the trees.

10.9 The trail quickly breaks into the open in Pigtail Meadows. Cross the creek and spin up a moderate grade for a couple miles to the subtle top of the draw.

12.8 Crest the saddle. Here comes one beautiful cruiser of a downhill trail. Take a moment along the way to enjoy the views of the Sawtooths, and *please*, be ready to stop and yield to uphill horseback riders, motorcycle riders, and mountain bikers.

16.1 Trail breaks into a meadow and crosses several wooden bridges. One more short climb to go. The trail switchbacks and climbs at a steep gradient for a short distance.

16.5 Crest the final summit. It's a short descent before rounding the corner into the Sawtooth Valley.

18.0 Arrive at the Williams Creek Trailhead. The biggest disappointment is that the ride has to be over . . . like a good movie or a dream you never want to end.

Knapp Creek–Valley Creek Cruiser

Location:	15 miles west of Stanley.
Distance:	19.5-mile loop.
Time:	2 to 3 hours.
Tread:	11.8 miles of singletrack, 4.6 miles of doubletrack, 3.1 miles of gravel road.
Aerobic level:	Moderate to easy. The only strenuous section of the trail runs for 0.3 mile. Total trip distance may make this ride a bit daunting for novice riders.
Technical difficulty:	1+ to 2 on buffed singletrack and doubletracks.
Highlights:	Beautiful cruise up and down the lush high-elevation meadows of Knapp Creek and Valley Creek. Good potential for seeing wildlife.
Hazards:	Please yield to horseback riders, hikers, and motorcyclists. This loop is bound to become more popular as people discover it.
Land status:	Challis National Forest, Sawtooth National Recreation Area.
Maps:	USGS Langer Peak, Elk Meadows.

Knapp Creek–Valley Creek Cruiser

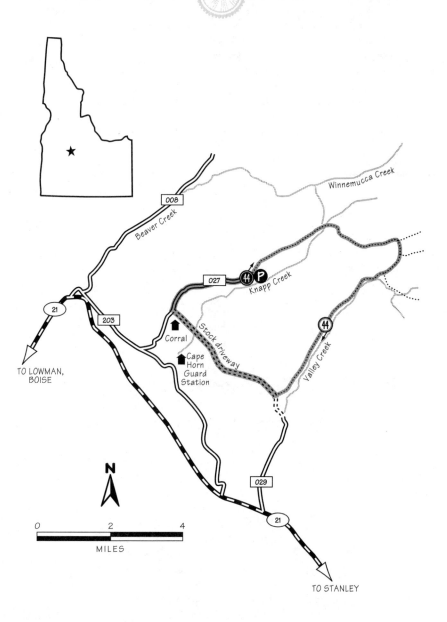

Access: From Lowman, follow Idaho Highway 21 toward Stanley. About 8 miles after Banner Summit, watch for a signed left-hand turnoff to Lola Creek Campground and the Bradley Memorial Camp. Turn left and then take an immediate right. Follow Forest Road 203 for 2.5 miles to a signed left-hand turn for Knapp/Asher creeks (FR 027). Turn left and follow the main road 4.3 miles to the Knapp Creek Trailhead. Park. The ride starts here. Shuttle: To trim 8 miles off this ride, plant a vehicle along the Valley Creek road (FR 029). It's a decent jeep trail road that leads to the Valley Creek Trailhead.

Notes on the trail: This is a sweet one, folks. The Knapp Creek–Valley Creek Loop takes you through some gorgeous wilderness-quality, high-mountain meadow country—elk haven in the spring and fall. The trail tread is wide-track singletrack, which winds through the meadows bordered by lodgepole pine forests and the rounded mountains above. There are several easy stream crossings (potentially gnarly in the spring), one steep descent for 0.3 mile at the summit, and then a real buffed zoom down Valley Creek. Please keep your speed in control on the way down Valley Creek; other people may be coming up the trail. Anglers may want to pack along a fly rod.

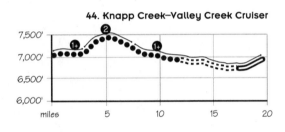

44. Knapp Creek–Valley Creek Cruiser

THE RIDE

0.0 Jump on the Knapp Creek Trail on the east side of the parking lot and spin up a gentle incline on a narrow-gauge doubletrack trail in a lodgepole forest, which dissolves into wide-track singletrack.

1.9 Ignore a trail on the left. Bear right. The trail continues to cruise above the Knapp Creek meadow on the forest edge at a slight incline.

2.0 Emerge in a beautiful meadow. Trail jumps up on the shoulder of the meadow to avoid resource damage.

2.9 Trail comes up alongside Knapp Creek. Good place to take a breather and water the dogs.

3.1 Junction with Winnemucca Creek on the left. Go right and cross a fork of Knapp Creek. There's a steep hill coming up; gear down and climb for a mile or so.

5.4 Come to the Valley Creek connector trail. Go right and cross Knapp Creek (the water level is so deep, even in the fall, that it's a wade-and-carry situation). Get into your small ring and climb a steep hill with tree roots across it for an added challenge.

5.7 Reach the crest of the hill. Now it's time to cruise downhill! Don't get carried away off the top because the Valley Creek Trailhead (Trail 039) is coming up quickly.

6.0 Turn right on Valley Creek. The junction is signed on a tree. Now you're home free to cruise downhill for nearly 6 miles! Wahoo! Please be prepared to slow down and yield to other trail users. This trail is buffed for big fun. Be sure to stop along the way to look for wildlife in the meadows. If you're really lucky, you might see a giant Chinook salmon in Valley Creek, digging a redd.

11.8 Reach the end of the Valley Creek singletrack. If you left a vehicle here, you're done! If not, send a couple strong riders to fetch the vehicle at the Knapp Creek Trailhead. To get there, head left toward the powerlines at the trailhead area and then turn right under the powerlines and head west. You're now on the Center Stock Driveway in the Stanley Basin. It's a wide dirt road that follows the powerline corridor to a corral alongside Knapp Creek. Bear right at several junctions to avoid going to Cape Horn Guard Station.

15.3 Cross a bridge over Kelly Creek.

16.3 The road peels left and right near the corrals. Go left, cross the creek, and go straight to the Knapp Creek Road (FR 027). Turn right and it's 3.1 miles to the trailhead.

19.5 Arrive at the trailhead.

Stanley Lake–Elk Meadows Loop

Location:	5 miles west of Stanley.
Distance:	12.5-mile loop.
Time:	1.5 to 2 hours.
Tread:	1.8 miles of gravel road, 4.4 miles of singletrack, 6.3 miles of doubletrack.
Aerobic level:	Mostly very moderate. None of the climbs on this loop lasts for long.
Technical difficulty:	2+ on the first part of the Elk Meadows singletrack (very rocky), but it's pretty smooth the rest of the way (1+ to 2).
Highlights:	Sweet singletrack riding in elk meadows. Drop-dead gorgeous views of the north face of the Sawtooth Mountains.
Hazards:	Rocky descent into Elk Meadows.
Land status:	Sawtooth National Recreation Area.
Maps:	USGS Stanley Lake, Elk Meadows.

Access: From Stanley, go west on Idaho Highway 21 about 5 miles to the well-signed left-hand turn for Stanley Lake. Proceed toward Stanley Lake Campground on Forest Road 455. As you approach the lake, notice Forest

Stanley Lake–Elk Meadows Loop

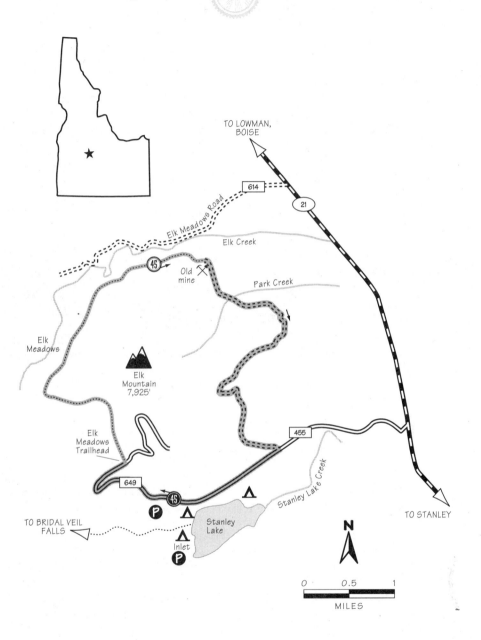

TO LOWMAN,
BOISE

614

21

Elk Meadows Road

Elk Creek

45

Old
mine

Park Creek

Elk
Meadows

Elk
Mountain
7,925'

455

Elk
Meadows
Trailhead

Stanley Lake Creek

649

45

TO STANLEY

P

TO BRIDAL VEIL
FALLS

Stanley
Lake

Inlet

P

N

0   0.5   1

MILES

Road 649 peeling off to the right. This is the start of the ride. The Forest Service plans to develop a new trailhead parking area at the beginning of the road. Please park here unless you've already got a campsite at Stanley Lake.

Notes on the trail: The Stanley Lake–Elk Meadows Loop has been a local standard in the Stanley area for years. It was one of the first mountain bike trails signed and developed by the Stanley Ranger District. The loop trail is an excellent activity as part of a weekend campout at Stanley Lake, and it's a worthwhile ride to pick off as part of a multiday mountain bike and white-water adventure in the Stanley area. Strong intermediate riders and teenagers should be able to handle the loop because of the lack of continuous strenuous climbing. Be sure to pay attention to trail junctions: the route can be a little confusing in and as you leave Elk Meadows, pass by some old mining areas, and follow jeep trails back toward Stanley Lake.

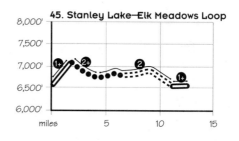

THE RIDE

0.0 Head up FR 649 and watch for a signed trailhead for the Elk Meadows Trail on the left.

1.8 Elk Meadows Trailhead. Go left and exercise caution as you ride over lots of baby head-shaped rocks and tree roots. Don't worry, the trail will get smoother ahead.

3.3 Enter Elk Meadows, a spacious lush meadow that's home to hundreds of elk in the spring and fall. Turn right on the faint trail on the right (east) side of the meadow. Please do not cross the fragile meadows on your bike.

4.9 Pass by a shallow lake next to some lodgepole trees.

5.3 Go right on the trail next to Elk Creek. This is the old Elk Meadows doubletrack. As the trail passes through the trees, it becomes a doubletrack tread. You'll pass by an old mine here.

6.5 Drop into Park Creek for a moment and confront a junction. Go straight and enjoy some nice meandering through meadows and lodgepole pines.

9.8 Go left at a trail junction and climb over a little bluff on the doubletrack. After you crest the hill, it's a fun descent back to the Stanley Lake road.

11.3 When the descent ends, you'll emerge into a primitive camping area next to Stanley Lake road. Ride through the area, turn right on the main road, and head back to your rig.

12.5 Complete the loop at FR 649.

Pocatello: Convenient Riding
Close to Town

Riding in the Portneuf Mountains, on the edge of Pocatello, is so convenient that locals ride directly from their home to the trail. Even if you're just visiting, the trails are close to Idaho State University, hotels, and campgrounds.

All of the trails in this area are nestled in the Portneuf Mountains—angular, steep mountains with lots of singletrack. Tree cover is thick in the draws and sparse on open mountain slopes. The season for riding in the Pocatello area is pretty typical of most mountain locations—May through October. The lower City Creek trails open up before the Mink Creek trails. Camping opportunities are extensive in the Caribou National Forest in the Mink Creek Recreation Area. Be sure to stock up on supplies in town before heading off into the forest.

As for other activities, Pocatello has a rich history as a gateway city for Native American trappers and, later, the Union Pacific Railroad. The Pocatello Zoo, Bannock County Historical Museum, and a replica of Fort Hall, a key trading center during the beaver-trapping era, are all located at upper Ross Park. Lava Hot Springs, a private spa and resort near Pocatello, has three restaurants, a museum, and a nine-hole golf course. The Fort Hall Indian Reservation presents a number of powwows during the summer, complete with dancing, song, drums, and colorful native dress.

City Creek Beginner Loop

Location:	Pocatello.
Distance:	3-mile loop.
Time:	30 minutes or less.
Tread:	1.8 miles of singletrack, 1.2 miles of doubletrack.
Aerobic level:	Easy. There is one short hill on this ride that can be walked, if necessary.
Technical difficulty:	1 +. The City Creek singletrack may present a few technical challenges for beginning riders.
Highlights:	Enjoyable ride on the edge of Pocatello.
Hazards:	None.
Land status:	City of Pocatello, Port Neuf Greenways Foundation.
Maps:	USGS Pocatello South.

Access: Take Benton Street to the southwest side of the city of Pocatello. Turn right on Grant Street. Follow Grant a few blocks to a Latter-Day Saints church next to the signed City Creek Trail. Park next to the fence on the southeast side of the church parking lot. The ride starts here.

Notes on the trail: The City Creek Beginner Loop will acquaint new riders with a wonderful place to ride on the edge of Pocatello. The ride follows the City Creek Trail for a short way before it switchbacks to an open sagebrush slope and climbs at a very moderate gradient to a point where you drop into City Creek and loop back to the start. If you want to continue climbing at the loop junction, just keep going up as far as you please. The trail gets progressively steeper and more technical as it proceeds up the tree-lined draw.

THE RIDE

0.0 Head up the City Creek Trail. The doubletrack dissolves into singletrack in the first 0.1 mile.

0.3 Junction with trail on left as the City Creek Trail crosses a wooden bridge. Go left and switchback up the grassy hillside to a sagebrush flat.

0.4 Reach the top of the hill. Ride up the doubletrack trail.

0.8 Junction with singletrack. Bear right on the doubletrack.

1.6 Drop off the ridge into City Creek. Turn right, cross a wooden bridge, and ride downhill.

1.7 Bear right on the singletrack.

City Creek Beginner Loop

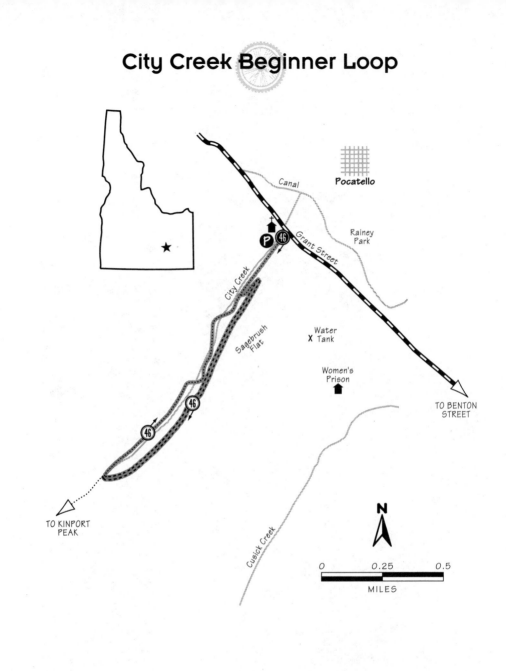

Pocatello

Canal

Rainey Park

Grant Street

City Creek

Sagebrush Flat

Water
X Tank

Women's Prison

TO KINPORT PEAK

TO BENTON STREET

Cusick Creek

N

O   0.25   0.5
MILES

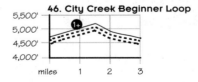

46. City Creek Beginner Loop

5,500'
5,000'
4,500'
4,000'

miles   1   2   3

The City Creek beginner ride features very moderate climbing on a sage and grassy mountain slope on the west side of Pocatello.

2.2 Technical descent into the creek bottom. Cross several wooden bridges.

2.4 Pass through wooden posts.

2.6 Loop junction. Continue heading back to the parking area.

3.0 Reach the bottom of the trail and the parking area.

47

City Creek–Outlaw Springs Loop

Location:	Pocatello.
Distance:	9.9-mile loop.
Time:	1.5 hours.
Tread:	3.6 miles of singletrack, 2.7 miles of doubletrack, 3.6 miles of paved road.
Aerobic level:	Moderately strenuous on the climb up City Creek singletrack and doubletrack to the saddle above Outlaw Springs.
Technical difficulty:	Mostly level 2. The downhill singletrack to Outlaw Springs rates a 3+ because of the steepness, ruts, and loose gravel.
Highlights:	Great loop ride linking City Creek and Trail Creek on the edge of Pocatello.
Hazards:	Please yield to hikers, joggers, horseback riders, motorcyclists, and other mountain bikers on this loop ride.
Land status:	City of Pocatello, BLM.
Maps:	USGS Pocatello South, Michaud Creek.

Access: Take Benton Street to the southwest side of the city of Pocatello. Turn right on Grant Street. Follow Grant a few blocks to a Latter-Day Saints (LDS) church next to the signed City Creek Trail. Park next to the fence on the southeast side of the church parking lot. The ride starts here.

Notes on the trail: The City Creek–Outlaw Springs Loop is a great after-work ride or destination ride on the edge of Pocatello. Riders will get a taste for the City Creek singletrack, open sagebrush hills overlooking the city, and high ridges between City Creek and Trail Creek canyons. It's an advanced ride because of sustained climbing and a technical descent into Outlaw Springs. Because this is a popular trail, please watch out for and yield to hikers, joggers, dogs, children, horseback riders, and motorcycle riders as you ride the loop.

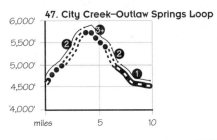

169

City Creek–Outlaw Springs Loop

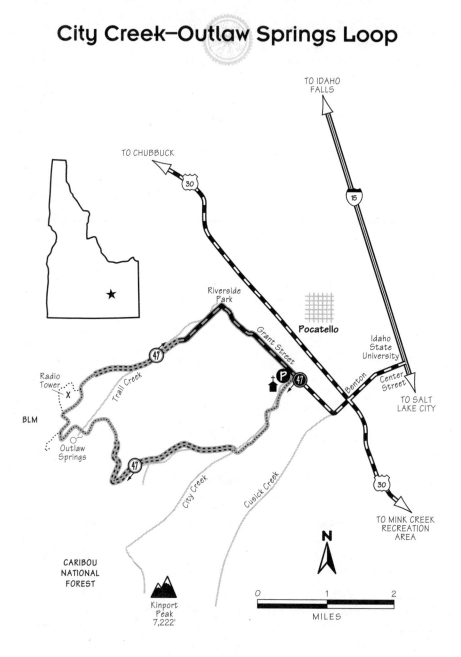

TO IDAHO FALLS

TO CHUBBUCK

30

15

Riverside Park

Pocatello

Grant Street

47

Radio Tower

X

BLM

Trail Creek

47

P

47

Benton

Center Street

Idaho State University

TO SALT LAKE CITY

Outlaw Springs

City Creek

Cusick Creek

30

TO MINK CREEK RECREATION AREA

N

CARIBOU NATIONAL FOREST

Kinport Peak 7,222'

0   1   2

MILES

Mark Lisk pedals into a rare opening on the tree-covered City Creek singletrack.

0.0 Head up the City Creek Trail. The doubletrack dissolves into singletrack in the first 0.1 mile. Follow the singletrack as it winds up and down in the narrow creek bottom, crossing a number of wooden bridges over the creek.

0.3 At a two-way junction by a wooden bridge, go right, cross a wooden bridge, and stay on the City Creek singletrack.

1.3 Singletrack dissolves into dirt road for a second and then continues again to the left.

1.7 Encounter three-way junction at the edge of the City Creek Trail. Go right, cross the City Creek dirt road, and pick up a doubletrack trail that heads up a side draw in the sagebrush hills.

3.3 Two-way junction at a switchback. Go right to climb to a saddle and head over to Outlaw Springs.

3.7 Crest the saddle. Bear left on the singletrack trail in front of you. Enjoy the highline contour ride to the next saddle.

4.2 Reach the next saddle. Stay on the singletrack as it crosses a faint doubletrack.

4.3 Bend left on singletrack by the sign pointing the way to Outlaw Springs. Here comes the technical steep drop into the spring. Hang on for a squirrelly descent.

4.9 Reach the spring (stock tanks full of water). Follow the singletrack into a gully, climb up the other side of the gully, and turn right, crossing a yellow cattle guard. Continue to climb on the singletrack.

5.6 Singletrack climbs to a large two-pole powerline. Now it's time to drop into the main dirt road below. Bear right and follow the eroded doubletrack road under the powerlines for a bit and then curve left.

5.9 Drop into main dirt road in the bottom of Trail Creek. Go right and descend.

6.3 Dirt road gives way to pavement. Ride down into the city to Riverside Street.

8.0 Turn right on Riverside Street next to a park. Follow Riverside Street and a number of other streets southeast to Grant Street. You're heading back toward the LDS church.

9.9 Arrive at the church parking lot.

48

Gibson Jack–West Fork Mink Loop

Location: Pocatello
Distance: 19.2-mile loop
Time: 3 hours
Tread: 9.8 miles of paved road, 7.8 miles of singletrack, 1.6 miles of doubletrack.

Gibson Jack–West Fork Mink Loop

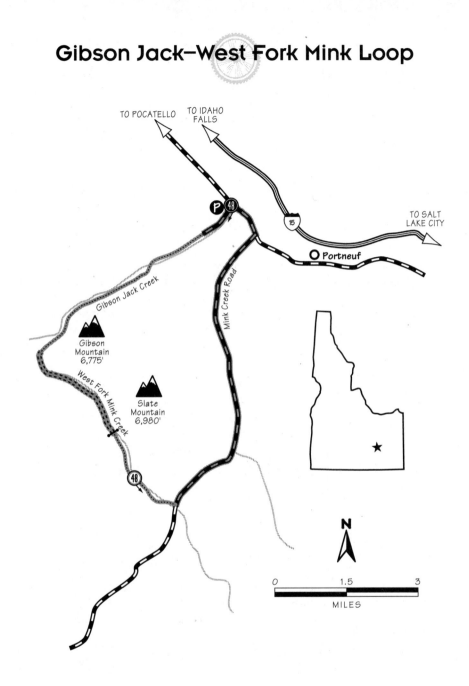

Aerobic level:	Strenuous to begin with on the Gibson Jack singletrack but moderate thereafter.
Technical difficulty:	2+ overall. A few rocky, technical sections rate 3.
Highlights:	Scenic riding in the Gibson Jack and West Fork Mink Creek areas.
Hazards:	Please watch out for and yield to other trail users on the popular West Fork Mink Trail.
Land status:	Caribou National Forest.
Maps:	USGS Pocatello South, Clifton Creek.

Access: From Pocatello, head south on the Bannock Highway (Old U.S. Highway 30) to the Pocatello Country Club, at the base of Gibson Jack Creek. Park. The ride starts here.

Notes on the trail: The Gibson Jack–West Fork Mink Loop features excellent singletrack riding in both the Gibson Jack and West Fork Mink draws. The ride also provides a backcountry tour of the Caribou National Forest near Pocatello with good views of Gibson Mountain (6,775 feet) and Slate Mountain (6,990 feet). Don't be dissuaded by the amount of paved road mileage here—most of it is downhill after the West Fork Mink singletrack descent.

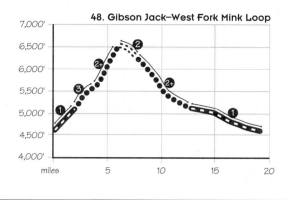

48. Gibson Jack–West Fork Mink Loop

THE RIDE

0.0 Head up the Gibson Jack paved road (Forest Road 008) for about 2 miles to a gate.

2.2 Trailhead for Gibson Jack Creek Trail. Get ready for a short, rocky climb at the beginning. It won't last long, however, and the singletrack climbs at a moderate pace up the canyon.

4.2 Singletrack crosses a bridge.

6.1 Encounter a gate at the top of Gibson Jack Trail. Pass through the gate and continue on the trail.

6.4 Two-way doubletrack junction. Go left and follow the jeep trail on a contour at the top of the West Fork drainage.

7.7 Encounter another gate on the left. This is the top of the West Fork Mink singletrack by a number of springs. Now begins a very cool descent, all on singletrack. Please yield to uphill traffic on the trail. Slate Mountain looms above on the left.

11.6 Arrive at the bottom of the West Fork Mink Trail. Turn left and rip down the pavement to town.

19.2 Arrive in the Pocatello Country Club parking lot.

South Fork Mink–Valve House Loop

Location:	15 miles southeast of Pocatello.
Distance:	9.5-mile loop.
Time:	2 hours.
Tread:	0.7 mile of paved road, 3.1 miles of doubletrack, 5.7 miles of singletrack.
Aerobic level:	Moderate climb up the South Fork of Mink Creek, followed by a strenuous steep climb at the top of Box Canyon. Then it's all downhill.
Technical difficulty:	2. Nearly all the singletrack on this ride is sweet and buffed. A few rough spots at the top of Box Canyon rate 3+.
Highlights:	Gorgeous tour of the South Fork Mink and Valve House draws, with splendid views of Scout Mountain off in the distance.
Hazards:	Please watch out for and yield to all trail users. Traffic is heaviest in the Valve House Creek area, going both ways.
Land status:	Caribou National Forest.
Maps:	USGS Clifton Creek.

Access: Take Interstate 15 south of Pocatello to the Portneuf exit. Note signs for the Mink Creek Recreation Area. Turn right off the freeway and head back toward Pocatello for about 2 miles to the signed turnoff for Mink Creek Road. Turn left and head up the paved road about 7 miles to a small parking area on the left side of the road at the Valve House Creek Trailhead. Park. The ride starts here.

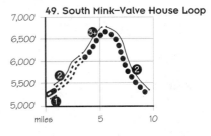

Notes on the trail: The South Fork Mink–Valve House Loop is a real treat for advanced riders. The climbing is very moderate on the South Fork Mink Creek doubletrack, followed by a few supersteep pitches in Box Canyon to

South Fork Mink–Valve House Loop

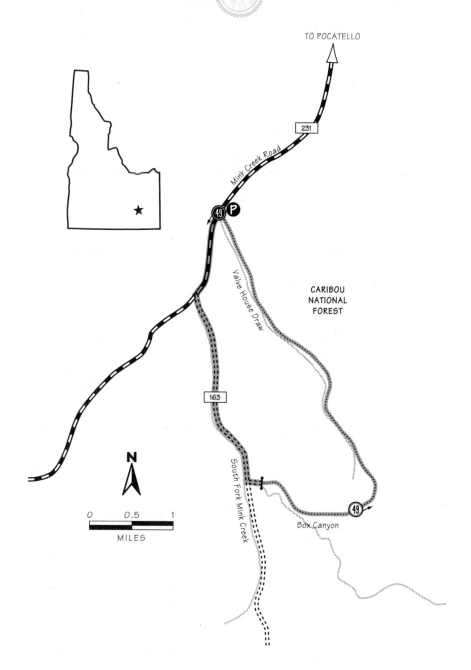

TO POCATELLO

231

Mink Creek Road

49 P

CARIBOU
NATIONAL
FOREST

Valve House Draw

163

South Fork Mink Creek

N

0   0.5   1
MILES

49

Box Canyon

Scout Mountain looms in the distance as riders climb Box Canyon on the way to Valve House draw.

the summit point of the loop. Then it's a real cruiser down the Valve House singletrack through tall grass, wildflowers, and aspen trees. Don't get carried away on the way down, however, because motorcyclists, horseback riders, mountain bikers, and hikers could be coming up the trail.

THE RIDE

0.0 Head up the paved road and watch for a signed turnoff for the South Fork of Mink Creek on the left.

0.7 Turn left on South Fork Mink Creek doubletrack. Cruise up the doubletrack for several miles.

3.2 Turn left into a doubletrack circle and follow the doubletrack behind the circle to a gate. This is the beginning of the Box Canyon singletrack. The trailhead is not signed.

3.8 Pass through a gate. Cattle graze in this area. The impressive peak looming in front of you is Scout Mountain.

4.7 Supersteep pitch will likely force you to walk. The trail is quite steep but mostly ridable for the next mile.

5.4 Singletrack merges with doubletrack road. Bear left and climb a little more through the aspen trees.

5.6 Reach a gate at the summit. Go through it and bend to the left on the main trail, which returns to singletrack. You're at the top of Valve House draw. Here comes the best part of the ride! All downhill now.

6.3 Pass covered-wagon cattle trough. Keep going down on the singletrack.

9.5 Arrive at the Valve House Trailhead and your vehicle. What a hoot!

Variation 1: Reverse the loop.

Variation 2: Try Dan's Potpourri Loop. It's a longer version of this ride with more singletrack and a foray into the East Fork of Mink Creek.

Dan's Potpourri Loop

Location:	15 miles southeast of Pocatello.
Distance:	15.6-mile loop.
Time:	3 hours.
Tread:	0.7 miles of paved road, 6.2 miles of doubletrack, 8.7 miles of singletrack.
Aerobic level:	Moderate with several strenuous interludes.
Technical difficulty:	2+. Nearly all the singletrack on this ride is sweet and buffed. A few rough spots rate 3+.

Dan's Potpourri Loop

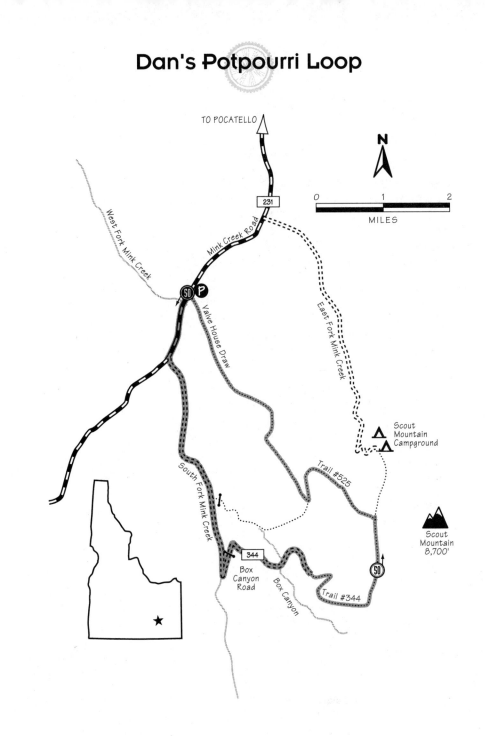

TO POCATELLO

N

0   1   2
MILES

231

West Fork Mink Creek

Mink Creek Road

50 P

Valve House Draw

East Fork Mink Creek

South Fork Mink Creek

Scout Mountain Campground

Trail #525

Scout Mountain 8,700'

344

Box Canyon Road

Box Canyon

50

Trail #344

	Highlights:	Gorgeous tour of the South Mink, East Mink, and Valve House draws, with splendid views of Scout Mountain off in the distance.
	Hazards:	Please watch out for and yield to all trail users. Traffic is heaviest in the Valve House Creek area, going both ways.
	Land status:	Caribou National Forest.
	Maps:	USGS Clifton Creek, Scout Mountain.

Access: Take Interstate 15 south of Pocatello to the Portneuf exit. Note signs for the Mink Creek Recreation Area. Turn right off the freeway and head back toward Pocatello for about 2 miles to the signed turnoff for Mink Creek Road. Turn left and head up the paved road about 7 miles to a small parking area on the left side of the road at the Valve House and West Fork Mink Creek trailheads. Park. The ride starts here.

Notes on the trail: Long-time Pocatello resident Dan Talley fashioned this loop ride as part of his many mountain biking forays in the Pokey area. We call this Dan's Potpourri Loop because it offers a little bit of everything in the vast Mink Creek Recreation Area. Look forward to some short but tough climbs, great singletrack, and rocky technical riding. This ride covers some of the same territory as the South Fork Mink–Valve House ride, but it's longer and it provides a peek into the East Fork Mink area. Dan's loop culminates in the same awesome downhill in Valve House Canyon. Wahoo! Be sure to keep your speed under control so you can yield to uphill traffic.

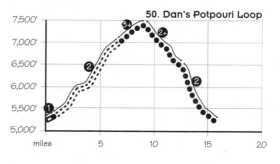

THE RIDE

0.0 Head up the paved road and watch for a signed left-hand turn for the South Fork Mink Creek Trail on the left.

0.7 Turn left on the South Fork Mink doubletrack road.

4.1 Turn left on the Box Canyon Road. Enjoy cool views of the Arbon Valley.

6.9 Road ends and singletrack begins on the right. The trail climbs at a steep gradient for the next mile.

8.2 Junction with East Fork Mink Creek Trail. Turn left and go down. The trail is technical in some areas, so stay on your toes.

9.2 Encounter a fork in the trail. Bear left and keep bearing left. You're descending now and the trail widens to a doubletrack tread.

11.0 Trail crosses a creek (ridable) and climbs to the top of Valve House draw.

11.5 Encounter the gate at the top of Valve House. Proceed through the gate and enjoy the descent in Valve House, a beautiful singletrack with tall grass and aspens bordering the trail.

15.6 Arrive at the Mink Creek Road and Valve House/West Mink parking area.

Upper Snake: Scenic and Secluded

The predominantly Mormon town of Idaho Falls may be Idaho's second-largest city, but riders will find plenty of solitude on a variety of trails in the Upper Snake region. Several rides in this area also provide a peek at spectacular scenery: the Idaho side of the magnificent Teton Range, the wildlife-rich Snake River bottoms near Swan Valley, and Mesa Falls—a 114-foot curtain of water on the Henrys Fork. It's also important to point out that the rides in this corner of the state will take you to destinations where fly-fishing is world-class—the Henrys Fork, the South Fork Snake River, and the Lemhi River. A drift boat might come in handy.

The singletrack riding season in the Upper Snake doesn't start until early May due to high-elevation snowpack and cold, blustery weather. The Idaho Falls Greenbelt, the Victor-Driggs Paved Trail, and the Warm River Rail-Trail are located at lower elevations than the mountain trails, providing an opportunity for early-season training.

Other activities in this corner of the state include visiting Yellowstone National Park, Jackson Hole, Wyoming, Harriman State Park in Island Park, and the St. Anthony Dunes. If you don't have your own boat, guided fishing trips are available on the South Fork Snake in Swan Valley or Henrys Fork in the Island Park area. In the tiny town of Arco, you can visit our nation's first nuclear reactor, built at the nearby Idaho National Engineering and Environmental Laboratory.

51

Idaho Falls Greenbelt Loop

Location:	Idaho Falls.
Distance:	4.5-mile loop.
Time:	30 minutes, depending on distance and speed of travel.
Tread:	4.5 miles of paved urban pathway.
Aerobic level:	Easy.
Technical difficulty:	1.
Highlights:	Nice paved pathway along the Snake River in Idaho Falls.
Hazards:	None.
Land status:	Idaho Falls City Parks and Recreation Department.
Maps:	None available.

Access: Take Broadway Street about a quarter-mile east of Interstate 15 to River Parkway Street, on the west side of the Snake River. Public parking and restrooms are available adjacent to the river. The ride starts and ends here.

Notes on the trail: The Idaho Falls Greenbelt has grown from a short, out-and-back paved path in front of the Latter-Day Saints (LDS) church to an enjoyable loop ride that links both sides of the Snake River and a city park at University Place on a small hill overlooking the city. The full loop is only 4.5 miles long, so you may want to extend the ride by trying the loop counterclockwise after riding it clockwise.

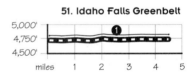

51. Idaho Falls Greenbelt

THE RIDE

0.0 Follow the sidewalk adjacent to River Parkway. Go slow to avoid pedestrians milling about along the side of the river.

0.3 Paved path begins and runs on the river frontage side of "hotel row" in Idaho Falls.

0.8 Path crosses parking lot and continues on the other side.

1.0 Pathway ends by a stairway leading to the U.S. Highway 20 bridge. Carry your bike up the stairs and cross the river on the highway bridge. On the other side, carry your bike down to the funky floating underpass and ride under the bridge in a northerly direction toward Freeman Park and University Place.

Idaho Falls Greenbelt Loop

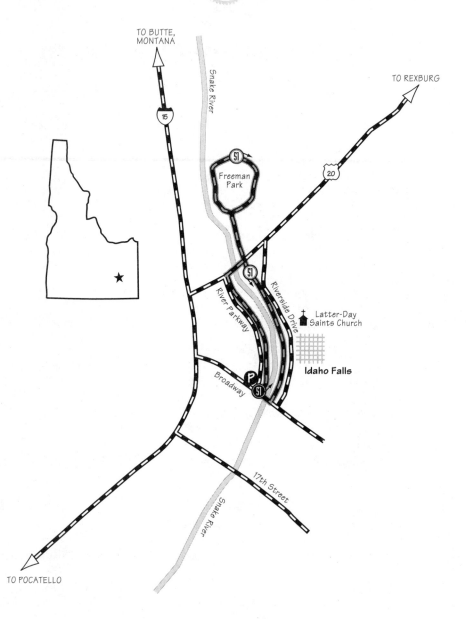

TO BUTTE, MONTANA

TO REXBURG

15

Snake River

51

Freeman Park

20

51

River Parkway

Riverside Drive

Latter-Day Saints Church

Idaho Falls

Broadway

P 51

17th Street

Snake River

TO POCATELLO

The Idaho Falls Greenbelt passes in front of the Mormon church along the Snake River, a signature scene in Idaho's second-largest city.

1.7 Arrive at a two-way T-junction in Freeman Park. Go left and ride along the river. The path courses through the grassy park and passes by a Vietnam War Memorial. The path does a complete loop around the park in exactly 1 mile.

2.7 Close the loop and return to T-junction. Go left and head back toward the LDS church.

3.2 Follow underpass beneath US 20 and ride the sidewalk on the same side of the river.

3.7 Pathway resumes on east side of the river near the LDS church. Cruise along the water's edge underneath towering fir and spruce trees.

4.3 Arrive at Broadway Bridge. Turn right and ride the sidewalk across the river bridge and turn right on River Parkway.

4.5 Complete the loop at River Parkway.

Variation: Reverse the loop.

52

Kelly Canyon Loop

Location: 24 miles east of Idaho Falls.
Distance: 5.4 miles, out and back; several loop options are also possible.
Time: 1 hour or more.
Tread: 5.4 miles of doubletrack.
Aerobic level: The initial climb up to the top of Kelly Mountain is strenuous but only a half-mile long, so it's over quickly.
Technical difficulty: 2 for rocks and ruts on jeep trail.
Highlights: Fun, scenic jeep trail riding 30 minutes from Idaho Falls.
Hazards: None.
Land status: Targhee National Forest.
Maps: USGS Heise, Hawley Gulch.

Access: From Idaho Falls, take the striplike Yellowstone Boulevard east of town toward Swan Valley. The road turns into Idaho Highway 26 several miles east of downtown and heads for Heise and Swan Valley. About 16 miles east of town, turn left on the well-marked turnoff for Heise Hot Springs and Kelly Canyon ski area. Proceed about 3 miles north, turn right on the paved Kelly Canyon Road, and continue about 5 miles to the base area. When the pavement ends, continue about a half-mile to the four-way junction of Forest Roads 218 and 217 and a jeep trail heading up to Kelly Mountain. Park off to the side of the road. The ride starts here.

Notes on the trail: Kelly Canyon is a decent mountain biking area close to Idaho Falls. The trails are pretty short, but, after riding this loop, you'll see that other options add diversity and challenge to the ride. Once on top of Kelly Mountain, a jeep trail provides skyline views in all directions, including the unique landscape of dry farms and yellow rapeseed fields on the rims above the South Fork of the Snake River, a world-renowned fly-fishing stream (see Ride 54 for Snake River singletrack). The Stinking Springs variation is an expert-level ride, so novice mountain bikers should not attempt that loop.

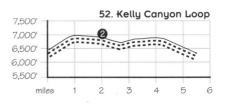

Kelly Canyon Loop

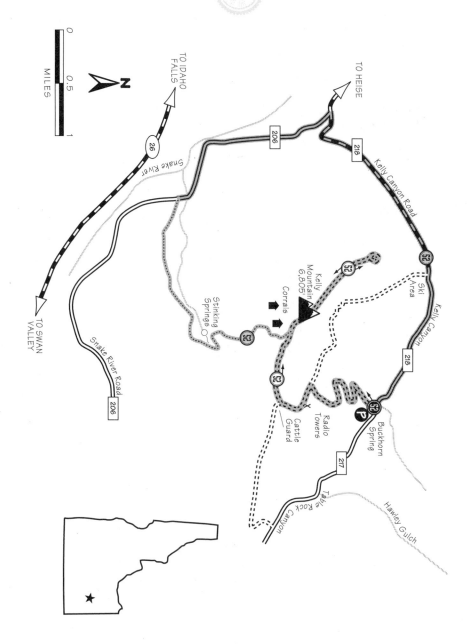

MILES

N

TO IDAHO FALLS

TO HEISE

Snake River

26

206

218

Kelly Canyon Road

TO SWAN VALLEY

Snake River Road

206

Stinking Springs

Corrals

Kelly Mountain 6,805'

Ski Area

Kelly Canyon

218

Radio Towers

Cattle Guard

Buckhorn Spring

217

Table Rock Canyon

Hawley Gulch

0.0 Gear down for some steep climbing and head up the mountain on the doubletrack jeep trail. The doubletrack will switchback several times as it climbs up Kelly Mountain. You will climb about 800 vertical feet in less than a mile.

0.6 Crest the broad ridge of Kelly Mountain. Now it's time to cruise the ridgetop and check out the scenery. Turn left to check out the views to the west first.

1.5 Pass the radio towers and come to a cattle guard. From here, the Snake River Plain, Big Southern Butte (Craters of the Moon National Monument), and the Lemhi and the Lost River mountains are visible on clear days. Turn around now and ride the ridge toward some corrals.

2.0 Arrive at three-way junction at a corral. Keep going straight to a dead end on the high-line jeep trail.

2.7 Reach dead end. Check out the views, turn around, and ride back to the corrals.

3.4 Here you've got a choice. You can either turn left at the corrals and take a steep jeep trail down the ski slope to the bottom of the hill or go back to the cattle guard. For this ride, go back to the cattle guard.

3.9 Return to cattle guard, turn left toward the radio towers, and descend the mountain back to your rig. Another option is to descend on the jeep trail into Table Rock Canyon; the downside of this approach is that you have to climb back to your rig.

5.4 Arrive at the bottom of the mountain.

Variation: At the corrals junction, you plunge off the mountain to the south on a steep trail to Stinking Springs. The trail will drop out on the South Fork Snake River road. So you'll either have to ride back to Kelly Canyon to pick up your rig, or you'll have to leave a shuttle rig near Stinking Springs. The trail is deeply rutted, so it's an expert-only type of trail.

Fall Creek–Echo Canyon Loop

Location:	35 miles east of Idaho Falls.
Distance:	21.7-mile loop.
Time:	5 to 7 hours.
Tread:	3.9 miles of gravel road, 3 miles of doubletrack, 14.8 miles of singletrack.
Aerobic level:	Strenuous. The difficulty meter rises dramatically first as you climb a narrow singletrack to the head of the South Fork of Fall Creek and then on a number of steep climbs near the top of Deadhorse Ridge.
Technical difficulty:	3 +. The trail tread becomes increasingly challenging in the singletrack uphill and downhill sections.

Fall Creek–Echo Canyon Loop

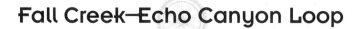

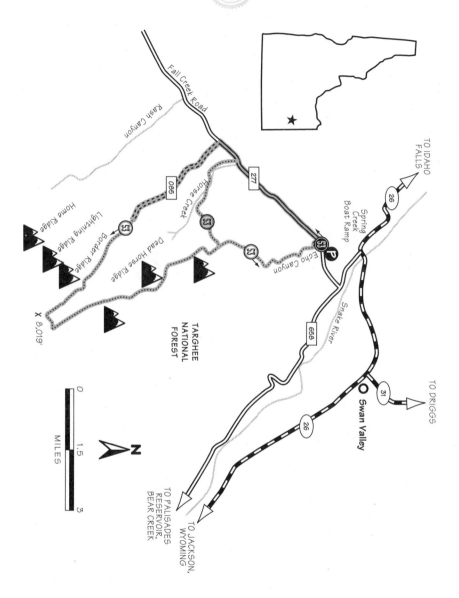

Fall Creek Road

Kaah Canyon

277

085

Horse Creek

53

Dead Horse Ridge

53

53

Border Ridge

Lightning Ridge

Home Ridge

X 8,019'

TARGHEE
NATIONAL
FOREST

Echo Canyon

Spring
Creek
Boat Ramp

53
P

TO IDAHO
FALLS

26

Snake River

658

31

TO DRIGGS

Swan Valley

26

TO PALISADES
RESERVOIR,
BEAR CREEK

TO JACKSON,
WYOMING

N

MILES

0   1.5   3

After toiling up and down steep slopes on Deadhorse Ridge, it's a relief to cruise down the singletrack in Echo Canyon.

Highlights:	Killer views of the Snake River Mountains, the Idaho side of the Tetons, and the Palisades Mountains from the top of Deadhorse Ridge. Nearly 15 miles of singletrack riding.
Hazards:	Watch out for obstacles on the trail. At certain times of the year, the mosquitos can be fierce. Domestic sheep and cattle graze this country in the summer.
Land status:	Targhee National Forest.
Maps:	USGS Conant Valley, Commissary Ridge, Red Ridge; Targhee National Forest map.

Access: From Idaho Falls, drive east on U.S. Highway 26 about 32 miles to the signed turnoff to Fall Creek and the Spring Creek boat launch site. The turn comes up after the South Fork Lodge in Conant Valley, just before the highway bridge crosses the South Fork of the Snake River. Turn right and head up the dirt road about 2 miles to the Fall Creek turnoff, Forest Road 107. Turn right and go 2 miles to the Echo Canyon Trailhead. The ride starts here.

Notes on the trail: The Fall Creek–Echo Canyon Loop is an excellent around-the-world expert ride. It's a good idea to pack a lunch and a bunch of energy bars for this ride and allow a full day to complete the loop. It's important to be mentally prepared for a difficult climb to the top of Deadhorse Ridge as well as a number of very steep climbs on the way down the humpbacked ridge. Mountain bikers might rename the ridge "Heartbreak" for the hidden steep uphill climbs over the top of many humps on the way to Echo Canyon. The views from the top, the challenge of cleaning the humps on the ridge, and the fast singletrack descents, however, make this trip well worth the effort for riders who like to punish themselves.

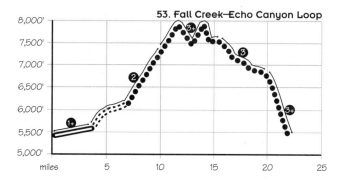

THE RIDE

0.0 Head out of the Echo Canyon Trailhead parking lot, turn left, and proceed up the Fall Creek gravel road. Spin and conserve energy.

3.9 Junction with the signed South Fork Fall Creek turnoff. Go left on Trail 085 and cross the creek (ridable except during high flows). The trail tread is a doubletrack for the next 3 miles.

4.1 Second crossing. Deep water may require walking.

4.4 Pass through barbed-wire gate.

4.7 Cross old rickety bridge. Be careful: it's missing some planks.

5.2 Cross creek (ridable).

7.1 Trail dissolves into singletrack in mountain meadow setting. Wildflowers everywhere.

7.9 Junction with trails to Rash Canyon, Home Ridge, and Lightning Ridge. Go left toward the North Fork of Bear Creek. Be ready for steeper climbing on narrow singletrack.

8.8 Treacherous divotlike crossing.

9.2 Cross left fork of upper section of creek (ridable).

10.3 Divotlike crossing (ridable).

10.9 Crest saddle junction. Go left and hike-a-bike 0.1 mile to a left-hand junction for Deadhorse Ridge. The trail is ridable again to the top of the ridge (mile 11.6). Good lunch spot.

11.8 Pass hunting camp.

12.1 Hike-a-bike down steep rutted section.

12.5 Hike up short pitches of steep hill.

13.9 Ridgetop hump summit. Enjoy brisk descent on banked singletrack.

14.4 Ignore minor trail on right and bear left on main trail.

15.6 Saddle junction with Horse Creek trail, the short loop (see variation). You've got another gut-buster climb ahead that requires hiking in places.

16.1 Crest the hump and descend.

16.5 Bear right at trail junction and descend some more.

16.7 Bear left at unsigned junction.

17.3 Pass through barbed-wire gate and descend. Watch out for deep ruts.

19.5 Junction with top of Echo Canyon and connector to Indian Creek Trail. Stay on main trail and descend some more.

20.4 Go far right at three-way junction, pass by cattle trough, and continue straight down the canyon.

20.9 Junction with gravel road. Go left and descend to the trailhead.

21.7 Arrive at parking area. You may want to cool off in Fall Creek.

Variation: Locals shorten this loop considerably by climbing about 5 miles on a singletrack trail up Horse Creek (located a mile before the South Fork doubletrack turnoff on the Fall Creek Road) to a junction with the Deadhorse Ridge singletrack as it approaches Echo Canyon. Turn left at a gate at the top of Horse Creek and descend the winding Echo Canyon singletrack back to the Fall Creek Road. This variation is about 12 miles long.

South Fork Snake River Trail

Location:	51 miles east of Idaho Falls.
Distance:	7.8 miles, one-way (with shuttle); 15.6 miles, out and back.
Time:	1.5 hours one-way.
Tread:	1.3 miles of doubletrack, 6.5 miles of singletrack. The narrow route winds along a rocky riverbank like a goat trail. It's buffed and flat in a few rare spots but is mostly technical and rutted, with loose rocks, tree roots, and supersteep pitches that will cause most to hike-a-bike.
Aerobic level:	Moderate to strenuous. Short, steep pitches with loose rock tax the legs and stretch the lungs to the redline zone. Lack of shade adds to the sweat factor in the hot summer months. Hence this ride is best in the spring and fall.
Technical difficulty:	3 +. Steep technical sections with death cookies (large, mobile rocks) will test the best. A few of the flat sections are level 2 smooth singletrack.
Highlights:	Fetching views of the South Fork Snake River canyon with its blue-ribbon trout stream bordered by a dense cottonwood forest. Chance sightings of wildlife—especially moose, bald eagles, and osprey—are likely here.
Hazards:	Rattlesnakes in hot weather; loose rocks.
Land status:	Targhee National Forest.
Maps:	Targhee National Forest; USGS Wheaton Mountain.

Access: From Idaho Falls, take Yellowstone Boulevard, U.S. Highway 26, to the eastern edge of town. Follow US 26, a two-lane paved road, 37 miles to Swan Valley. In the tiny 'burb of Swan Valley, turn left on Idaho Highway 31, heading for Victor and Driggs. Proceed 5 miles on ID 31 to Pine Creek Bench Road. Turn left and follow the 2WD dirt road 5 miles to the obvious point where county maintenance ends and the road becomes rutted. The South Fork/Dry Creek trailhead is a quarter-mile away at the fence line. Alternative access: Take Idaho Highway 26 to the turnoff for Heise and Kelly Canyon Ski Area. Turn left and follow the paved road across the river. At the junction with Forest Road 206, turn right and follow the gravel road along the South Fork of the Snake River about 10 miles to the Black Canyon Trailhead. The first access route takes you to the east end of the trail; the second one takes you to the west end.

South Fork Snake River Trail

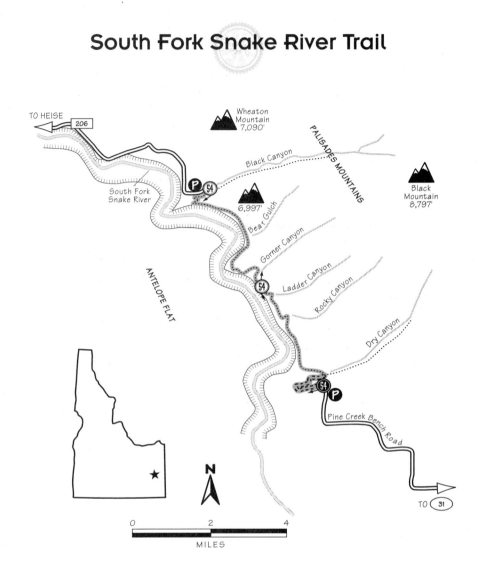

TO HEISE
206

Wheaton
Mountain
7,090'

Black Canyon

PALISADES MOUNTAINS

Black
Mountain
8,797'

P 54

South Fork
Snake River

6,997'

Bear Gulch

Gorner Canyon

Ladder Canyon

Rocky Canyon

Dry Canyon

54

ANTELOPE FLAT

54

P

Pine Creek Bench Road

N

TO 31

0   2   4

MILES

54. South Fork Snake River Trail

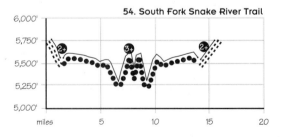

6,000'
5,750'
5,500'
5,250'
5,000'

2+   3+   2+

miles   5   10   15   20

Amy Stahl spins along the South Fork singletrack amid big sagebrush, tall grass, and a rainbow of wildflowers on a bench above the Snake River Canyon.

Notes on the trail: The South Fork Snake River canyon is a special place. It's one of the most biologically rich cottonwood riparian ecosystems in the Rocky Mountain West. With awesome fishing and wildlife viewing, it's a worthy place to visit. That said, the South Fork singletrack is a fairly arduous mountain bike ride. The narrow trail rolls up and down along the north bank of the South Fork, fairly close to the river, but often about 250 to 500 feet above it. The trail also provides a short tour of five different side canyons, taking riders into the welcome shade of aspen and Douglas-fir groves. It's getting in and out of each side canyon, plus avoiding steep rock cliffs bordering the river, that sends the trail up some abrupt, very steep pitches. Some of the hills feature a trenched-out singletrack with death cookies lying in the middle, just to make sure that your back tire will spin out. The trail is short enough, however, that a few hike-a-bike sections aren't the end of the world. If you're doing this as a shuttle ride, it's easier to ride from Black Canyon to the Pine Creek Bench. If you're going out and back, it's easier to knock off the hard part first and enjoy an easier trip on the way back.

THE RIDE

0.0 Head downhill from the scenic farm country on the Pine Creek Bench and follow the gnarly trenched-out 4WD jeep trail down to the Dry Creek junction.

1.3 Bear left at the creek junction, ride across the creek in low gear, and continue on the South Fork Trail.

1.6 Bear right at trail junction and get into your small front chain ring for a steep climb to a bench above the river.

2.0 Reach top of bench. Enjoy killer views of the South Fork canyon and the adjacent farmland. Trail will wind in and out of several small gulches ahead.

4.0 Ride into Ladder Canyon.

5.0 Descend into Gormer Canyon, the largest of the side draws. A big climb looms ahead; some hiking may be required.

5.4 Reach the top of the hill.

6.2 Technical descent into Bear Gulch. Trail dips closest to the river ahead; if you're planning to take a dip, this is the spot.

7.0 Trail begins climb over bluff into Black Canyon.

7.8 Fast descent into Black Canyon, cross creek, and ride into trailhead. If you shuttled a vehicle to this point, you're done. Otherwise, cool off in the creek, turn around, and head back the way you came.

15.6 Finish climb back to Pine Creek Bench.

Variation: Shuttle a vehicle to the Pine Creek Bench and ride the trail starting at the Black Canyon Trailhead.

Victor–Driggs Paved Trail

Location:	Victor, Driggs, and points in between.
Distance:	7.3 miles, one-way; 14.6 miles out and back.
Time:	30 minutes one-way.
Tread:	7.3 miles of paved pathway.
Aerobic level:	Easy, depending on headwinds.
Technical difficulty:	1.
Highlights:	Nice paved pathway in the Big Hole Valley on the Idaho side of the Tetons.
Hazards:	None. Please yield to walkers, in-line skaters, and others on the pathway.
Land status:	Highway right-of-way, old railroad right-of-way.
Maps:	USGS Victor, Driggs.

Access: Take Idaho Highway 31 to Victor, a little town at the junction of ID 31 and the road over Teton Pass to Jackson Hole, Wyoming. Turn left at the blinking light and head for Driggs on Idaho Highway 33. The pathway starts on the north end of Victor, by Cedron Street and the highway. There is a parking area here.

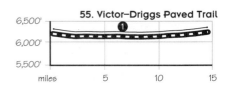

Victor–Driggs Paved Trail

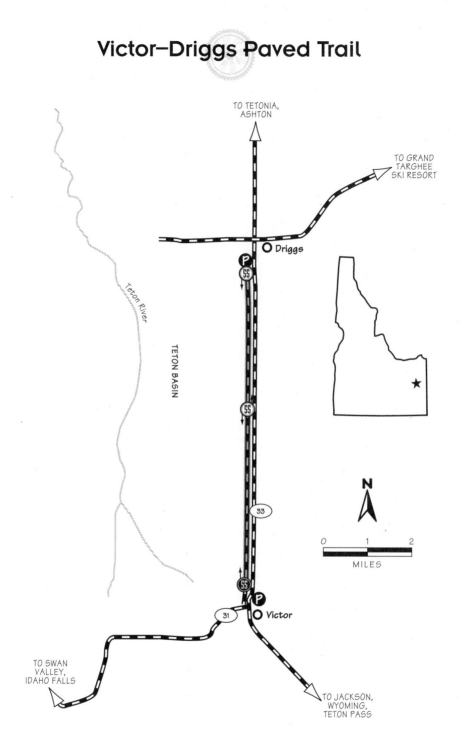

TO TETONIA, ASHTON

TO GRAND TARGHEE SKI RESORT

Driggs

Teton River

TETON BASIN

55

55

33

N

0 1 2
MILES

31 Victor

TO SWAN VALLEY, IDAHO FALLS

TO JACKSON, WYOMING, TETON PASS

Amy Stahl winds along the Victor-Driggs paved trail, a level pathway with big views of the Tetons.

Notes on the trail: The Victor-Driggs paved pathway is a new addition to the scenic, low-key Teton Valley. It follows the old Union Pacific Railroad right-of-way between the two towns. Veteran Greenbelt Trail enthusiasts will notice that the pathway is a little narrower than some, about 4 feet wide. The gradient of the valley pathway is slightly downhill from Victor to Driggs, but the prevailing winds of the day are more likely to be a factor in your ride, depending on their speed. In the summertime, the winds usually blow from the south, so traveling from Victor to Driggs should give you a tailwind. But nothing about weather is guaranteed in the mountains. Plans call for building a pathway from Main Street in Driggs toward Grand Targhee ski area.

THE RIDE

0.0 Head north on the pathway toward Driggs. You will pass by a number of new homes and a drive-in movie screen along the way.

7.3 Arrive in the southern end of Driggs at a public parking area. Cross a bridge going over a little creek. Turn around and return to Victor.

14.6 Arrive in Victor.

Warm River Rail-Trail/Mesa Falls Scenic Loop

Location:	9 miles northeast of Ashton.
Distance:	14.7-mile loop.
Time:	2 hours, depending on speed of travel and length of stay at Mesa Falls scenic overlooks.
Tread:	5 miles of rail-trail, 3.4 miles of doubletrack, 6.3 miles of paved road.
Aerobic level:	Moderate uphill climbing on the Warm River Rail-Trail. Easy, flat riding in lodgepole forests and rolling up-and-down terrain on paved road to visit Mesa Falls overlook.
Technical difficulty:	1+ to 2. Tread is smooth with a few bumps and rocks.
Highlights:	Scenic tour of Warm River area, towering Mesa Falls, and the Targhee National Forest.
Hazards:	Watch out for vehicles on the paved road to Mesa Falls overlook, and watch out for other people on the rail-trail.

Warm River Rail-Trail/Mesa Falls Scenic Loop

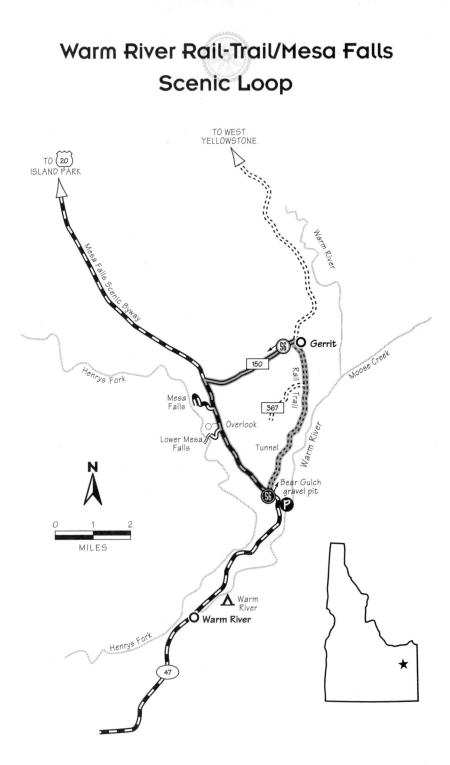

The author emerges from a short but interesting tunnel on the Warm River Rail-Trail.

Land status: Targhee National Forest.

Maps: USGS Warm River, Snake River Butte; Targhee National Forest map.

Access: Take U.S. Highway 20 to Ashton. Head east on Idaho Highway 47 to the Warm River junction. Stay on ID 47, the Mesa Falls scenic route, for 3 miles to the Bear Gulch gravel pit and parking area. You'll see the Warm River Rail-Trail on the right side of the highway. Take a dirt road out of the parking area to the rail-trail.

Notes on the trail: This is a scenic loop that combines the most scenic part of the Warm River Rail-Trail (including a short tunnel), a dirt doubletrack cruise on mostly flat terrain in the Targhee National Forest, and a scenic tour of upper and lower Mesa Falls on the way back to Bear Gulch. The Warm River Rail-Trail runs from the Idaho-Montana border near West Yellowstone all the way to Warm River, a distance of 60 miles, but few beginning or intermediate riders would attempt to tackle that kind of distance. So here's a shorter, scenic alternative.

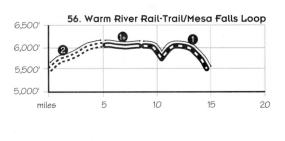

56. Warm River Rail-Trail/Mesa Falls Loop

THE RIDE

0.0 Head north on the Warm River Rail-Trail toward the tunnel portal that's visible ahead.

0.4 Enter tunnel. A light may be handy, but the tunnel is short enough that you can wing it without one.

0.5 Exit tunnel and continue riding uphill.

3.8 Pass through junction with Forest Roads 154 and 367.

5.0 Junction with Forest Road 150 near an old townsite of Gerrit. Turn left and follow the gravel road in a westerly direction toward the Mesa Falls scenic drive. Bear right at the junction with FR 153 and stay on FR 150.

8.4 Arrive at Mesa Falls scenic drive, marked by a stop sign on FR 150. Turn left and head for Mesa Falls.

9.4 Turn right to drop down to an Idaho Parks and Recreation overlook at the brink of the main (upper) falls. It's about 1 mile down to the overlook and 1 mile back.

11.4 Back on the main road. Turn right and head for Bear Gulch. Stop at the lower falls overlook if you wish. This falls is smaller but spectacular.

14.7 Arrive at Bear Gulch Parking Area.

Backcountry Byway

Stephen Ambrose, author of the best-seller *Undaunted Courage*, singled out a night he spent with his family at Lemhi Pass as "the most glorious night of our lives. You could reach out and touch the stars. Except for a logging road, the place was unchanged since Lewis was there."

That's the whole point of this backcountry byway adventure—to get a rare personal feel for American frontier history. For those who haven't read Ambrose's book on Lewis and Clark's adventure, be sure to take a copy along on your trip to Lemhi Pass.

57

Lemhi Pass Scenic Byway

Location:	Tendoy, 21 miles south of Salmon.
Distance:	39.1-mile loop.
Time:	Two days.
Tread:	39.1 miles of gravel road.
Aerobic level:	Strenuous major uphill pull on the Warm Springs Woods Road with a climb of 3,000 vertical feet over 11 miles. Vehicle support (sag wagon) is possible for the entire length of the ride.
Technical difficulty:	1+.
Highlights:	Interesting historical and recreational ride to Lemhi Pass and Sacajawea Memorial in the Beaverhead Mountains on the Idaho-Montana border.
Hazards:	Watch out for vehicles traveling the Lewis and Clark Backcountry Byway.
Land status:	Salmon National Forest.
Maps:	USGS Baker, Goldstone Mountain, Lemhi Pass, Agency Creek.

Access: From the town of Salmon, head southeast on Idaho Highway 28 to the Tendoy post office and store. Turn left on the dirt road next to the store. Right away, you'll come to a T-intersection. Turn left and follow signs for the Warm Springs Woods Road and Lewis and Clark Backcountry Byway. The clockwise loop ride starts here.

Notes on the trail: The Lewis and Clark Backcountry Byway loop to Lemhi Pass is one of two historic, recreational dirt-road rides in this book that trace portions of the route followed in 1805–6 by the Corps of Discovery. The Forest Service developed the Lemhi Pass loop as a scenic drive. I recommend it as a two-day campout adventure for groups of riders, whether families or friends. Day 1 features an arduous 3,000-foot-vertical climb up Warm Springs Woods Road into heavy timber on the Idaho-Montana divide in the

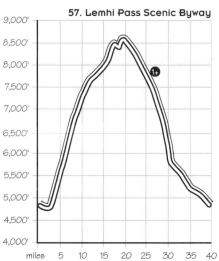

Lemhi Pass Scenic Byway

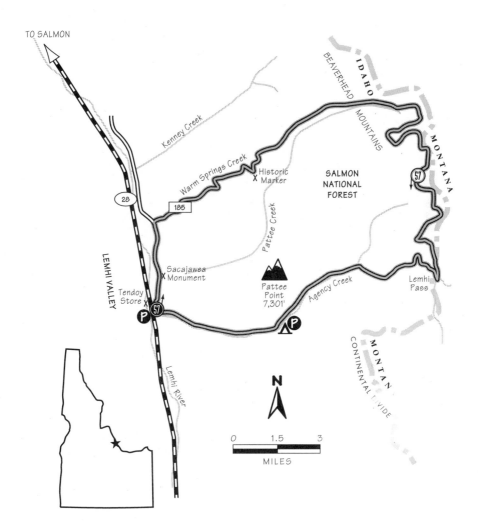

TO SALMON

Kenney Creek

Warm Springs Creek

Historic
X Marker

Pattee Creek

BEAVERHEAD MOUNTAINS

IDAHO

MONTANA

SALMON
NATIONAL
FOREST

57

28

185

LEMHI VALLEY

Sacajawea
X Monument

Tendoy
Store X

P 57

Pattee
Point
7,301'

Agency Creek

Lemhi
Pass

P

MONTANA

CONTINENTAL DIVIDE

Lemhi River

N

0   1.5   3

MILES

Take a moment to read up on Lewis and Clark at Lemhi Pass, a grassy saddle on the Idaho-Montana border along the Continental Divide.

Beaverhead Mountains. Parties can camp at numerous primitive (self-support) camping areas in the forest at the top of the loop or near Lemhi Pass itself. Day 2 involves a ripping descent down the Agency Creek Road back to Tendoy.

The Salmon-Challis National Forest office in Salmon has several brochures with details about the Lewis and Clark route in the Lemhi Pass area. In short, the Continental Divide crossing at Lemhi Pass had special significance for three key reasons: The party discovered that an inland waterway did not exist from St. Louis to the Pacific Ocean; Sacajawea was reunited with her home tribe, the Lemhi band of the Shoshone; and Lewis and Clark learned that the Salmon River would be too dangerous to navigate (it was known as the River of No Return). So the expedition pushed north, to Lolo Pass, and traveled overland along the north ridge of the Lochsa River in late September in miserable cold and snow. (Pick up the story at Ride 59 as part of a three-day, 72.9-mile trip that retraces the gnarly ridgetop route.

THE RIDE

0.0 Follow the dirt road at the base of the mountains. Watch out for ranch vehicles.

3.0 Turn right on Warm Springs Woods Road. Here comes the long strenuous climb! The sagebrush-dotted slopes are wide open with no shade. Start the climb early in the day to avoid getting hammered by the sun.

3.7 Pass interpretive sign. Take a breather and soak in some history.

4.2 Ignore junction on right.

6.2 First of many switchbacks.

8.6 Take a breather at rock monument to Lewis and Clark expedition.

9.9 Signed junction with Kenney Creek Road. Bear right on the byway.

11.0 Finally enter timber zone after climbing 2,800 feet. Now the grade begins to be moderate. Whew!

13.1 Pass corral and spring. Ignore road on left.

14.1 Ignore road on right. You're climbing again now.

15.7 Ignore road on left.

18.0 Road levels out at cattle guard. Now you're passing through some old lodgepole pine clearcuts. If you want to camp in the trees (and shade), find a spot between here and mile 21.5.

20.4 Pass junction with Continental Divide National Scenic Trail. This is a hiking trail. Byway climbs again for a bit.

21.5 Road begins major descent to Lemhi Pass.

24.0 Byway is rough, with washboard sections here.

26.5 Arrive at four-way road junction at Lemhi Pass. Here you can look into low sloping hills in western Montana and look back at the Lemhi and Beaverhead mountains in Idaho. Take some time to soak in the information on interpretive signs here. A jeep trail heads south on the ridge toward the trees (another possible camping area). To continue, head down the Agency Creek Road to complete the loop. The downhill gradient is steep in the next couple miles.

29.2 Pass by Copper Queen Mine. The road gradient moderates to a more gentle downhill slope.

31.2 Note the evidence of beaver activity on Agency Creek as you pass by an old cabin and corral.

33.8 Rocky walls of canyon close in next to the road.

34.3 Restroom and picnic area. If riders are getting tired, this would be good place to jump in the rig. The road is less scenic now as you descend back toward Tendoy.

38.7 Turn right at T-intersection.

39.0 Back at junction behind the Tendoy store. Go left to ID 28.

39.1 You've completed the loop. Now I hope you're psyched to try Ride 59 and retrace the Lewis and Clark route in north-central Idaho along the Lolo Motorway.

Variation: The most direct route to Lemhi Pass is to ride up the Agency Creek road from Tendoy to the pass, a distance of 13 miles. The vertical gain on this route is 2,100 feet.

The Palouse and Clearwater Country: Big Timber, Wheat Fields, and Head-High Ferns

High-quality singletrack riding in a densely forested setting is waiting for you in north-central Idaho.

In Grangeville, located on the edge of North Idaho's Camas Prairie, the Fish Creek Loops provide gentle but highly entertaining singletrack riding in the Nez Perce National Forest. At one point on the loop, the Gospel Hump Wilderness is plainly visible on a clear day.

Several hours east of Grangeville, riders must sample at least a portion of the 72.9-mile Lewis and Clark Trail on the north ridgetops above the Lochsa River. I recommend a three-day vehicle-supported ride to sample the full experience. Near Lowell, the Coolwater Ridge Jungle Ride will test the best expert riders.

Farther to the north, near the wheat fields of the Palouse, ridgetop singletrack riding on Moscow Mountain provides views of the Palouse to the south and of heavy forest to the north. Check out Idaho's largest known white pine trees at the Giant White Pine Campground, near Potlatch, where a serpentlike singletrack provides a loop tour of the Piah Creek drainage.

The riding season in the Palouse and Clearwater areas begins in May and ends in October. Snow and rain are common in the winter, and the area receives so much moisture that the forest undergrowth (ferns and brush) is uncommonly thick.

Other activities include camping, hiking, backpacking in the Nez Perce and Clearwater national forests, white-water boating on the Lochsa River, and canoeing on the lower Selway and Clearwater rivers. On the way to Grangeville at Whitebird Hill, you can take an audio tour of Nez Perce National Park. Check out Jerry Johnson and Weir Creek hot springs along the Lochsa River—huge cedar trees surround these popular primitive pools.

58

Clearwater and Snake River National Recreation Trail (Lewiston Levies)

Location:	Lewiston; Clarkston, Washington; and Asotin, Washington.
Distance:	7 miles, one-way, on Idaho side (10 miles on Washington side).
Time:	2.5 hours max, depending on ride distance and speed of travel.
Tread:	Paved urban recreation trail.
Aerobic level:	Easy.
Technical difficulty:	Easy.
Highlights:	Impressive vistas of the mighty Snake and Clearwater rivers; year-round use.
Hazards:	Please yield to pedestrians, in-line skaters, dogs, etc.
Land status:	U.S. Army Corps of Engineers/cities of Lewiston, Clarkston, and Asotin.
Maps:	U.S. Army Corps of Engineers, Clearwater and Snake River National Recreation Trail.

Access: You can access the Clearwater and Snake River National Recreation Trail in many ways. The following ride description starts at the east end of the Lewiston Levies Parkway, at Locomotive Park, and points out other access points along the way to Hells Gate State Park, the south end of the trail on the Idaho side. Locomotive Park lies adjacent to the junction of U.S. Highway 12 and twenty-first Street in Lewiston, on the river side of the street. Pull off US 12 in front of Hahn Plumbing and Heating Supplies and park. Ride behind the plumbing store on a paved street that crosses the railroad tracks and leads to the beginning of the levy trail. The ride starts here.

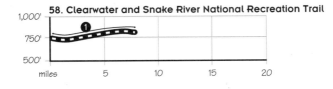

58. Clearwater and Snake River National Recreation Trail

Clearwater and Snake River National Recreation Trail (Lewiston Levies)

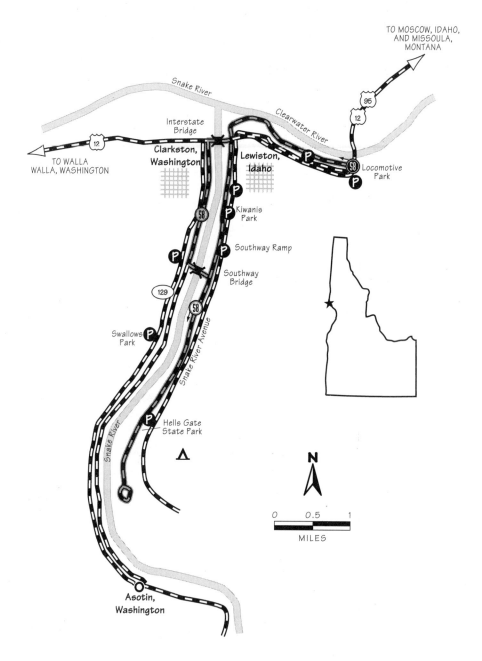

Notes on the trail: The Clearwater and Snake River National Recreation Trail is a nifty paved trail system that runs along the crest of protective 18-foot levies bordering the two rivers. The trail also knits together a series of parks on the Idaho and Washington sides of the Snake River, much like the Boise River Greenbelt in Boise. Because of Lewiston's mild weather and low elevation—at 700 feet above sea level, the lowest point in Idaho—the paved trail is typically snow-free year-round, except for the occasional fluke snowstorm. By crossing the Interstate Bridge or the Southway Bridge, it's possible to create a loop as part of your ride. Take a moment to stop at the interpretive sites to learn a few fun facts about the Lewis and Clark expedition and the Lower Snake/Columbia waterway. The Port of Lewiston is the uppermost inland shipping port from the Pacific Ocean, about 350 miles from the sea.

Hells Gate State Park has several miles of mountain trails open to hikers, mountain bikers and equestrians. As this book went to press, the trails were overgrown with weeds and in very poor condition. The trails may be improved in the summer of 1999, according to state park officials. After new trail work is completed, these mountain trails may be worth exploring. Inquire at the Hells Gate Park Headquarters (for more information, call 208-799-5015).

THE RIDE

0.0 Jump on the pathway next to the river and climb a short ramp to the top of the levy. You are riding along the Clearwater River in a westerly direction.

0.3 Parking access.

0.7 Parking access and restrooms at Clearwater Landing.

1.3 Parking area by giant drawbridge.

1.7 Lewis and Clark interpretive site at the confluence of the Clearwater and Snake rivers; restrooms. Cyclists can take a skybridge over the highway here to ride into the city of Lewiston. The Corps of Discovery camped at this location October 5, 1805, on their way to the Pacific. The path bends to the south here and proceeds up the Snake River.

2.0 Path runs under Interstate Bridge (possible loop junction).

2.6 Lewiston Levy Parkway access area and park.

3.2 Parking area and boat launch site.

4.0 Cross under Southway Bridge (possible loop junction).

4.8 Parkway leaves the levy and runs along the highway for a short section before dropping down along the dike.

5.3 Small park and restrooms.

5.6 Enter Hells Gate State Park marina area. Stay to the right on the parkway next to the river until the path ends temporarily in the parking lot. Keep heading south across the parking lot and pick up the path as it continues south into the state park campground.

7.0 Parkway ends in campground. It's possible to ride another half-mile to the south on campground roads if you wish. Otherwise, turn around to head back to Locomotive Park.

Variation: On your way back to Locomotive Park, cross the Southway Bridge and ride the Greenbelt Trail on the Washington side in the northerly direction to the Interstate Bridge in Clarkston. Cross back to the Idaho side on the Interstate Bridge (use the narrow bike lane on the north side of traffic) and ride back to Locomotive Park. This loop ride adds about 1 mile to the out-and-back ride from Locomotive Park to Hells Gate State Park, making for a 15-mile loop.

Lewis and Clark Trail/Lolo Motorway

Location:	Powell Junction, 168 miles east of Lewiston or 65 miles west of Missoula, Montana.
Distance:	72.9 miles, one way.
Time:	Three to four days.
Tread:	72.9 miles of single-lane dirt road. Surface is rocky with many ruts, divots, and washboard bumps.
Aerobic level:	Most strenuous on Day 1 with 2,000-vertical-foot climb; Day 2 features more rolling up-and-down terrain; Day three is easiest with long downhill to the finish. Vehicle support is recommended for the entire distance.
Technical difficulty:	2 for many rocky, rough, rutted, and washboard-prone sections.
Highlights:	Historic recreational ride on a tree-lined ridge road high above the Lochsa River. The route follows the overland route of the Corps of Discovery in 1805— the single most arduous portion of their journey from St. Louis, Missouri, to the Pacific Ocean.
Hazards:	Watch out for vehicles and log trucks on the road.
Land status:	Clearwater National Forest.
Maps:	East to West: USGS Rocky Point, Cayuse Junction, Indian Post Office, Horseshoe Lake, Lookout Peak, Holly Creek, Liz Butte, Weitas Butte, Snowy Summit, Boundary Peak, Musselshell, Syringa.

Access: Take U.S. Highway 12 east from Lewiston or west from Missoula to well-marked Powell Junction, a tiny wilderness 'burb with a hotel (Lochsa Lodge), restaurant, and ranger station. This is the rendezvous point for the beginning of the trip. From Powell Junction, take Forest Road 569 to the

Lewis and Clark Trail/Lolo Motorway

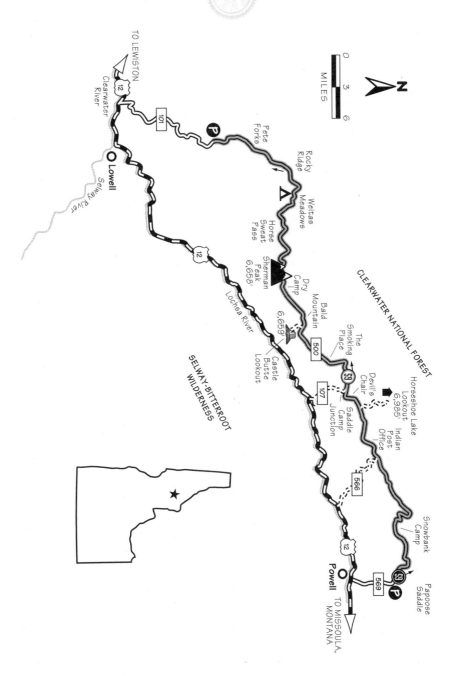

Mountain bike guides Heidi MacDonald and John Indrehus soak in the scenery of the Clearwater National Forest from the "Smoking Place," a lofty ridge with special spiritual meaning to the Nez Perce Indians, along the Lewis and Clark Trail.

Thirteen Mile Camp site at Papoose Saddle to start the ride. If you only have enough time to sample a portion of the ride, a number of Forest Service roads tie into the Lolo Motorway, known locally as the 500 Road, from US 12. Alternative routes include FR 566, 107, and 101. Note: The Clearwater National Forest may put a quota on vehicle use of the 500 Road in the future, depending on tourist use during the bicentennial of the Lewis and Clark expedition (2004–6). Call the Lochsa Ranger District for information on restricted use (see appendix).

Notes on the trail: It's a real treat to retrace the approximate route that Lewis and Clark's Corps of Discovery followed along a craggy ridgeline that bobs up and down along the north side of the Lochsa River canyon. I rode this route in the early 1990s with Lewis and Clark Trail Adventures (see appendix), a Missoula-based outfitter that was just starting to offer guided trips on the Lolo Motorway. It's best to do this three-day ride with vehicle support so you can ride without the burden of carrying all of your food and camping gear, and you can live it up in camp with Dutch oven meals, lawn chairs, and coolers full of beverages—you know what I mean. Make sure that your support vehicle is a 4WD—the 500 Road is very rough in places. A second spare tire would be a good idea, too. For riders who want to carry their camping gear on this route, you may want to extend the time period for the ride to four or five days. Be sure to take at least one book on Lewis and Clark's journey so you can fully appreciate the arduous near-death experience they had passing through this rough country. A number of interpretive signs are located along the 72.9-mile route to provide historical information about the expedition. The ridgetop route also served as a Nez Perce buffalo trail prior to Lewis and Clark's adventure.

Please remember: All singletrack trails peeling off the 500 Road are restricted to foot and stock traffic. No mountain biking on these trails.

Outfitted trips: To inquire about an outfitted trip on the Lolo Motorway, call Lewis and Clark Trail Adventures (see appendix).

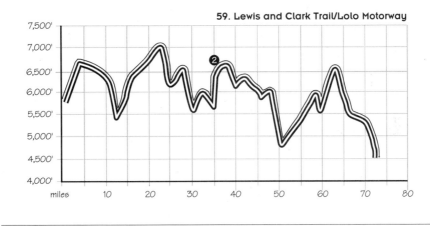

THE RIDE

0.0 Head up the 500 Road. The gradient is all uphill for the first 3 miles. Then it's level or downhill to Snowbank Camp and Cayuse Junction.

8.0 Arrive at Snowbank Camp, named for the snow that the Corps of Discovery had to trudge through as they climbed 3,000 vertical feet from the bottom of the Lochsa River to the ridge (their guide, Old Toby, goofed by taking the party from Lolo Pass down to the river bottom, instead of trying to stay high on the ridge). It's a ripping descent from Snowbank to Cayuse Junction. Enjoy it. There's a big climb ahead.

12.8 Cayuse Junction. Look off to the right to see Cayuse Lake. Now it's time to climb 9 miles and 1,400 vertical feet.

16.6 Pass by Bears Oil and Roots interpretive sign. The name provides hints about the supper menu at the historic campsite.

22.1 Arrive at Indian Post Office, a possible campsite for the first night. The name of this site comes from Indian lore: Nez Perce people used to leave messages in rock cairns for each other on their way east to hunt buffalo. Lonesome Cove Camp is across the road. To continue, ride downhill to Moon Saddle.

24.5 Moon Saddle, a possible campsite. Now you're climbing again to Howard Camp.

26.5 Arrive at Howard Camp, the site of a campsite picked by General O. O. Howard, who was chasing the Nez Perce tribe during the Nez Perce War. This is a broad flat with excellent spots for camping. If you want to take a side trip, ride 4 miles north by Horseshoe Lake to Horseshoe Lookout, where you'll feel on top of the world. After Howard Camp, you're climbing to Devil's Chair.

28.0 Pass by Devil's Chair, a granite rock formation resembling a chair. Now it's time to fly downhill to Saddle Camp. You'll drop 1,000 vertical feet in less than five minutes.

30.2 Major four-way saddle junction at junction with Saddle Camp Road (Forest Road 107). This road drops down to US 12 in 9 miles. Not a good spot for a campsite.

32.5 Interpretive sign for Sinque Hole Camp.

35.8 Junction with the Smoking Place, a high ridgetop with big views of the Lochsa Canyon and Selway Crags to the south. It's a worthwhile side hike.

39.8 Two-way junction. A left-hand turn provides an uphill side trip to Castle Butte Lookout (not recommended). Go right and climb toward Bald Mountain.

41.6 Pass grassy slope under the shadow of Bald Mountain. Enjoy the big open vistas. It's mostly level or downhill now for several miles.

43.7 Arrive at Dry Camp, an excellent spot for camping at the end of Day 2. It's mostly level or downhill from here to Sherman Peak.

45.4 Arrive at trailhead for Noseeum Meadows and Sherman Creek at a saddle junction. It's a nice 1-mile side hike from here to Sherman Creek to see the Weippe Prairie off to the west. This is the place where the Corps of Discovery finally saw a way out of the dark woods, cold, and snow, much to their delight. Hence the name: Spirit of Revival Ridge.

50.1 Horse Sweat Pass and Sherman Saddle. A rough up-and-down section, including three steep climbs, is coming up on the way to Rocky Ridge Peak.

53.6 Pass Deep Saddle and climb again.

56.9 Pass Green Saddle and climb one more time.

61.1 Arrive at Rocky Ridge Lake and Rocky Ridge Peak. A good potential campsite for the last night. There's one more big climb to the top of Rocky Ridge at 6,400 feet, and then, it's a fun gravity ride to the end of the trip. It's a blast to whiz by tall old-growth hemlock, fir, and cedar trees. Watch out for vehicles and log trucks coming up the road.

64.5 Whoa! Check out the interpretive sign for Patrick Gass.

66.4 Pete Creek junction on right, FR 104.

68.8 Junction with FR 485 to Boundary Peak Lookout. A potential side trip.

72.9 Reach Canyon Junction, where the 500 Road converges with FR 101 and 483. Time to load up the bikes and take FR 101 down to US 12, east of Kooskia. Hope you had a blast!

Coolwater Ridge
Epic Jungle Ride

Location: 98 miles east of Lewiston.

Distance: 24.7 miles, one-way, with shuttle; 35.2 miles without shuttle.

Time: 6 to 8 hours.

Tread: 17.7 miles of 2WD gravel road; 8.5 miles of gnarly doubletrack road; 9 miles of singletrack.

Aerobic level: Strenuous (big time). This ride features a whopping 5,400-foot climb over 12 miles and a grueling but rewarding 5,000-foot all-singletrack descent that will make your arms, neck, and hands quiver from fatigue.

Technical difficulty: 3 +. The tread on the Coolwater Ridge Road starts out very smooth, but it gets increasingly technical in the last 3 miles of the climb on a gnarly jeep road. The singletrack portion of the ride is fairly smooth, but heavy junglebrush makes visibility difficult in many places.

Highlights: Monster views of the Selway-Bitterroot Wilderness from the top of Coolwater Ridge; killer singletrack descent; awesome workout.

Hazards: High potential bonk factor; junglebrush in singletrack descent could cause you to lose the trail. Stay alert.

Land status: Nez Perce National Forest.

Maps: USGS Lowell, Coolwater Mountain, Stillman Point.

Access: Take U.S. Highway 12 east of Lewiston or west of Missoula, Montana, to Lowell, Idaho, a small community at the junction of the Selway and Lochsa rivers. Go south on the Selway River Road (FR 223) about a half-mile to the beginning of the Coolwater Ridge Road, Forest Road 317. If you want to eliminate a 10.5-mile slightly downhill ride back to the car along the bumpy and washboard-prone Selway River Road, shuttle a rig to the Boyd Creek Campground, 10.5 miles from Lowell.

Notes on the trail: The Coolwater Ridge Epic Jungle Ride should be reserved for those hardy souls who have the physical endurance necessary for not only a 5,400-foot climb but also a taxing, 5,000-foot singletrack descent through tall and overhanging ferns and brush. In fact, you might want to pack a machete (just kidding). It's best to ride this trail in cool, clear weather

Coolwater Ridge Epic Jungle Ride

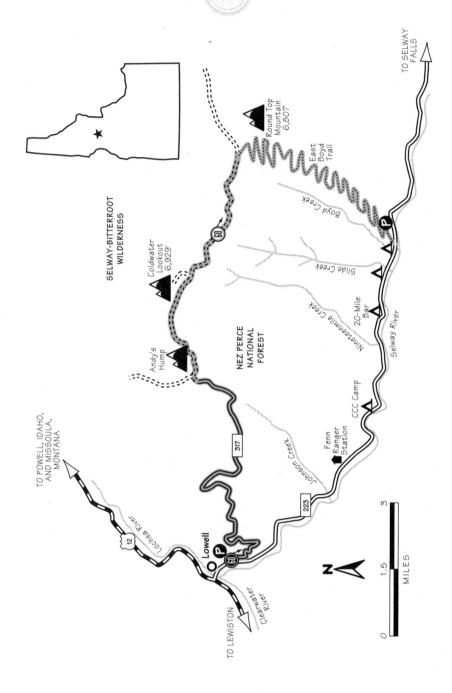

SELWAY-BITTERROOT WILDERNESS

Round Top Mountain 6,807'

East Boyd Trail

Boyd Creek

TO SELWAY FALLS

Coldwater Lookout 6,929'

Slide Creek

20-Mile Bar

Nineteenmile Creek

Selway River

Andy's Hump

NEZ PERCE NATIONAL FOREST

CCC Camp

317

Johnson Creek

Fenn Ranger Station

223

TO POWELL, IDAHO, AND MISSOULA, MONTANA

Lochsa River

12

Lowell

Clearwater River

TO LEWISTON

N

0   1.5   3

MILES

Harley Parson and Leo Hennessy struggle to stay with a narrow singletrack amid tall ferns and thimbleberry leaves in the Clearwater National Forest.

in September. To miss out on the summit views because of rain would be a shame. Carry a ton of water and take your time on the climb up Coolwater Ridge to the Coolwater Lookout. You can replenish water supplies at two coolwater springs just before the lookout.

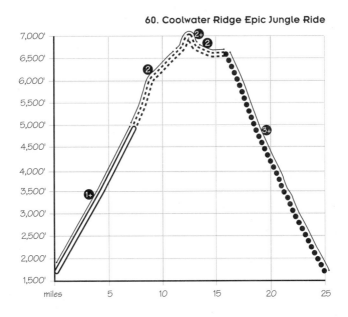

0.0 Head up FR 317 and spin easy gears to conserve energy. The road stays in the shade on a north slope for the first 7 miles.

1.2 First switchback. Are we having fun yet? A series of switchbacks keeps the road grade at a reasonable level.

7.2 The road breaks out of the trees on a first ridgetop saddle, providing awesome views of the Selway-Bitterroot country. Don't be fooled. It's still 5 miles of continuous climbing and 1,000 vertical feet to Coolwater Lookout. The tread becomes more primitive now on a doubletrack surface.

8.8 Road junction. Go right toward the lookout. The road surface will get increasingly rocky as it approaches the lookout.

9.0 Water spring! Time to cool off and fill up on water. You can see the lookout now off to the south.

11.7 Second spring.

12.0 Junction with spur road to top of lookout. It's a quarter-mile to the top, well worth it for the views of several high mountain lakes below, the Selway Crags, and a 360-degree view of the Clearwater National Forest.

12.5 Back at the lookout junction, continue south on the ridge (FR 317) as it cruises up and down for the next several miles.

14.5 Ignore junction on right and stay high on the ridge road.

14.7 Pass by wilderness trailhead on left. Stay on ridge road.

15.7 Junction on right with the East Boyd Trail. The sign for this trail was missing from the sign post when I rode this trail in July 1998. It is a well-trodden singletrack with rock water bars. Turn right on the singletrack and begin the huge descent. Use caution to avoid getting pitched by tall, abrupt rock and log water bars.

16.2 First of many switchbacks. Keep your speed down and your weight back to avoid getting pitched by the water bars, which may be hidden by increasingly thick brush on the upper slope.

17.0 The first of a number of tiny stream and boggy crossings like this one in the next few miles. The crossings may or may not be ridable, depending on the time of year and mush factor. Use caution.

20.0 Trail begins to enter tree cover in places, providing welcome shade in the heat of the summer, and the brush factor is less extreme.

24.7 Trail dumps out at Boyd Creek Campground. Turn right to head down the Selway River Road back to your rig. If you shuttled a vehicle to this point, you're done! Take a swim in the Selway River. You deserve it.

35.2 Return to the Coolwater Ridge Road junction on the Selway River Road. Wahoo!

Fish Creek Loops

Location:	7 miles south of Grangeville.
Distance:	6.6-mile (or less) loop.
Time:	1.5 hours or less.
Tread:	6.6 miles of singletrack.
Aerobic level:	Easy to moderate.
Technical difficulty:	2. Mostly smooth tread with a few bumps, rocks, and ruts.
Highlights:	A rare find in Idaho: very moderate rolling terrain in the mountains. Big views of the Gospel-Hump Wilderness.
Hazards:	Watch out for equestrians, hikers, and other cyclists.
Land status:	Nez Perce National Forest.
Maps:	USGS Goodwin Meadows, Whitebird Hill.

Access: From downtown Grangeville, head to the east end of town and turn south at the signed turnoff to Snowhaven ski area. Follow the narrow two-lane paved road 7 miles to the Fish Creek park-and-ski area and campground (1 mile past the entrance to Snowhaven). Turn right into the trailhead parking area and park near the covered pavilion.

Notes on the trail: The Fish Creek Loops contain a delightful network of trails in a shady, forested setting. This is an excellent area for beginning mountain bikers, families, and kids.

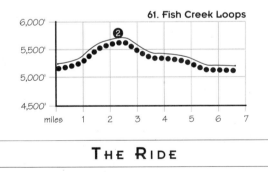

THE RIDE

0.0 Pick up the trail to the south of the pavilion and trailhead sign. Cross the meadow and ride across the campground paved driveway to continue on the trail.

0.1 Cross the creek on a small bridge and go through a gate. At the junction of the Fish Creek Loops, bear right to ride the loop counterclockwise, the easiest way.

Fish Creek Loops

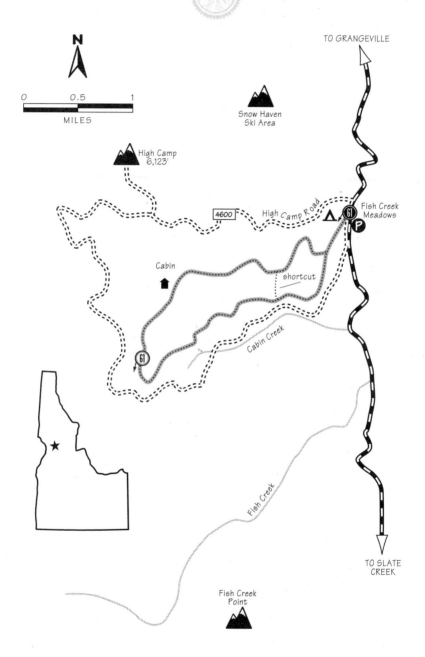

N

0   0.5   1
MILES

TO GRANGEVILLE

Snow Haven
Ski Area

High Camp
6,123'

4600   High Camp Road

Fish Creek
Meadows

61

P

Cabin

shortcut

61

Cabin Creek

Fish Creek

TO SLATE
CREEK

Fish Creek
Point

Harley Parson spins across one of a number of wooden bridges in a boggy area of the Fish Creek Loop Trail.

0.6 Follow the Fish Creek loop to the right.

1.4 Junction with shortcut loop. Ignore shortcut unless you're ready to head back to the parking lot.

1.6 Junction with meadow cutoff trail. Follow sign for Fish Creek loop and cabin.

1.8 Bear left at unsigned junction.

2.3 Junction with cabin trail loop. Stay on Fish Creek loop.

2.5 Junction with boundary cutoff trail. Stay on Fish Creek loop.

3.4 Bear left at unsigned junction. Then go straight at four-way junction. If in doubt, follow the blue diamonds on the trees.

3.9 Cross boggy area.

4.2 Bear left at unsigned junction.

4.6 Bear right at meadow cutoff sign.

5.1 Bear left at unsigned junction.

5.4 Bear right at unsigned junction.

5.8 Bear left at unsigned junction.

6.0 Ignore junction on left and go straight.

6.4 You've completed the loop. Mix it up and try another loop if you've got the energy, or repeat the loop in the opposite direction.

6.6 Return to the parking lot.

Bill Chipman Palouse Trail

Location:	Moscow to Pullman, Washington.
Distance:	8.7 miles, one-way; 17.4 miles, out and back.
Time:	30 minutes to 1.5 hours.
Tread:	8.7 miles of paved pathway.
Aerobic level:	Easy, depending on headwinds.
Technical difficulty:	Easy.
Highlights:	Nice paved pathway that links the border towns of Moscow and Pullman, Washington. There is a Starbucks coffee house at the end of the pathway in Pullman, next to the Washington State University campus.
Hazards:	Please yield to walkers, joggers, dogs, children, etc.
Land status:	Whitman County, Washington.
Maps:	None available at press time. A pathway map may be produced in 1999. You can't get lost: The trail runs from the University of Idaho along Idaho Highway 8 the whole way.

Access: The Palouse Trail can be accessed next to Starbucks in Pullman, along Sixth Street in downtown Moscow, or at the western edge of the University of Idaho campus in Moscow, across from Wendy's and Stinker gas station. The campus parking lot across from Wendy's has several reserved parking slots for the Palouse Trail (4 hours maximum).

Notes on the trail: The Palouse trail offers a convenient and popular paved pathway for greenbelt riders. It's a good early-season destination for local mountain bikers, too.

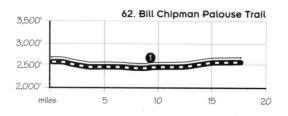

Bill Chipman Palouse Trail

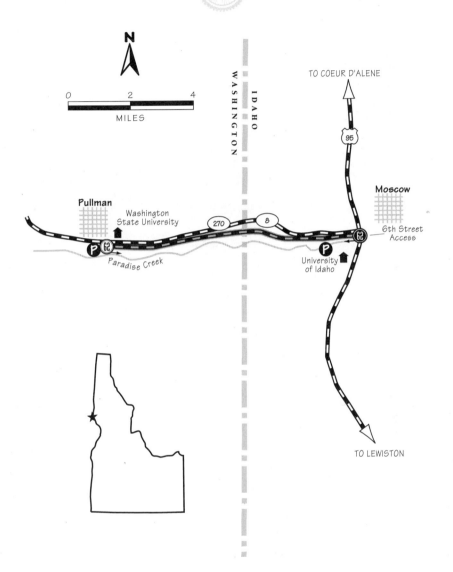

The author takes an early-morning cruise on the Palouse Trail, an urban pathway that links the university towns of Pullman, Washington, and Moscow, Idaho.

THE RIDE

0.0 From the end of the pathway on Sixth Street in Moscow (by the railroad tracks), pick up the paved pathway and follow it through the University of Idaho campus.

1.0 Intersect University of Idaho parking area across ID 8 from Wendy's.

2.0 Reach Moscow city limits.

3.2 Pass wooden bridge and public restroom. Parking access.

8.7 Reach end of trail next to Starbucks, a Quality Inn, and Washington State University. Have a beverage, turn around, and go back.

Moscow Mountain Majesty

Location: 5 miles northeast of Moscow.

Distance: 13.2-mile loop.

Time: 2 hours.

Tread: 2.7 miles of gravel road, 4.6 miles of doubletrack, 5.9 miles of singletrack.

Moscow Mountain Majesty

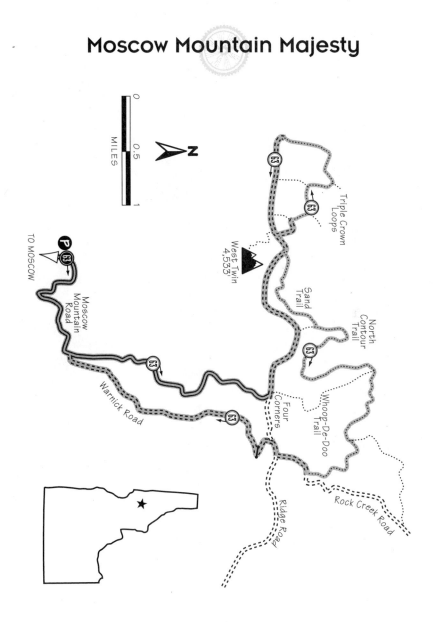

MILES

0 0.5 1

N

TO MOSCOW

Moscow Mountain Road

Warnick Road

West Twin 4,535'

Triple Crown Loops

Sand Trail

North Contour Trail

Four Corners

Whoop-De-Doo Trail

Ridge Road

Rock Creek Road

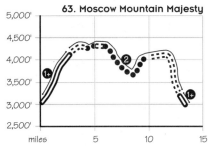

63. Moscow Mountain Majesty

5,000'
4,500'
4,000'
3,500'
3,000'
2,500'

miles   5   10   15

Marci Stephens rides the super-buffed Sand Trail on Moscow Mountain.

Aerobic level:	Moderately strenuous. Riders climb only one section of supersteep singletrack in this ride, but they must have the endurance to climb up to the top of Moscow Mountain to access the best singletrack trails, and, after a number of descents, be prepared to climb back over the mountain spine before the final descent.
Technical difficulty:	Level 1 or 2 most of the way.
Highlights:	The sweetest singletrack surface imaginable on the North Contour Trail and portions of the Sand Trail. Cool views of the Palouse to the south and dark old-growth cedar forests looming overhead on the north side of Moscow Mountain.
Hazards:	A labyrinth of dirt roads, doubletrack roads, and singletrack creates vast potential for getting lost. Pay attention to directions and, if in doubt, ask local riders for assistance. None of the trails or junctions is signed.
Land status:	Private forest land, University of Idaho Experimental Forest, Clearwater National Forest.
Maps:	USGS Moscow Mountain, Robinson Lake.

Access: Follow U.S. Highway 95 to the north end of Moscow and head east on D Street. In a mile, turn left on Mountain View Road. Mountain View Park is a good place to rendezvous with friends and leave extra vehicles. One mile east of the park, turn right on the gravel Moscow Mountain Road, (the turn is not marked, nor is there a road sign). Follow Moscow Mountain Road about 5 miles to a little parking area next to a hairpin turn. Park off to the side of the road. Do not block a driveway with a brown gate and a yellow "Private Drive" sign.

Notes on the trail: Local riders have created a beautiful trail system on top of Moscow Mountain, with the cooperation of a private timberland owner. This ride description takes you on a tour of the best singletrack riding on the mountain, covering the Triple Crown loops, the North Contour Trail, and the Sand Trail. This is only a glimpse of the full potential of Moscow Mountain, however. For more information, see the local book, *Mountain Bike Guide to Hog Heaven*, by Jim LaFortune, or explore on your own. As noted above, however, it's wise to be cautious on Moscow Mountain because there are so many unmarked trails and intersections—it'd be a cinch to get lost.

THE RIDE

0.0 Head up the dirt road in a comfortable spinning gear. It's a 1,300-vertical-foot climb over 2.7 miles to Four Corners Junction, a key intersection on the ridge spine of Moscow Mountain.

0.9 Bear left at two-way junction.

2.7 Confront Four Corners Junction, a major four-way junction with other road offshoots nearby. Go straight through the blue gate and turn left on the Ridge Road. You're headed west on the Ridge Road to the first ring of the Triple Crown loop.

3.2 Sand Trail peels off to the right. Note junction for future reference. Keep going straight.

4.0 North Contour Trail peels off to the right. Note junction for future reference. Keep going straight on the Ridge Road.

4.1 Turn right on doubletrack to begin a counterclockwise tour of the Triple Crown loops. Bear right and then left immediately after making the initial turn. You'll pass by a green cabin.

4.3 Go directly across a skid trail and then bear right on a doubletrack road.

4.4 Bear left onto a grassy doubletrack, and then right on a singletrack heading into the woods. The singletrack is currently marked by a pink ribbon tied to a pine tree. The ribbon may or may not be present in the future.

4.6 Bear right at two-way junction.

4.7 Bear right at two-way junction.

4.8 The singletrack drops back onto the Ridge Road. Turn left and head for the North Contour Trail.

4.9 Ignore a major dirt road on the right, which climbs to a number of radio towers.

6.0 Peel left off Ridge Road on the North Contour singletrack, a very buffed and smooth trail.

6.5 Contour Trail merges with Sand Trail. Bear left to ride the sweetest portion of the Sand Trail singletrack, a very smooth narrow pathway on a cushioned duff layer on the forest floor.

7.4 Reach possible bailout point at junction with Whoop-de-doo Trail. You can turn right to return to the Ridge Road at Four Corners junction. Go left to continue on the Sand Trail.

7.7 Take a hard right-hand turn in an open area.

8.7 Turn right at a trail junction marked by a wooden pallet on the right. This singletrack angles back toward Rock Creek Road at a continuous but moderate grade, at first.

9.1 At a four-way junction, turn left on the steep singletrack and climb through the woods to the Rock Creek Road.

10.3 Bear right on Rock Creek, a major dirt road, and climb to the ridge.

11.3 Reach a four-way saddle junction. Bear left on the doubletrack and pass by a blue gate. This is the Warnick Road descent back to the parking area. Stay on the main road and ignore minor roads shooting off to the left and right as you descend.

12.3 Merge with main Moscow Mountain Road.

13.2 Arrive in parking area.

Variation: For a shorter loop after the initial climb to Four Corners Junction, go straight on the Whoop-de-doo Trail and descend a half-mile or so to the Sand Trail. Turn left and follow the Sand Trail and North Contour Trail back to Ridge Road. Turn left on Ridge Road to return to Four Corners and descend back to the parking area. This loop is only about 8 miles long.

64

Piah Creek Loop

Location:	35 miles northeast of Moscow.
Distance:	14.8-mile loop.
Time:	2 hours and up, depending on speed of travel and food breaks.
Tread:	3.8 miles of doubletrack, 11 miles of singletrack.
Aerobic level:	Moderate to majorly strenuous on uphill singletrack sections from the Giant White Pine Campground to North-South ski area.
Technical difficulty:	2. Most of the singletrack is superbuffed, but there are a few technical sections with roots and ruts.
Highlights:	Very sweet singletrack riding in old-growth forest environment.
Hazards:	Please yield to hikers, horseback riders, and other riders.
Land status:	Clearwater National Forest, private timberland.
Maps:	USGS West Dennis, Emida; Clearwater National Forest map.

Access: From Moscow, head north on U.S. Highway 95 to the junction with Idaho Highway 6 to Potlatch. Turn right and follow ID 6 about 20 miles, past the Giant White Pine Campground to a pass. Forest Service signs point the direction to Palouse Divide Nordic Trails. Turn right on Forest Road 377, pull off to the side of the road and park. The ride starts here, at the site of the now defunct North-South ski area.

Notes on the trail: The Piah Creek Loop is bound to become an Idaho classic. It has some gorgeous sections of serpentlike singletrack in dark old-growth forest and some major climbing from the Giant White Pine Campground back to the start. Because of the length and amount of climbing involved in this ride, it's an advanced or expert ride. The only downside to this ride is that several logging projects have ripped up the singletrack trail, replacing it with logging road for the time being. Follow directions carefully in these sections. Some riders may wish to start the ride at the Giant White Pine Campground and ride

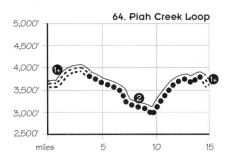

Piah Creek Loop

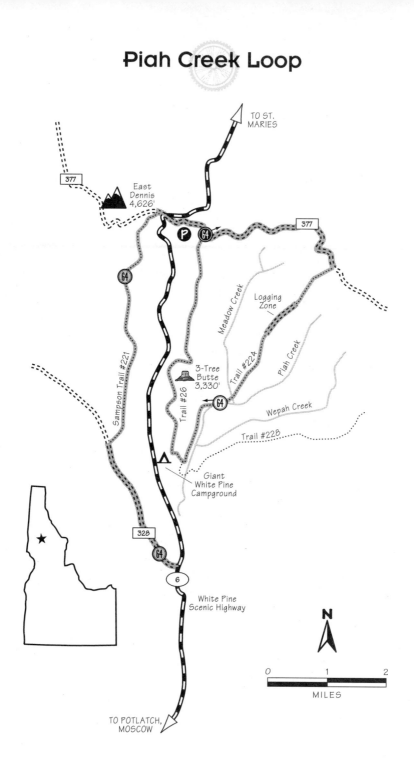

TO ST. MARIES

377

East Dennis 4,626'

377

P 64

Meadow Creek

Logging Zone

Trail #224

Piah Creek

Sampson Trail #221

3-Tree Butte 3,330'

Trail #26

64

Wepah Creek

Trail #228

Giant White Pine Campground

328

64

6

White Pine Scenic Highway

N

0   1   2
MILES

TO POTLATCH, MOSCOW

a major uphill climb first instead of ending the ride with a long climb. From the description below, you can figure out directions and make that decision on your own. Camping is available at the Giant White Pine Campground. Staying overnight is a good idea for out-of-town riders because there are many other trails to explore in the area, including the Sampson Trail 221 across the highway (see variation).

THE RIDE

0.0 Head up the dirt road. By a gate, bear right immediately toward the park-and-ski trails.

0.3 Bear left on FR 377. Get ready for a fast downhill on the doubletrack dirt road.

3.8 Whoa! Turn right at signed junction with Trail 224. The gorgeous singletrack begins here, on the right side of the gated doubletrack road.

4.7 Bear left on the singletrack and follow a logging road through a recent logging zone. Pick up the trail as the logging road ends.

5.3 Follow singletrack onto a logging road. Follow the road to the top of the next hill.

5.4 Peel right by an orange ribbon and pick up the singletrack again. (The ribbon marks the turn, but, the ribbon may or may not be present in the future.)

5.6 Trail crosses dirt road to three-way junction on other side. Take the middle route and climb.

6.0 Bear left at two-way singletrack junction.

6.4 Go directly across dirt road and pick up trail on other side. Big descent ahead.

7.7 After crossing a wooden bridge, get into your little ring to climb.

7.8 Go left at trail junction.

8.3 Trail climbs uphill.

8.6 Go straight at junction.

9.3 Go right on Beason Meadow Trail 228. Now you're heading into the Giant White Pine Campground.

9.6 At the campground junction, go right on Trail 224A.

10.6 Bear left at major trail junction on Trail 26, your climbing buddy, heading for Three Tree Butte and North-South ski area. The worst uphills are in the next 0.7 mile.

12.6 Cross FR 1443. Two more miles of climbing ahead.

14.6 Trail 26 ends at a T-intersection with FR 377. Go left and ride back to your vehicle.

14.8 Reach the vehicle.

Variation: If you're camping at the Giant White Pine Campground, try riding the Sampson Trail 221 on the other side of the highway. Ambitious riders could ride the Sampson Trail uphill to North-South ski area, cross the highway, and ride Trail 26 downhill to the Giant White Pine Campground. To access the Sampson Trail, cross ID 6 and pick up Forest Road 328. Climb 328 to Sampson Trail 221. Climbing on this trail is easier than climbing Trail 26.

The Panhandle:
Lakeview Singletracks Galore

The Panhandle region of Idaho is almost like a different world. The rivers run smooth, the heavily forested mountains appear molded into soft rounded curves, and many beautiful lakes, including Lake Coeur d'Alene and Lake Pend Oreille, add a measure of delight to trailside views.

The mere presence of so much water should warn riders that precipitation is common in this part of Idaho, especially in the fall, winter, and spring. In midsummer, however, high pressure can move in and provide a long string of bluebird days. The riding season runs from May through October, with a few exceptions.

A number of the rides in this region are on uncommonly gentle terrain, such as the trails in Farragut State Park and lakeshore trails along Priest Lake and Upper Priest Lake. It's rare to find such sweet singletrack without having to pay serious dues in the form of long gut-buster climbs. And this is the region where you'll find the popular Route of the Hiawatha Rail-Trail, near Wallace.

Other activities in the Panhandle include camping, swimming, and boating. Underground mine tours are available daily in Wallace and Kellogg. Check out the Cataldo Mission on the way to Silver Mountain. Silverwood, a family theme park north of Coeur d'Alene, has a roller coaster, many kids' rides, and air shows. Luxury accommodations and fine dining are available at the Coeur d'Alene Resort. Sandpoint has a number of uncommonly good restaurants for a small town.

North Idaho Centennial Trail

Location:	Coeur d'Alene–Post Falls–Spokane, Washington.
Distance:	23 miles, one-way, from Coeur d'Alene to Stateline; trail continues for 37 additional miles into Spokane.
Time:	Depends on length of trip and speed of travel.
Tread:	23 miles of paved urban pathway.
Aerobic level:	Easy.
Technical difficulty:	1.
Highlights:	Scenic urban pathway bordering Coeur d'Alene Lake.
Hazards:	Please watch out for and yield to pedestrians, dogs, children, etc.
Land status:	Mixed: City of Coeur d'Alene, Kootenai County, Idaho Department of Transportation, Federal Highways Administration.
Maps:	City of Coeur d'Alene has a good map of the Idaho portion of the trail; Friends of the Centennial Trail in Spokane has a nice map of the Washington portion.

Access: Multiple entry points. This ride description starts on the eastern end of the path and proceeds to Stateline, Idaho. Ride or drive on Lakeshore Drive to the eastern end of the path, just before Blue Creek Bay.

Notes on the trail: The North Idaho Centennial Trail is quite a gem, considering it runs for 23 miles in Idaho and 37 miles in Washington, making for a potential 60-mile one-way journey. The trail knits together a series of parks, waterways, and points of interest along the way. The only downside is that you've got to endure a less scenic windblown section of pathway along the freeway between Lake Coeur d'Alene and Post Falls. Things get decidedly more scenic when the trail runs alongside either Lake Coeur d'Alene or the Spokane River. Be aware that there are a few places in downtown Coeur d'Alene, Post Falls, and Spokane where the pathway ends temporarily and riders have to follow bike lanes in traffic. While this description is one approach to riding the trail, consider simply tapping into the Centennial Trail where it is most convenient for you and riding as far as you please.

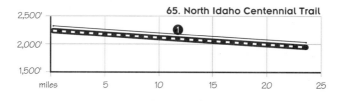

North Idaho Centennial Trail

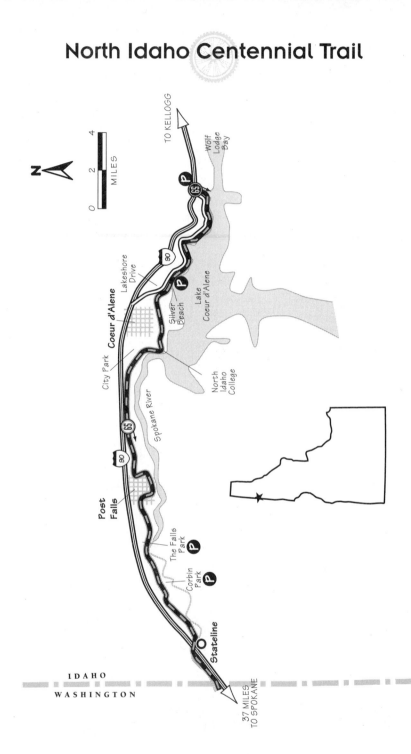

TO KELLOGG

Wolf Lodge Bay

Lakeshore Drive

Coeur d'Alene

Silver Beach

Lake Coeur d'Alene

City Park

North Idaho College

Spokane River

Post Falls

The Falls Park

Corbin Park

Stateline

IDAHO

WASHINGTON

37 MILES TO SPOKANE

N

MILES

0 2 4

Michelle Gilbertson takes a spin on the North Idaho Centennial Trail alongside Lake Coeur d'Alene.

THE RIDE

0.0 Head west on the Centennial Trail as it winds along Lakeshore Drive, offering excellent views of Lake Coeur d'Alene along the way.

3.0 Pass Bennett Bay.

4.6 Approach Silver Beach, a public beach and access point.

5.7 Pathway ends temporarily and follows bike lanes through downtown Coeur d'Alene. The path begins again in earnest at North Idaho College.

8.0 Access at North Idaho College.

8.5 Pass through City Park.

10.0 Pathway parallels the freeway.

11.7 Access and parking at Atlas Road.

14.5 Enter Post Falls area. Pathway ends temporarily and follows bike lanes on streets through town. Keep heading west.

17.5 Trail begins again prior to the Falls Park trailhead and parking area. Path follows bank of Spokane River for a piece here.

20.5 Pathway courses through Corbin Park.

21.0 Enter Riverbend Commerce Park.

23.0 Centennial Trail enters Stateline, a border town, and passes under Interstate 90 at Gateway Bridge. It's 39 miles from here to Spokane.

Mount Coeur d'Alene Loop

Location:	15 miles south of Coeur d'Alene.
Distance:	8.1-mile loop.
Time:	1 hour.
Tread:	8.1 miles of gravel road.
Aerobic level:	Easy to moderate on gentle uphill sections.
Technical difficulty:	1+.
Highlights:	Scenic loop ride around the top of Mount Coeur d'Alene with overlook views of Coeur d'Alene Lake. Family special.
Hazards:	None.
Land status:	Panhandle National Forests, Coeur d'Alene National Forest.
Maps:	USGS Mount Coeur d'Alene.

Access: From Coeur d'Alene, take Interstate 90 east to exit 22 to Idaho Highway 97 and Harrison. Turn right and head south on ID 97. In 2 miles, turn left on Forest Road 438. Follow the paved road for 8.3 miles and turn right on FR 453. At a T-junction, go right, pull off the road, and park. The ride starts here.

Notes on the trail: This is a low-key scenic ride around the top of Mount Coeur d'Alene (elevation 4,439 feet) for families and beginning riders. You will get some nice views of Lake Coeur d'Alene, the city of Coeur d'Alene, Canfield Mountain, and Tubbs Hill as you ride the loop. You'll also pass by a picnic area with tables but no restrooms. The loop starts on a logging road on the south side of Mount Coeur d'Alene and then wraps around to the north side of the mountain on FR 439. For a change of pace on the drive home, take FR 439 down to Turner Bay and follow the lakeshore back to the freeway.

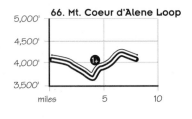

THE RIDE

0.0 Go back to the T-intersection and go left on the logging road. You'll pass by a gate. The doubletrack road is quite smooth as it contours along the mountain.

0.7 Ignore logging road on left and bear right.

Mount Coeur d'Alene Loop

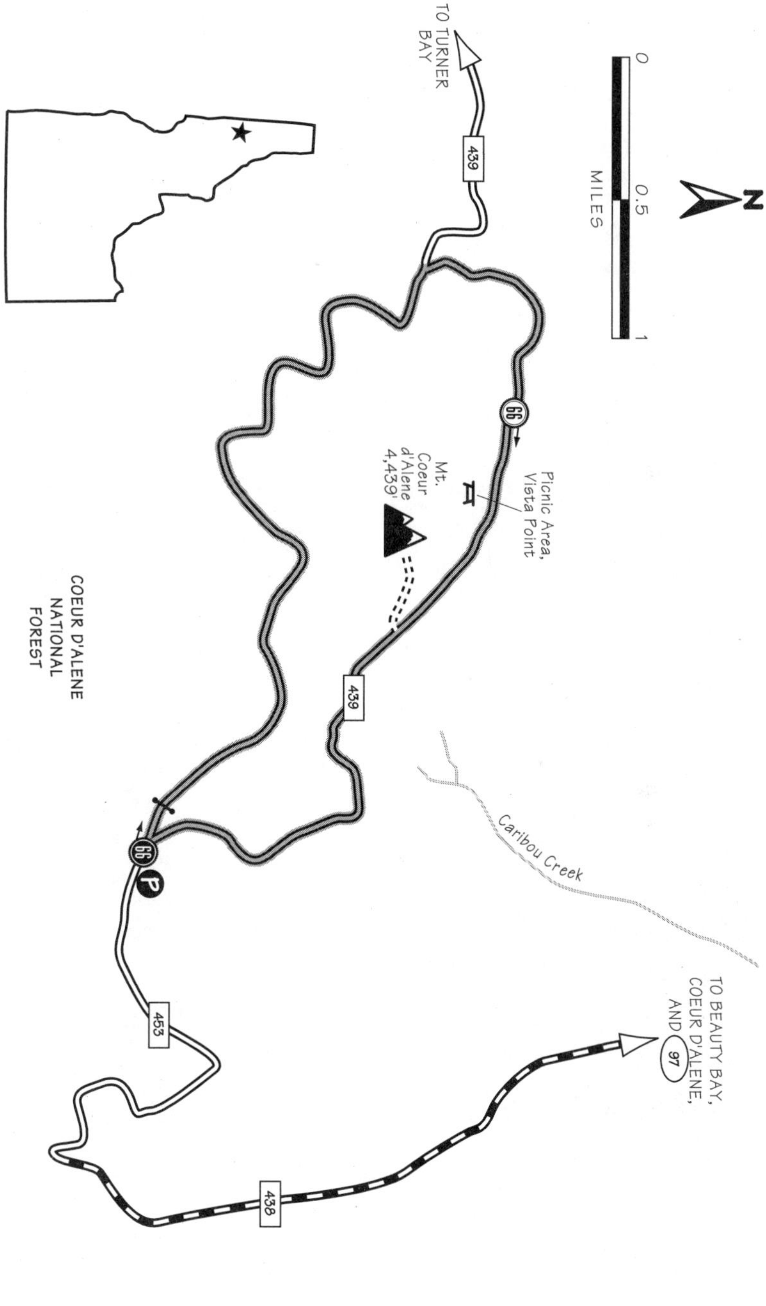

TO TURNER
BAY

439

MILES

0   0.5   1

N

COEUR D'ALENE
NATIONAL
FOREST

99

Mt.
Coeur
d'Alene
4,439

Picnic Area,
Vista Point

439

Caribou Creek

99

P

453

438

TO BEAUTY BAY,
COEUR D'ALENE,
AND
97

Mount Coeur d'Alene provides a perfect perch about 2,500 feet above the lake and city of the same name.

3.9 Junction with FR 439 as logging road ends. Turn right and head for the picnic area. Ignore logging roads on left.

5.2 Ignore logging road on left.

5.4 Enter picnic area. The remains of a fountain and interpretive sign indicate vandalism. Take a food break and enjoy the views.

6.1 Junction with road to the top of the mountain (the road is blocked by heavy brush, and there is no view from the flat-topped peak). Continue on the dirt road—downhill now—back to your vehicle.

8.1 Arrive at the T-intersection and your vehicle.

Canfield Mountain Mecca

Location:	North end of Coeur d'Alene.
Distance:	17.7-mile loop; potential variations up here are endless.
Time:	2.5 to 3 hours.
Tread:	9.5 miles of singletrack, 7.7 miles of doubletrack
Aerobic level:	Moderate most of the way, with the exception of a couple short, steep strenuous sections.
Technical difficulty:	2 overall. Steep downhill singletrack from the top of Trail 5 rates 3 + to 4.
Highlights:	Awesome network of singletrack and doubletrack trails in proximity to the city of Coeur d'Alene. Ride out of your driveway to enjoy the area.
Hazards:	Canfield Mountain is a popular destination for hikers, mountain bikers, horseback riders, and motorcyclists. Please exercise caution and yield to other trail users.
Land status:	Coeur d'Alene National Forest, Panhandle National Forests.
Maps:	USGS Fernan Lake. Free color map on Canfield Mountain trail system is available from the Forest Service and local outdoor stores.

Access: From downtown Coeur d'Alene, head east to Fifteenth Street, a north-south street on the north side of Interstate 90. Take Fifteenth Street north of the freeway 1 mile to Nettleton Gulch Road. Turn right and head up the road for 2 miles to the trailhead.

Notes on the trail: Canfield Mountain offers a huge variety of rides close to downtown Coeur d'Alene. The loop ride described here was recommended by Mark Beattie, owner of Vertical Earth bike shop (see appendix) in Coeur d'Alene. The loop will give riders an excellent overview of the trails on

Canfield Mountain Mecca

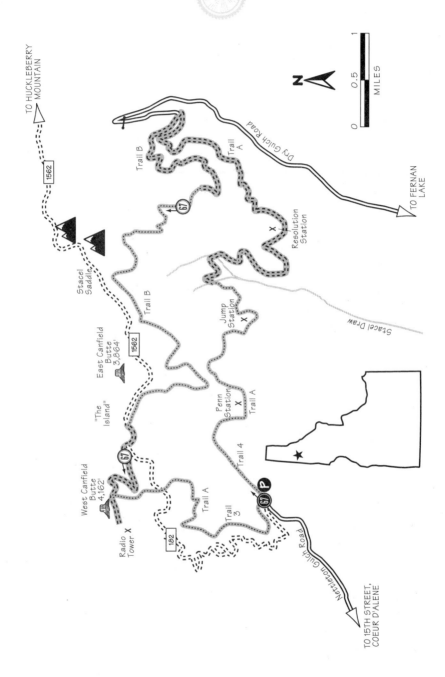

TO HUCKLEBERRY MOUNTAIN

1562

Stacel Saddle

Trail B

67

Trail A

Dry Gulch Road

TO FERNAN LAKE

Resolution Station

East Canfield Butte 3,864'

1562

"The Island"

Trail B

Jump Station

Stacel Draw

67

West Canfield Butte 4,162'

Penn Station

Trail A

Radio Tower X

182

Trail A

Trail 4

Trail 3

67 P

67

Nettleton Gulch Road

TO 15TH STREET, COEUR D'ALENE

N

MILES

0   0.5   1

Canfield Mountain because it takes you across the front side of the mountain on a long uphill contour on Trail A, then back across the mountain toward the top on Trail B, and then down some steep technical singletrack back to the Nettleton Gulch Trailhead. Local motorcycle

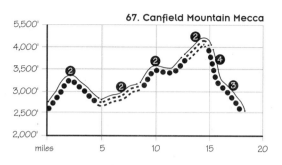

riders deserve credit for working with the Forest Service to develop the vast network of trails on the mountain and for posting signs at nearly every trail junction. If you get a chance, thank them for their efforts.

THE RIDE

0.0 From the Nettleton Gulch Trailhead, head up Trail 4, an uphill singletrack, to start the ride. It's the middle trail of the three singletracks that depart from this area. You should see a trail sign on the left before climbing several tight switchbacks.

0.2 Steep gradient moderates a bit as the trail follows a creek.

0.6 Cross creek (ridable).

1.0 Turn right at junction of Trail 4 and Trail A. Now you're going to contour across the mountain on Trail A, riding a moderate uphill grade on singletrack.

1.7 Arrive at Penn Station, a major junction. Go right on Trail A.

2.5 Arrive at Jump Station junction. Bear left on Trail A.

3–3.4 Encounter serious mud bog (may be unridable, depending on weather).

3.8 Cross creek (ridable).

4.3 Trail widens to doubletrack through logging zone.

5.0 Junction with Trail 9. Keep going straight on Trail A.

5.6 Junction with Trail 10 at Resolution Station. Mountains to the north come into view.

7.0 Turn left at junction with Trail B on left (not signed). The Dry Gulch trailhead is 0.5 mile straight ahead (alternative access on Forest Road 1562). After you make the turn on Trail B, you'll see a trail sign. Trail is doubletrack surface to begin with; it climbs for the top of East Canfield Butte at a moderate pace.

8.6 Junction with Trail B and Trail 11. Go straight on Trail B.

9.0 Junction with Trail B and Trail 10. Bear right on Trail B and Trail 10. Trail narrows to singletrack tread.

9.6 Trail B peels off to the left from Trail 10.

10.4 Trail B levels off a bit now on a high contour.

11.7 Junction with Trail B and Trail 9. Stay on Trail B.

12.0 Ignore first junction with Trail 8, and then bear left on Trail 7 at junction of Trail 8, Trail B, and Trail 7. Now you're climbing on Trail 7 to the viewpoint saddle.

12.8 Reach junction with Forest Road 1562. Go left and follow the road to the top of West Canfield Butte by a radio tower.

13.1	Bear right at two-way road junction to go to the lookout.
14.3	Reach the top of West Canfield Butte (4,162 feet). Take a breather, munch some food, and enjoy the views of Lake Coeur d'Alene and the city. Turn around and head back down the road.
14.5	Turn right on Trail 5 and ride down the steep eroded singletrack. You will have to do some hemorrhoid polishing on the descent.
15.5	Turn right on Trail A. The downhill grade is not as steep but still fun.
16.0	Bear right at junction with Trail 6 and Trail A.
16.3	Go left on Trail 3 at junction with Trail A. This is the final descent to the trailhead.
17.7	Arrive at trailhead. What a ride!

Farragut State Park: Shoreline Trail

Location:	20 miles north of Coeur d'Alene.
Distance:	3.5 miles, one-way.
Time:	30 minutes and up.
Tread:	Wide-track singletrack and paved pathway.
Aerobic level:	Easy.
Technical difficulty:	1+ for gravel and dirt surface.
Highlights:	Mostly flat well-maintained trail next to Lake Pend Oreille.
Hazards:	Watch out for and yield to hikers and other trail users.
Land status:	Idaho Department of Parks and Recreation.
Maps:	Farragut State Park has free trail maps.

Access: Take U.S. Highway 95 north to the little town of Athol. Turn right and follow Idaho Highway 54 to Farragut State Park and Bayview. After passing the park entrance, turn right on South Road and park at the Highpoint Trailhead. The Highpoint Trail provides access to the western end of the Shoreline Trail. Plan to pay a day use fee to ride the trails if you're parking a vehicle in the park.

Notes on the trail: Farragut State Park offers a rare opportunity for novice mountain bikers and families with young children to ride a moderate to flat trail next to Lake Pend Oreille. You can visit the park for a day trip

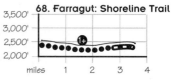

Farragut State Park: Shoreline Trail and Northside Loop

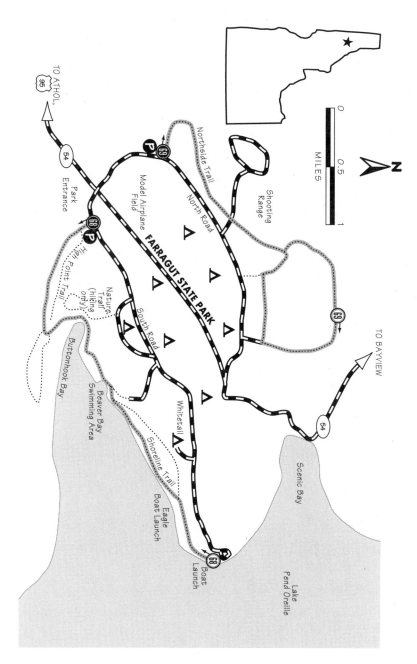

The Shoreline Trail in Farragut State Park rolls along Lake Pend Oreille at a mostly level grade, making it a perfect family trail.

or make reservations well in advance (this is a popular car camping mecca) and plan a major camp-out adventure. The park has public beaches and boat launch facilities, too, so there's lots to do. The Shoreline Trail follows a bench just above the shoreline of Lake Pend Oreille. Much of the trail is graveled or paved and easy to ride.

THE RIDE

0.0 Follow the Highpoint Trail as it enters dense timber and heads southeast.

0.6 At the second junction, turn left on the well-signed Shoreline Trail. In short order, the trail will leave the trees and wind along Buttonhook Bay.

1.0 Buttonhook Bay trail access. Go straight on the Shoreline Trail.

1.5 Pass Beaver Bay swimming area.

2.3 Encounter three-way junction. Trail access to Whitetail Campground and short loop possibilities. Go straight and stay on the Shoreline Trail.

2.8 Trail emerges at parking area for the Eagle Boat Launch. Shoreline Trail is paved from here to the Willow day use area.

3.5 Trail ends at eastern end of Willow day use area. Turn around and retrace your tracks, take a swim, or try a variation on the way back.

69

Farragut State Park: Northside Loop

See Map
on Page 245

Location:	20 miles north of Coeur d'Alene.
Distance:	4.7-mile loop.
Time:	45 minutes to 1 hour.
Tread:	Singletrack.
Aerobic level:	Easy.
Technical difficulty:	2 for rocks, ruts, and roots.
Highlights:	Mostly flat, well-maintained, and signed forest trail in large state park.
Hazards:	Watch out for and yield to hikers, horseback riders, and other trail users.
Land status:	Idaho Department of Parks and Recreation.
Maps:	Farragut State Park has free trail maps.

Access: Take U.S. Highway 95 north to the little town of Athol. Turn right and follow Idaho Highway 54 to Farragut State Park and Bayview. After passing the park entrance, turn left on North Road and watch for a trailhead

Gary Gilbertson and a young friend follow a rare open section of the mostly forested singletrack on the north side of Farragut State Park.

on your left where the paved road takes a hard right. The trails on the north side of the park are labeled horse trails on the map. The ride starts here.

69. Farragut: Northside Loop

[Elevation profile chart showing elevation from 2,000' to 3,500' over 5 miles, with point ② marked near mile 3]

Notes on the trail: Farragut State Park offers a rare opportunity for novice mountain bikers and families with young children to ride a moderate to flat trail next to Lake Pend Oreille. You can visit the park for a day trip or make reservations well in advance (this is a popular car camping mecca) and plan a major camp-out adventure. The park has public beaches and boat launch facilities, too, so there's lots to do. The Northside Loop is more like a genuine mountain trail than the wide, buffed Shoreline Trail. It passes through thick timber, often lodgepole pine, and breaks out into open grasslands occasionally. Some locals ride this loop in the winter, depending on weather.

THE RIDE

0.0 Follow the trail out of the parking area.

0.3 Bear right at the first trail junction. Now you're heading for the shooting range road.

1.3 Cross shooting range access road and continue on the Northside Loop.

2.0 Turn left at junction 5 and begin a 2-mile loop, going clockwise.

3.6 Pass by junction 3. Ignore trail on the left.

3.8 At junction 2, turn right.

4.4 At junction 6, bear right again.

4.7 Return to junction 5. You've closed the loop. Now you can ride the loop in a counterclockwise direction or retrace your tracks back to the start.

Bernard Peak Loop

Location:	Near Bayview.
Distance:	18.5-mile loop.
Time:	3 hours.
Tread:	4.4 miles of gravel road, 8.9 miles of doubletrack, 5.2 miles of singletrack.
Aerobic level:	Mostly moderate gradient climbing to the top of Bernard Peak, but it's still 2,650 feet of vertical gain to get there. After that, it's all downhill.

Bernard Peak Loop

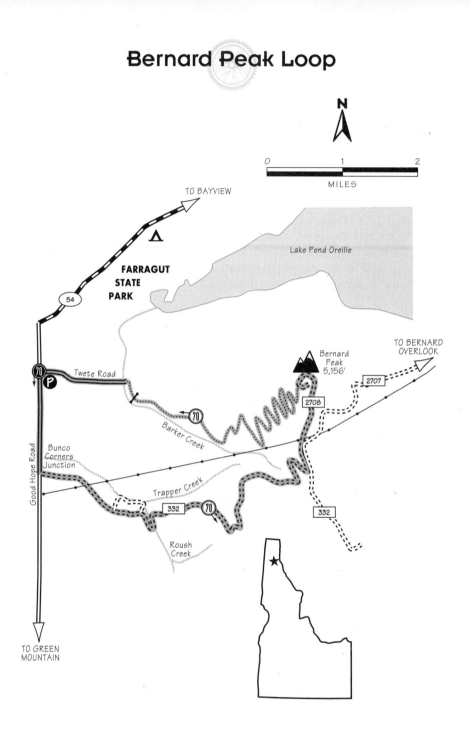

N

0   1   2

MILES

TO BAYVIEW

Lake Pend Oreille

FARRAGUT
STATE
PARK

54

70

Twete Road

P

Barker Creek

70

Bernard
Peak
5,156'

2707

2708

TO BERNARD
OVERLOOK

Good Hope Road

Bunco
Corners
Junction

Trapper Creek

332

70

332

Roush
Creek

TO GREEN
MOUNTAIN

Gary Gilbertson descends a lovely singletrack below Bernard Peak.

Technical difficulty:	2. Nearly all of the singletrack is premium and buffed, except for a tiny steep section with mobile death cookies and loose soil right off the top (3 + for 0.1 mile).
Highlights:	Beautiful loop ride within sight of Lake Pend Oreille.
Hazards:	Watch out for trees and limbs hanging into the singletrack as you're whizzing by.
Land status:	Panhandle National Forests.
Maps:	USGS Bayview; Panhandle National Forests, North.

Access: Take U.S. Highway 95 north to Athol. Turn right on Idaho Highway 54 and head for Farragut State Park. Just before the park entrance, turn right on a dirt road. In a half-mile, watch for Twete Road on the left. Park next to the road sign in a vehicle pullout. The ride starts here.

Notes on the trail: The Bernard Peak Loop is an excellent advanced ride near Farragut State Park and Bayview. The loop starts with a pretty hefty 10-mile climb to the top of Bernard Peak on a smooth doubletrack dirt road. On top, take a moment to hike through the brush to view the southern end of Lake Pend Oreille and the surrounding countryside. Then it's time to enjoy some beautiful singletrack that winds through the dark woods on the west slope of Bernard Peak for 5 miles. The ride finishes out on doubletrack dirt roads and county roads back to your vehicle.

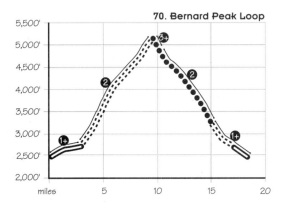

THE RIDE

0.0 From the Twete Road junction, head dead south on the wide dirt road known as Good Hope Road.

1.4 Reach turnoff to Bunco Road. Turn left and ride up Bunco.

3.0 Bear right on Forest Road 332. The road climbs at a continuous but moderate grade. Spin gears to conserve energy.

7.6 Bear left on FR 2707.

8.0 Bear left on FR 2708. The grade gets steeper now to the top.

9.7 Reach the top of Bernard Peak (5,156 feet). Take a break and enjoy the view. Note the evidence of a fire lookout that has since been removed. On the west side of the broad opening at the summit, a singletrack trail heads down to the gravel road and crosses it. This is your trail heading downhill. Exercise caution on the first 100 feet of the trail—it's nasty.

9.8 Cross the gravel road and descend on the singletrack. The delightful trail winds through the dense forest.

11.5 Encounter nasty switchback. You may want to walk. This is the first of a series of switchbacks.

12.4 Good spot to pull off the trail to enjoy a view of the lake.

14.9 Singletrack ends on doubletrack road. Ignore logging spurs on the left.

16.2 Pass by a gate.

17.1 Doubletrack dumps out on gravel road next to pasture. This is Twete Road. Go straight (west) and head back to your vehicle.

18.5 Arrive at your vehicle at Twete and Good Hope junction.

71

Silver Mountain Nature Trail

Location:	Kellogg.
Distance:	2.8-mile loop.
Time:	30 minutes.
Tread:	0.5 mile of doubletrack, 2.3 miles of singletrack.
Aerobic level:	Moderate.
Technical difficulty:	2. Singletrack is very rocky in a couple places, and the singletrack switchbacks provide a measure of challenge.
Highlights:	Best singletrack loop at the top of Silver Mountain ski area. See Ride 72 for the best long ride off the top.
Hazards:	Watch out for large rocks, and yield to hikers and mountain bikers on the trail.
Land status:	Silver Mountain Resort.
Maps:	USGS Polaris Peak, Coeur d'Alene National Forest, Silver Mountain trail map.

Access: Take Interstate 90 to Kellogg city center exit 49. Turn right and drive into town. You'll see the Silver Mountain gondola building and the parking lot across the street. Park. Take the gondola to the top of the mountain. Lift fee in 1998 was $9.95 for a full-day lift ticket for adults or teens.

71. Silver Mountain Nature Trail

Silver Mountain Nature Trail

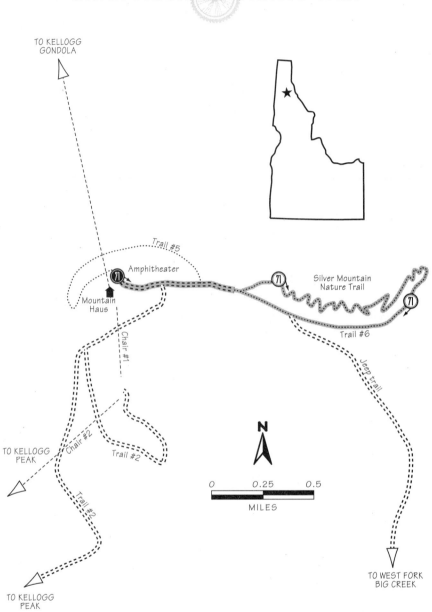

TO KELLOGG
GONDOLA

Trail #5

Amphitheater

Mountain
Haus

Silver Mountain
Nature Trail

Chair #1

Trail #6

Jeep trail

Chair #2

TO KELLOGG
PEAK

Trail #2

Trail #2

N

0   0.25   0.5

MILES

TO KELLOGG
PEAK

TO WEST FORK
BIG CREEK

Classic views of Kellogg Mountain open up on the Silver Mountain Nature Trail.

Notes on the trail: The Silver Mountain Nature Trail is the best self-enclosed loop at the top of the gondola lift. The loop is short but sweet, and you can stop and read about nature along the way. You can ride the loop clockwise and counterclockwise and then sample the lift-served gravel roads on the mountain if you wish. Then check out Ride 72 for very cool singletrack from the top of Kellogg Mountain down the West Fork of Big Creek, ending at the bottom of the valley.

THE RIDE

0.0 After arriving at the Mountain Haus, at the top of the gondola, ride over to the amphitheater. This is a common starting point for several short loop trails near the Mountain Haus. Follow signs for Nature Trail 6.

0.5 Veer left to pick up the singletrack Nature Trail.

1.2 Ride a number of switchbacks on a moderate uphill grade.

2.2 Encounter a number of interpretive signs after riding over some rough thick-diameter rocks.

2.7 You've completed the loop. Now turn around and ride the loop counterclockwise if you've got the interest or the energy, or ride back to the amphitheater.

2.8 Arrive at the amphitheater.

Silver Mountain–Big Creek Banzai

Location:	Kellogg.
Distance:	14.8 miles, one-way.
Time:	1 hour and up.
Tread:	1.8 miles of doubletrack, 5.2 miles of singletrack, 0.7 mile of gravel road, 7.1 miles of paved road.
Aerobic level:	Moderate for death-grip braking on downhill singletrack.
Technical difficulty:	2 to 3+ on most technical portions of singletrack—loose dirt, steep pitch, multiple opportunities to crash.
Highlights:	This is the best all-gravity singletrack ride from the top of Silver Mountain ski area to Kellogg.
Hazards:	Watch out for large rocks, and yield to hikers, horseback riders, and mountain bikers on the trail.
Land status:	Silver Mountain Resort, Coeur d'Alene National Forest, Panhandle National Forests.
Maps:	USGS Polaris Peak, Kellogg East, Coeur d'Alene National Forest, Silver Mountain trail map.

Access: Take Interstate 90 to Kellogg city center exit 49. Turn right and drive into town. You'll see the Silver Mountain gondola building and the parking lot across the street. Park. Take the gondola to the top of the mountain. Lift fee in 1998 was $9.95 for a full-day lift ticket for adults or teens.

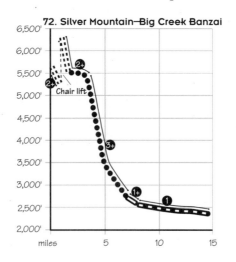

Silver Mountain–Big Creek Banzai

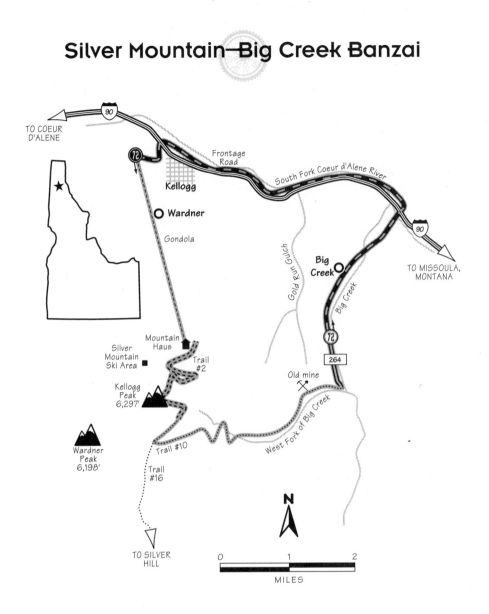

TO COEUR
D'ALENE

90

72

Frontage
Road

South Fork Coeur d'Alene River

Kellogg

O **Wardner**

Gondola

90

TO MISSOULA,
MONTANA

Gold Run Gulch

**Big
Creek** O

Big Creek

Mountain
Haus

Silver
Mountain
Ski Area

Trail
#2

72

264

Kellogg
Peak
6,297'

Old mine

West Fork of Big Creek

Wardner
Peak
6,198'

Trail #10

Trail
#16

N

TO SILVER
HILL

0   1   2

MILES

The Big Creek singletrack descends at a steep grade amid big timber and ferns in the Coeur d'Alene National Forest.

Notes on the trail: This ride is a total hoot for advanced riders. Steep downhill sections will scare less experienced riders to the point where they may walk and wish they hadn't tried this ride. The lift-served mountain biking is pretty limited on Silver Mountain proper, so the mountain managers are savvy enough to suggest out-of-bounds singletracks that wind down from Kellogg Peak to the valley. You will need a lift to the Mountain Haus on the gondola, and then you'll need to take a chair lift to the top of Kellogg Peak to get in position to begin the long descent. The following ride description follows Trail 10 from Kellogg Peak down the West Fork of Big Creek to the old mining town of Big Creek. Then you'll ride downhill on flat paved roads back to Kellogg. If there's a headwind, it could be a bit of a strain along the freeway.

THE RIDE

0.0 After arriving at the Mountain Haus, at the top of the gondola, ride over to the amphitheater. Follow signs for Trail 2 and follow a gravel road down to the bottom of a chair lift that takes riders to the top of Kellogg Peak.

1.0 Arrive at chair lift. From the top of Kellogg Peak, take Trail 2 downhill. Don't go too fast—there's a turn coming up quickly on the right.

1.4 At saddle junction, turn right on access road to Trail 16 and Trail 10. It runs downhill to start with.

1.8 Road dissolves to singletrack and climbs an abrupt short ridable pitch.

2.1 Trail levels out and begins to descend through rough large-diameter rocks. Spin easy gears for best stability through the rough stuff. Here comes the big descent!

3.0 Go left at junction with Trail 16 and stay on Trail 10.

4.1 Enter series of steep switchbacks. Be sure to use your front brake and feather both brakes to avoid skidding and crashing.

4.8 Cross creek (ridable).

5.7 Gnarly creek crossing. Probably smartest to walk—or you might get slammed into the creek bed on slippery rocks.

6.2 Pass by portal of old mine shaft.

7.0 Trail comes to Big Creek jeep trail. Take the foot bridge across the creek and go left on the dirt road.

7.7 Dirt road hits pavement. Ride downhill by the old town of Big Creek.

10.2 Ride under the freeway bridge and turn left on the Frontage Road on the other side. You're heading back to Kellogg.

14.0 As you enter the outskirts of Kellogg, go straight on the Frontage Road.

14.2 Turn left and then right on Bunker Street.

14.8 Arrive at the base of the gondola lift. You survived!

Variation: There is an even more challenging long ride off the top, Trail 16, which features a series of major climbs to follow a ridge over to Silver Hill.

Route of the Hiawatha

Location:	15 miles northeast of Avery.
Distance:	12.7 miles, one-way.
Time:	1 hour and up, depending on speed of travel, lunch stops, etc.
Tread:	12.7 miles of rail-trail.
Aerobic level:	Easy (all downhill with shuttle).
Technical difficulty:	1+.
Highlights:	All-downhill rail-trail passes through eight—count 'em, eight!—tunnels and over seven high trestles. Experienced riders can ride the trail uphill to double the pleasure.
Hazards:	Riding in the dark. Be sure to bring a bright light (flashlights and headlamps do poorly in pitch-black tunnels). Watch out for people inside the tunnels.
Land status:	Panhandle National Forests, St. Joe National Forest.
Maps:	USGS Shefoot Mountain.

Access: Freeway is the quickest way to reach the top of the rail-trail. Take Interstate 90 east of Coeur d'Alene about 50 miles to Taft exit 5 in Montana. Follow signs to Roland Trailhead. To reach the Pearson Trailhead at the bottom of the trail, take Forest Road 456 south of Wallace over Moon Pass, or drive up the St. Joe River from St. Maries. Directions from downtown St. Maries: Follow Idaho Highway 97 toward Harrison and Coeur d'Alene. After crossing the St. Joe River, turn right on FR 50, a paved road, to Calder and Avery. It's 43 miles to Avery, which has fuel and a general store. Just past Avery, turn left on FR 456 to the well-marked Pearson Trailhead. Park. The ride starts here. The Forest Service charges a trail fee; in 1998 it was $5 for adults and $3 for children. Tickets can be purchased from trail marshals at the trailhead. Shuttle: If you can't arrange your own two-vehicle shuttle, call ahead (208-744-1392) to arrange a shuttle between the two trailheads for a fee.

Notes on the trail: The Route of the Hiawatha is, without a doubt, one of the most fun and unique rail-trail mountain biking trips in the Northwest. Following the historic route of the Old Milwaukee Road, the rail-trail passes through eight tunnels and over seven high trestles (equipped with guard rails for safety) as part of a 12.7 mile adventure. As mentioned above, high-beam lights are essential for the ride to navigate the pitch-black tunnels, and helmets are required. It's an understatement to say this rail line is rich with history. Check out the interpretive signs along the way. By the

Route of the Hiawatha

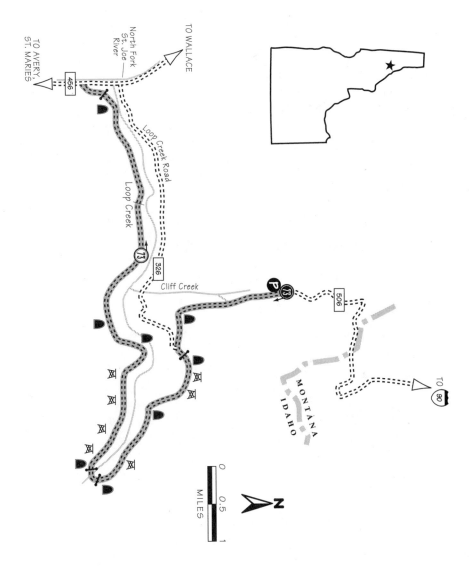

Be sure to take a bright light for the thrilling 12.8-mile descent through eight tunnels on the Route of the Hiawatha Rail-Trail.

year 2001 or 2002, the 1.7-mile Taft Tunnel on the Idaho-Montana border is expected to be ready for public use. Then riders will be able to lengthen the ride from the top, starting with a very cool and exciting ride through the long tunnel. Ambitious riders eventually will be able to ride sections of the Route of the Hiawatha in Montana. All told, the trail will run 46 miles, from the Pearson Trailhead in the upper St. Joe in Idaho to St. Regis, Montana. In the meantime, fire up the high beams and ride! By the way, don't forget to take your sunglasses off in the tunnels.

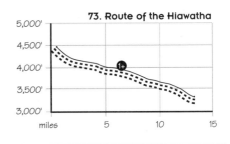

73. Route of the Hiawatha

THE RIDE

0.0 Head downhill from the west portal of the Taft Tunnel. It's a 2 percent downhill grade the whole way.

1.5 Enter the first tunnel. Turn on the lights.

1.7 Exit tunnel. Enjoy views of the upper St. Joe River country as the rail route unfolds before your eyes. Yes, you will be riding over those 200-foot-high trestles below.

2.3 Pass by Cliff Creek Road junction, FR 506 (shuttle route to the bottom). Bear left on rail-trail.

2.4 Enter second tunnel.

2.8 Exit tunnel.

3.3 Route bypasses a tunnel under repair.

3.4 Enter third tunnel. After you emerge on the other side, cross first high trestle. Note the large wooden beams above you. This rail line was electrified at one time.

3.8 Pass over second trestle.

4.4 Pass over the Kelly Creek trestle, the longest one.

5.3 Cross creek and enter fourth tunnel. This one has a bend in it, as the rail-trail begins a major hairpin turn.

5.5 Exit tunnel and cross the Loop Creek Road.

5.6 Enter fifth tunnel.

5.7 Exit tunnel.

6.3 Cross over Turkey Creek trestle.

6.9 Cross over No-Name trestle.

7.4 Cross over Bear Creek trestle.

7.7 Cross over the Clear Creek trestle, the highest one at 246 feet. This one is quite scenic as it spans a small creek winding down from steep mountains above.

8.1 Enter sixth tunnel and exit.

8.2 Enter seventh tunnel and exit. Now you've got 4 miles of fairly level riding to the next tunnel.

12.0 Enter and exit eighth and final tunnel, a short one.

12.7 Arrive at Pearson Trailhead.

Variation: Start from the bottom and ride uphill on the Route of the Hiawatha—and then ride back down, to double the fun. Experienced riders will enjoy the challenge of riding uphill on the easy grade. See if you can make it in less than an hour (you must average 14 m.p.h. going uphill; it's doable).

Sagle Community Trail

Location:	Sandpoint.
Distance:	4.8 miles, one-way.
Time:	30 minutes.
Tread:	4.8 miles of paved pathway.
Aerobic level:	Easy.
Technical difficulty:	1.
Highlights:	Nice pathway adjacent to beautiful Lake Pend Oreille.
Hazards:	Please watch out for and yield to walkers, joggers, children, and others using the pathway.
Land status:	Idaho Department of Transportation.
Maps:	USGS Sandpoint, Sagle.

Access: From the city of Sandpoint, head to the south end of town on U.S. Highway 95. Next to a Texaco gas station is a parking area for pathway users. Park. The ride starts here.

Notes on the trail: Though not nearly as extensive as the North Idaho Centennial Trail, the Sandpoint Greenbelt is almost 5 miles long, making for a 10-mile round-trip. It starts out by running alongside US 95 on the long bridge across Lake Pend Oreille, a deep lake framed by mountains. Then it runs south to Sagle and the road to Garfield Bay. Sandpoint is a nifty resort town with an eclectic mix of restaurants and shopping as well as a public beach—a cool place to visit, to be sure.

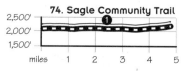

THE RIDE

0.0 Head south on the pathway.

1.0 Begin the trek across the US 95 long bridge. The path is very wide here for lots of pedestrian traffic.

Sagle Community Trail

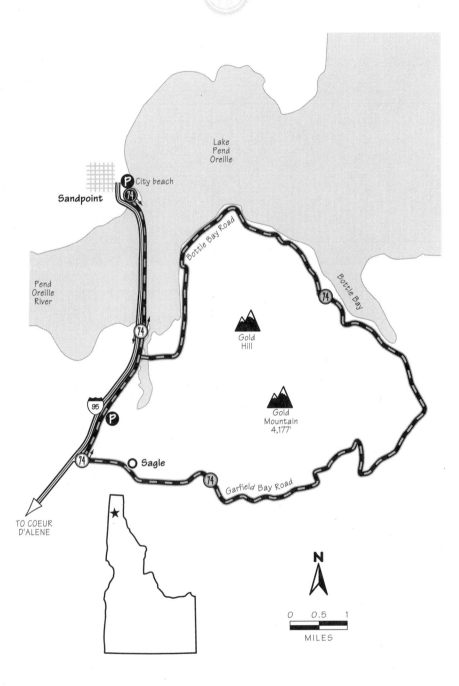

Lake
Pend
Oreille

City beach

Sandpoint

P

74

Bottle Bay Road

Bottle Bay

74

Pend
Oreille
River

74

Gold
Hill

Gold
Mountain
4,177'

95

P

74

Sagle

74

Garfield Bay Road

TO COEUR
D'ALENE

N

0   0.5   1

MILES

The Sagle Community Trail is uncommonly wide as it crosses the U.S. 95 "long bridge" into Sandpoint.

- **2.0** Bridge ends and path runs on a berm parallel to the highway. Cool up and down terrain ahead.
- **2.5** Pass turnoff to Bottle Bay on left.
- **4.1** Parking area for pathway.
- **4.8** Junction with Sagle Road and road to Garfield Bay on left. End of pathway. Turn around and head back to town.

Variation: Instead of retracing your tracks on the bike path, at Sagle Road turn left on the paved road to Garfield Bay and do a loop around Gold Hill and Gold Mountain to the Bottle Bay Road. Then take the Bottle Bay Road back to the bike path and ride to Sandpoint. This is a highly scenic paved road loop about 20 miles long.

Gold Hill Switchback Delight

Location:	8 miles southeast of Sandpoint.
Distance:	10.6 miles, one-way.
Time:	1.5 hours.
Tread:	5.5 miles of singletrack, 5.1 miles of doubletrack road.
Aerobic level:	Strenuous due to fifty-plus switchbacks on the climb to Gold Hill.
Technical difficulty:	2 +. Good riding skills required to navigate hairpin corners.
Highlights:	Entertaining singletrack climb to the top of Gold Hill, which offers splendid views of Lake Pend Oreille. Fast and fun downhill.
Hazards:	Watch out for other trail users and vehicles on the dirt road sections.
Land status:	Panhandle National Forests, Sandpoint District.
Maps:	USGS Oden Bay, Sagle, Talache.

Access: From Sandpoint, ride or drive 3 miles south on U.S. Highway 95 to Bottle Bay Road. Turn left. Bear left at the railroad tracks. Follow Bottle Bay Road 5 miles to a signed trailhead and parking area for Trail 3. Park. The ride starts here. Shuttle: If you're not riding from town, you may want to plant a vehicle at the end of this ride at the junction of Garfield Bay Road and Forest Road 2642.

Notes on the trail: Riders who get dizzy from riding switchbacks had better not attempt this ride. Most advanced riders will enjoy the challenge of trying to ride fifty-plus switchbacks over 4 miles (1,800 feet of vertical gain) to the top of Gold Hill. Although the challenge sounds daunting, the trail is quite smooth and well-engineered—so if you're having a good day, you won't have to make a single dab, much less have to hike. On the way to the summit, be sure to take a moment to enjoy a gorgeous overlook (with picnic tables) of Lake Pend Oreille.

After reaching the summit, you'll be rewarded with a short but fun singletrack downhill and a quick dirt-road descent to Garfield Bay Road. Then it's an easy spin on paved roads back to Sandpoint or to the trailhead. If you're doing this ride with friends, have a contest on counting the number of switchbacks to the top.

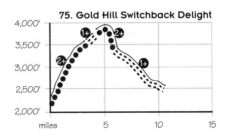

Gold Hill Switchback Delight

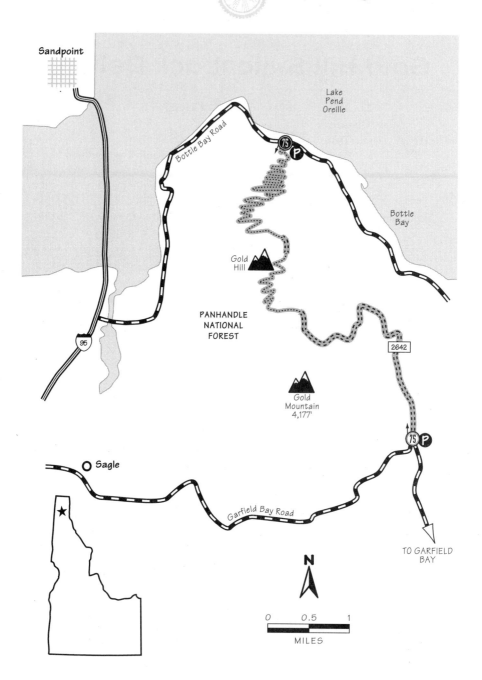

Sandpoint

Lake Pend Oreille

Bottle Bay Road

95

75

P

Bottle Bay

Gold Hill

PANHANDLE NATIONAL FOREST

2642

Gold Mountain 4,177'

75

P

Sagle

Garfield Bay Road

TO GARFIELD BAY

N

0   0.5   1

MILES

Jolanda Van Ooyen leads Tim Boden and Bill Mullane up the Gold Hill switchbacks. Boden jokes that when guys ride with Van Ooyen, they expect to get passed.

The Ride

0.0 Head up Trail 3; spin a comfortable gear for maximum control.

1.3 Twenty switchbacks later . . .

3.0 Forty switchbacks and counting . . .

3.4 Stop a moment at the overlook.

3.9 Crest the summit as Trail 3 joins FR 2642. Go south on the dirt road.

4.4 Road fizzles and turns to singletrack. Go straight and climb.

5.0 Reach a second summit. Now it's a fun downhill ahead with a number of twists and turns, of course.

6.0 Trail dumps out on doubletrack dirt road. It's a zoomer down to Garfield Bay Road from here.

10.6 At the end of FR 2642, turn right and ride 5.5 miles back to Sagle (or go to Garfield Bay and take a swim). Then take the Sandpoint bike path north back to town or to Bottle Bay Road and your vehicle.

Variation: At the top of Gold Hill, turn around and ride the switchbacks downhill.

Green Bay–Mineral Point Loop

Location:	12 miles southeast of Sandpoint.
Distance:	7-mile loop.
Time:	1 hour.
Tread:	2.7 miles of gravel road, 4.3 miles of singletrack.
Aerobic level:	Moderate; a few uphill spurts rate strenuous.
Technical difficulty:	2 to 2+ in rocky sections with tree roots.
Highlights:	Cool, challenging singletrack follows shoreline of Lake Pend Oreille for much of the ride.
Hazards:	Several singletrack sections are perilously close to granite cliffs. Exercise caution!
Land status:	Panhandle National Forests, Sandpoint District.
Maps:	USGS Talache.

Access: From Sandpoint, take U.S. Highway 95 south for 5 miles to Sagle. Turn left on Garfield Bay Road and follow it about 7 miles to the Green Bay Campground. The singletrack starts here.

Notes on the trail: Locals adore this short but technical singletrack scenic tour. The ride starts out of a Forest Service campground and beach, so after youre done, you can take a swim or camp here (get a spot early). There won't be any major uphill pulls on this ride, just lots of up and down on a smooth well-traveled singletrack trail.

At Mineral Point is a rock monument dedicated to Brent "Jake" Jacobson, a Forest Service ranger who was killed in the course of trying to apprehend a fugitive in January 1989.

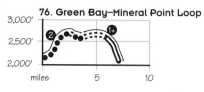

THE RIDE

0.0 Pick up Trail 82 and spin up the trail in low gear.

1.1 Pass a major overlook of the midsection of Lake Pend Oreille, Idaho's largest natural lake.

1.3 Caution: Nasty switchback with exposure.

1.7 Enter interpretive trail area. Bear right and ride around the edge of the interpretive loop. Then bear right again as the trail switchbacks and climbs to the next knoll.

2.0 Rock monument to Forest Service ranger.

Green Bay–Mineral Point Loop

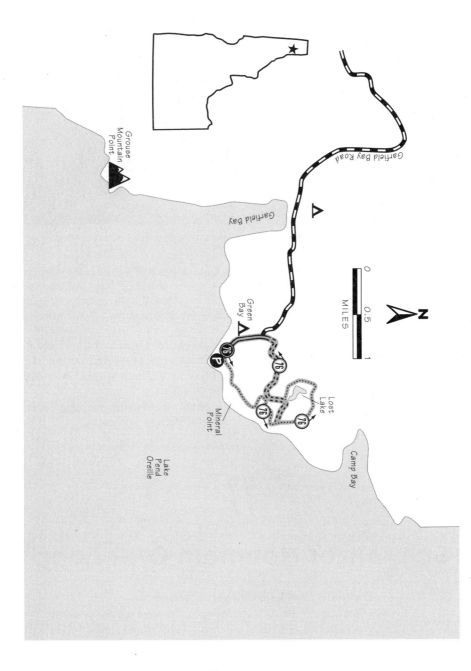

Jolanda Van Ooyen spins along Lake Pend Oreille on the Mineral Point singletrack.

2.3 Trail ends at dirt parking lot for Trail 82 and Forest Road 532. Go directly across the parking lot and watch for a singletrack bailing downhill into the trees. This is the way to Lost Lake—no pun intended. It's also possible to hook up with this singletrack off of FR 532. Follow the singletrack in a scenic winding loop through the trees.

3.3 Singletrack drops out on FR 532. You can take the road back to the parking lot. Or, better, turn around and ride the singletrack back, retracing your tracks.

4.3 Arrive back in parking lot. Turn right and take FR 532 back toward Green Bay Campground.

6.3 Arrive at junction of FR 532 and 2672. Go left to return to the campground. Or take Garfield Bay Road back to Sagle and ride back to Sandpoint.

7.0 Arrive in campground.

77

Schweitzer Mountain GRR Loop

Location: 9 miles northwest of Sandpoint.
Distance: 7.5-mile loop, several other loop options possible.
Time: 1.5 hours.
Tread: 6.5 miles of singletrack, 1 mile of doubletrack.

Schweitzer Mountain GRR Loop

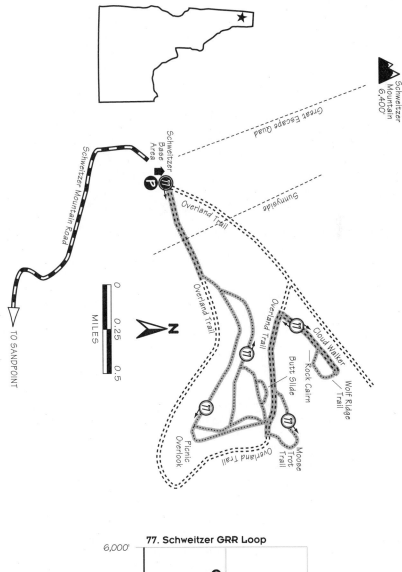

Schweitzer Mountain 6,400'

Great Escape Quad

Sunnyside

Schweitzer Base Area

Overland Trail

Schweitzer Mountain Road

TO SANDPOINT

MILES

0   0.25   0.5

N

Overland Trail

Overland Trail

Cloud Walker

Wolf Ridge Trail

Butt Slide

Rock Cairn

Picnic Overlook

Overland Trail

Moose Trot Trail

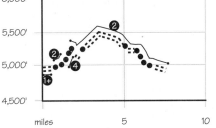

77. Schweitzer GRR Loop

6,000'

5,500'

5,000'

4,500'

miles   5   10

273

Joe Witty, left, and Tim Boden of the Grizzly Ridge Riders take a moment to peer at Lake Pend Oreille and the city of Sandpoint on the GRR Trail on Schweitzer Mountain.

Aerobic level:	Mostly moderate; a few uphill sections are strenuous, but they're short
Technical difficulty:	Most of the loop rates 2 to 3 for typical singletrack obstacles such as loose dirt, rocks, and ruts. The Butt-Slide Trail optional loop rates 3+ to 4 for very technical rock drops.
Highlights:	Delightfully diverse singletrack with great views of Sandpoint and Lake Pend Oreille.
Hazards:	Exercise caution on technical sections—there are multiple opportunities to get pitched or crash.
Land status:	Schweitzer Mountain Resort.
Maps:	Schweitzer Mountain Resort trail maps are best. Trails are too new to be shown on Forest Service or USGS maps.

Access: From downtown Sandpoint, follow signs for Schweitzer Mountain on U.S. Highway 95. At a traffic light junction for US 95 and Idaho Highway 200, go left on Schweitzer Mountain Road. It's 9 miles to the base of the ski area. Lifts run Friday through Sunday during the summer season. It's not necessary, however, to buy a lift ticket for the loop ride described here.

Notes on the trail: Local mountain bikers known as the Grizzly Ridge Riders have developed this nifty singletrack network of short, linked loop trails to enhance the singletrack opportunities at Schweitzer Mountain Resort. The trails provide an excellent after-work area for locals to ride, a race course for the summer season, and a premium destination for avid riders and tourists. The loop ride described below is a mixture of the Overland Trail, GRR (acronym for the club) Trail, Bear Ridge Trail, and Butt-Slide Trail. There are lots of potential combinations here, but this will give you an overall idea of the network.

THE RIDE

0.0 Starting from the Village (base) area, head off to the right (as you face the ski area) on a doubletrack dirt road, which serves as the Overland Trail.

0.1 Pass sign for Overland Trailhead.

0.6 Peel left onto the GRR Trail. Remember, you're in grizzly country. GRRR!

1.6 Pedal up to a picnic area viewpoint of Sandpoint and Lake Pend Oreille. What a view! Take a hard left after the picnic area and bear left on the Bear Ridge Trail.

2.2 Bear Ridge ends and merges with the Overland Trail.

2.3 Turn left and then right on an alternative shortcut expert trail called Butt-Slide Rock, a.k.a. Skid Row. It's a 0.4-mile technical loop. If in doubt, try it and walk anything questionable. After completing the loop, go left on the Overland Trail.

3.6 Go right on a doubletrack road at a two-way junction. You're riding on Cloud Walker to Wolf Ridge Trail.

3.9 Turn right on a singletrack by a rock cairn. And then turn left on a steep singletrack.

4.0 Singletrack pops out on Cloud Walker Trail. You're going downhill.

4.6 Go left at a two-way junction on the Overland Trail.

4.9 Go left on Moose Trot Trail.

5.4 Turn right on Cougar Gulch Road.

5.6 Veer to the right on Bear Ridge singletrack.

5.9 Follow the main trail as it takes a hard right-hand turn onto the GRR Trail by a large rock. Now you're going downhill on GRR toward the bottom of the trail network.

7.1 GRR ends and merges with Overland Trail. Take the doubletrack back to the base area.

7.5 Arrive at the Schweitzer Mountain Village.

Priest Lake Lakeshore Trail

Location:	Nordman.
Distance:	7.2 miles, one-way.
Time:	About 1 hour.
Tread:	7.2 miles of singletrack.
Aerobic level:	Mostly moderate, with a few abrupt steep pitches that rate strenuous.
Technical difficulty:	2. Singletrack is smooth and buffed, with a few roots here and there.
Highlights:	Gorgeous rolling singletrack in neat old-growth forest next to Priest Lake, one of the state's most pristine lakes.
Hazards:	None. Please yield to hikers, joggers, and other cyclists.
Land status:	Panhandle National Forests, Priest Lake District.
Maps:	USGS Priest Lake NW, Priest Lake NE, Panhandle National Forests, North.

Access: From Sandpoint, go west on U.S. Highway 2 to the town of Priest River. Turn north on Idaho Highway 57 heading for Priest Lake, Nordman, and Coolin. At a two-way junction at Coolin, bear left for Nordman. When you reach the tiny town of Nordman, turn right on the paved road to Reeder Bay. Follow the road about 3 miles past Reeder Bay Campground and turn right into a signed parking area for the Lakeshore Trail 294. Shuttle: Drop a vehicle at the northern end of the trail at Beaver Creek Campground if you want to avoid riding the trail or a paved road back to the start.

Notes on the trail: The Lakeshore Trail on the west shoreline of Priest Lake is one of my all-time favorite rides in Idaho. It's a gorgeous trail, being so close to Priest Lake, and the views of the Selkirk Mountains looming across the lake add visual spice to a beautiful setting. On top of the scenery, the singletrack trail tread is amazingly smooth, and it rolls up and down the shoreline, never climbing much before descending again. You'll be riding in an old-growth cedar forest, with ferns and little berry bushes sticking up here and there. Wooden bridges provide safe crossing at creeks. The trail is suitable for intermediate riders and up, and for children with good mountain biking skills. Riders who own a trailer should consider packing in their overnight gear and camping out on one of many white sandy beaches along the trail. After you finish this trail, you may want to ride the Navigation

Priest Lake Lakeshore Trail

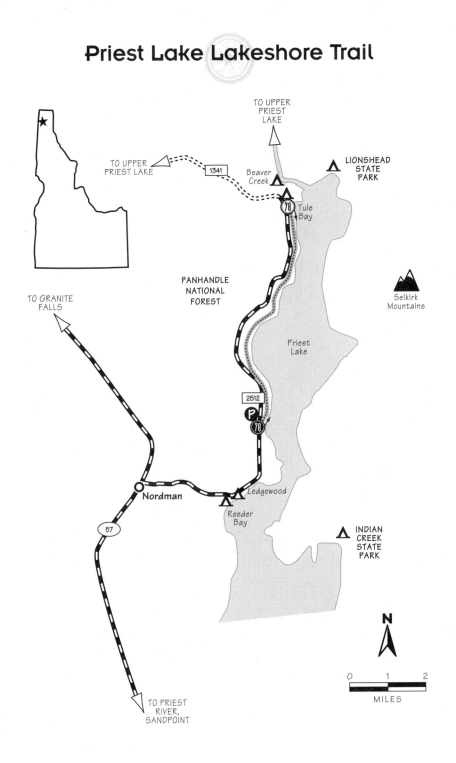

TO UPPER
PRIEST
LAKE

TO UPPER
PRIEST LAKE

1341

Beaver
Creek

LIONSHEAD
STATE
PARK

78 Tule
Bay

PANHANDLE
NATIONAL
FOREST

Selkirk
Mountains

Priest
Lake

TO GRANITE
FALLS

2512

P

78

Nordman

Ledgewood

Reeder
Bay

57

INDIAN
CREEK
STATE
PARK

N

0   1   2
MILES

TO PRIEST
RIVER,
SANDPOINT

The Lakeshore Trail weaves along the shore on the west side of Priest Lake, allowing riders like Tim Boden to stop and check out the view.

Trail to Upper Priest Lake (see Ride 79) or the Upper Priest River Trail (see Ride 80). Alternative activities in this area include boating, waterskiing, canoeing, camping, backpacking, hiking, waterfall driving-tours, and fishing.

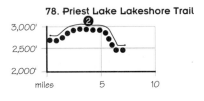

78. Priest Lake Lakeshore Trail

THE RIDE

0.0 To begin, ride out of the parking area and cruise up the trail.

1.1 Encounter two logs blocking the trail at neck (guillotine) level.

2.1 Cross wooden bridge, the first of many.

2.7 Caution: Trees block wooden bridge crossing.

2.8 Bear right at signed junction. This is another access point from the paved road above that runs parallel to the Lakeshore Trail.

3.1 Caution: Multiple trees blocking the trail in the next quarter-mile.

3.4 Encounter mud and roots. Please walk if it's wet and boggy.

4.5 Bear right at signed junction.

4.8 Pass by large campsite and picnic area.

6.0 Steep pitch. Get into your small ring and ride it.

6.7 Ride through another large campsite.

6.8 Big tree across trail.

7.2 Arrive at the end of the trail at a large beach area. There is a dirt boat ramp here at Tule Bay, just south of Beaver Creek Campground. If you left a shuttle vehicle here, you're done. Otherwise, turn around and ride back on the singletrack. If most of the group is tired, stay put and send one rider back to pick up the vehicle. Instead of riding the singletrack back to the trailhead, you can ride the paved road (Forest Road 2512) back to the start.

Variation: See the description for the Navigation Trail (Ride 79)—continue northwest to link with the incredibly beautiful buffed singletrack to Upper Priest Lake.

Upper Priest Lake Navigation Trail

Location: 10 miles northeast of Nordman.
Distance: 6 to 9.4 miles, one-way.
Time: About 1 hour or more.

Upper Priest Lake Navigation Trail

TO UPPER PRIEST RIVER

N

0   1   2
MILES

1013

TO NORDMAN

79 Navigation

Optional turnaround point

Upper Priest Lake

PANHANDLE NATIONAL FOREST

Plowboy

Beaver Creek Campground

79
P

2512

Priest Lake

TO NORDMAN

79. Upper Priest Lake Navigation Trail

3,000'

2,500'

2,000'

miles   5   10

Tread:	7.2 miles of singletrack, 2.2 miles of doubletrack.
Aerobic level:	Easy to moderate. Trail gets much more taxing after leaving Upper Priest Lake and going northwest to Forest Road 1013.
Technical difficulty:	1+ to 2. Singletrack is smooth and buffed, with a few roots and bogs here and there.
Highlights:	Gorgeous rolling singletrack in old-growth cedar forest next to Upper Priest Lake, one of the state's most treasured lakes.
Hazards:	Several creek crossings require slow, cautious approach. Please yield to hikers, joggers, and other cyclists.
Land status:	Panhandle National Forests, Priest Lake District.
Maps:	USGS Priest Lake NE, Upper Priest Lake, Panhandle National Forests, North.

Access: From Sandpoint, go west on U.S. Highway 2 to the town of Priest River. Turn north on Idaho 57 heading for Priest Lake, Nordman, and Coolin. At a two-way junction at Coolin, bear left for Nordman. When you reach Nordman, turn right on the paved road to Reeder Bay. Follow the road about 10 miles to a parking area in the north end of Beaver Creek Campground. The trailhead is signed. Shuttle: If you wish to drop a vehicle at the northern end of the trail, go north from Nordman on FR 302 for about 15 miles to a three-way junction at Granite Pass. Take the middle route, FR 1013, and follow it about 5 miles to the north end of the Navigation Trail. The trailhead is just past the junction with FR 662.

Notes on the trail: The Navigation Trail (Trail 291) is equally as sweet as the Lakeshore Trail (Ride 78) except it is even more buffed (if that's possible) and remarkably level for an Idaho mountain trail. This is a perfect trail for families and kids, but it's so scenic and smooth that advanced riders will want to sample it too. You might say this trail has the quality of a honeymoon-like, full-moon experience. Bring along some wine and cheese and take your time. Trail 291 starts at Beaver Creek Campground, runs north alongside the channel connecting Upper Priest Lake and Priest Lake, and then, upon reaching Upper Priest Lake, the views of the Selkirk Mountains and the lake itself open up. This is another prime candidate to ride and camp. Alternative activities in this area include boating, waterskiing, canoeing, camping, backpacking, hiking, waterfall driving-tours, and fishing. Because of the scenery along Upper Priest Lake, I recommend riding to Navigation campsite at the northern end of the lake and riding back, athough a shuttle is possible if you prefer that approach. It's about 3 miles past the lake to a jeep trail and the northern trailhead on FR 1013.

0.0 To begin, ride out of the parking area and cruise up the trail. It's mostly flat and level. Don't get too carried away with speed and watch out for horseback riders, hikers, and other cyclists.

1.1 Whoa! Hazardous descent into creek crossing. Exercise caution.

2.4 Pass by an old cabin.

2.6 Another hazardous crossing. Upper Priest Lake comes into view by a primitive campsite called Plowboy.

2.8 Trail snakes along the lakeshore within 25 feet of the water. Lookout Mountain, a broad white-granite peak with a fire lookout on top, looms across the lake. Mollies Peak (elevation 6,512 feet) and Phoebe Tip (6,658 feet) are to the north of Lookout Mountain.

6.0 Reach the northern end of Upper Priest Lake at Navigation campsite. Here you can turn around and retrace your tracks or continue on to FR 1013. I recommend turning around for the best views and to avoid the shuttle.

7.0 Singletrack ends; tread widens to doubletrack. Trail switchbacks and climbs to the northern trailhead.

9.4 Arrive at a gate at the northern trailhead.

Upper Priest River Trail

Location:	25 miles northeast of Nordman.
Distance:	20.4 miles, out and back.
Time:	4 to 5 hours.
Tread:	20.4 miles of singletrack.
Aerobic level:	Increasingly strenuous as you ride up the singletrack over many tree roots and wooden bridges to reach the falls.
Technical difficulty:	2+ to 3. Singletrack is smooth and buffed in many places, but there are a number of sections with tree roots and rocks.
Highlights:	Wilderness-quality singletrack in high-canopy old-growth cedar forest next to Upper Priest River. Take a dip in Priest River Falls near the Canadian border.
Hazards:	Watch out for grizzly bears. Bring your pepper spray. Yield to horseback riders and backpackers.
Land status:	Panhandle National Forests, Priest Lake District.
Maps:	USGS Priest Lake NE, Upper Priest Lake, Panhandle National Forests, North.

Upper Priest River Trail

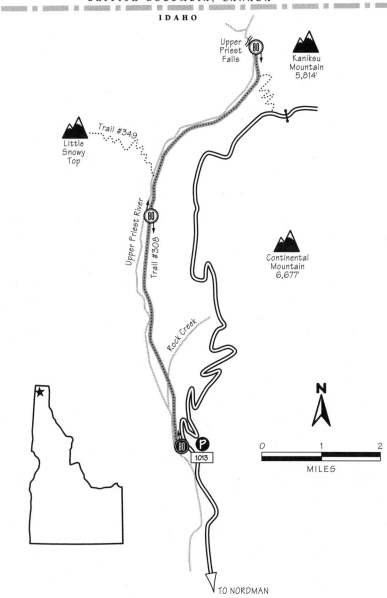

Upper
Priest
Falls

Kaniksu
Mountain
5,814'

Trail #349

Little
Snowy
Top

Upper Priest River

Trail #308

Continental
Mountain
6,677'

Rock Creek

N

1013

0   1   2

MILES

TO NORDMAN

Two members of the Grizzly Ridge Riders cross one of many wooden bridges they helped the Forest Service install along the Upper Priest River Trail.

Access: From Sandpoint, go west on U.S. Highway 2 to the town of Priest River. Turn north on Idaho Highway 57 heading for Priest Lake, Nordman, and Coolin. At a two-way junction at Coolin, bear left for Nordman. Stay on ID 57, which becomes Forest Road 302, to a three-way junction at Granite Pass. Take the middle route at the pass, Forest Road 1013, and follow it about 13 miles to the signed trailhead for the Priest River Trail on the left side of the dirt road. Park. The ride starts and ends here.

Notes on the trail: The Upper Priest River Trail is a truly unique experience. The scenic trail winds through a dark, old-growth cedar forest adjacent to the Upper Priest River. Most of the time the tall canopy prevents any significant sunlight from pouring through, so the darkness creates an eerie feeling. Combine that with the fact that grizzly bears roam this area and it makes you very alert for the duration of the ride. The Grizzly Ridge Riders and the Forest Service worked together to develop the trail, clear it, and install many wooden bridges across bogs and side streams. Many of the bridges are not flush with the ground, forcing you to lift your front tire about 3 or 4 inches as you approach. That adds to the strenuous factor, despite the fact that it's only 700 vertical feet of gain from the trailhead to Priest River Falls. Be sure to bring lots of water and food for the ride, so you can take a nice break at the falls. There is a deep, freezing cold pool here for the hardy to cool off. This trail is also the northernmost section of the Idaho State Centennial Trail, port of a 1,200-mile recreation trail that stretches from Nevada to Canada.

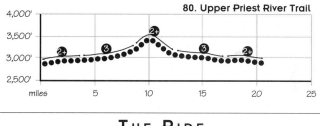

80. Upper Priest River Trail

THE RIDE

0.0 To begin, ride out of the parking area and cruise up the trail. It snakes toward the Priest River for a bit, and then it turns north to parallel the beautiful stream as you travel toward the falls. You will encounter many bridge crossings and technical tree root sections in the first 5 miles of the trail.

0.6 Four-way junction. Go straight.

7.0 Trail 349 junction comes up on the left. Stay on the main trail.

9.0 Junction with trail on the right. Go left and head for the falls. Only 1 mile to go!

10.2 Arrive at the falls. Park your bike and hike over to the falls for lunch and maybe a swim. When you're finished, turn around and head back the way you came. It's a blast to ride downhill, and remarkably easier!

20.4 Arrive in the trailhead parking area.

Appendix A: Resources

Bureau of Land Management Offices:

Idaho State Office
1387 Vinnell Way
Boise, ID 83709
208-373-4000

Owyhee Resource Area
3948 Development Avenue
Boise, ID 83705
208-384-3358

Pocatello Resource Area
1111 North Eighth Avenue
Pocatello, ID 83201
208-236-6860

Ridge-to-Rivers Trail System
BLM-Boise Front Office
3948 Development Avenue
Boise, ID 83705
208-384-3360

Snake River Birds of Prey National Conservation Area
3948 Development Avenue
Boise, ID 83705
208-384-3300

County Offices:

Blaine County Recreation District
P.O. Box 297
Hailey, ID 83333
208-788-2117

Teton County
89 North Main, Number 1
Driggs, ID 83422
208-354-2905

Miscellaneous Offices:

Cascade Field Office
U.S. Bureau of Reclamation
P.O. Box 270
Cascade, ID 83611
208-382-4258

Farragut State Park
East 13400 Ranger Road
Athol, ID 83801
208-683-2425

Friends of Weiser River Trail
2165 Seid Creek Road
Cambridge, ID 83610
208-549-1732

Hells Gate Park Headquarters
3620A Snake River Avenue
Lewiston, ID 83501
208-799-5015

Lewis and Clark Trail Adventures
Wayne Fairchild, owner
P.O. Box 9051
Missoula, MT 59801
800-366-6246
www.montana.com/lcta/index.htm

Ponderosa State Park
P.O. Box A
McCall, ID 83638
208-634-2164

Portneuf Greenways Foundation
P.O. Box 71
Pocatello, ID 83204
208-232-3711

Route of the Hiawatha concessionaires
208-744-1392

Sun Valley Trekking
P.O. Box 2200
Sun Valley, ID 83353
208-726-1002

U.S. Army Corps of Engineers
Snake-Clearwater National Recreation Trail
100 Fair Street
Clarkston, WA 99403
509-751-0240

Venture Outdoors
Hailey, ID 83333
800-528-5262

Mountain Bike Advocacy Groups

Grizzly Ridge Riders
P.O. Box 9
Sandpoint, ID 83664

Moscow Area Mountain Biking Association
710 East Seventh Street
Moscow, ID 83843
http://members.aol.com/lakook
lakook@aol.com

Southwest Idaho Mountain Biking Association (SWIMBA)
P.O. Box 1443
Boise, ID 83701
http://members.aol.com/jjlehn/SWIMBA
bigrins@micron.net

Wood River Trails
c/o Sun Summit Sports
791 Warm Springs Road
Ketchum, ID 83353

Ski Areas

Bogus Basin Ski Resort
2405 Bogus Basin Road
Boise, ID 83702
208-332-5100

Brundage Mountain Ski Resort
P.O. Box 1062
McCall, ID 83638
800-888-7544

Schweitzer Mountain Resort
10000 Schweitzer Mountain Road
Sandpoint, ID 83864
208-263-9555

Silver Mountain
610 Bunker Avenue
Kellogg, ID 83837
208-783-1111

Sun Valley Resort
P.O. Box 10
Sun Valley, ID 83353
208-622-4111

State of Idaho Offices:

Idaho Department of Lands
8355 West State Street
Boise, ID 83703
208-334-3488

Idaho Department of Parks and Recreation (Idaho City yurt rentals)
5657 Warm Springs Avenue
Boise, ID 83712
208-334-4199

Tourism and Travel Information

Boise Convention and Visitors Bureau
P.O. Box 2106
Boise, ID 83701
800-635-5240

Coeur d'Alene and Post Falls
Convention and Visitors Bureau
P.O. Box 908
Post Falls, ID 83854
Info@cda-pfcvb.com
208-773-4080 or 800-292-2553

Idaho Falls Convention and Visitors Bureau
P.O. Box 50498
Idaho Falls, ID 83405
208-523-1010 or 800-634-3246
ifcvb@ida.net

Idaho Department of Commerce
(free statewide travel guide)
P.O. Box 83720
Boise, ID 83720-0093
208-334-2470

Idaho Tourism and Travel
www.visitid.org

Lewiston Chamber of Commerce
2207 East Main Street
Lewiston, ID 83501
800-473-3543

Moscow Chamber of Commerce
411 South Main Street
Moscow, ID 83843
800-380-1801

Pocatello Chamber of Commerce
2695 South Fifth Street
Pocatello, ID 83204
208-233-1525

Priest Lake Chamber of Commerce
P.O. Box 174
Coolin, ID 83821
208-443-3191 or 888-774-3785
trav@myself.com

Salmon Valley Chamber of Commerce
200 Main Street, Suite 1
Salmon, ID 83467
208-756-2100

Sandpoint Chamber of Commerce
P.O Box 928
Sandpoint, ID 83864
208-263-2161
chamber@netw.com

Silver Country
Best Western Wallace Inn
100 Front Street
Wallace, ID 83873
888-326-4611

Stanley-Sawtooth Chamber of Commerce
P.O. Box 8
Stanley, ID 83278
800-878-7950

Sun Valley/Ketchum Chamber of Commerce
P.O. Box 2420
Sun Valley, ID 83353
800-634-3347
www.visitsunvalley.com
sunval@micron.net

Twin Falls Chamber/Visitors Center
858 Blue Lakes Boulevard North
Twin Falls, ID 83301
800-255-8946

USDA Forest Service Offices:

Ashton District
Targhee National Forest
Ashton, ID 83420
208-652-7442

Avery District
St. Joe National Forest
Panhandle National Forests
HC Box 1
Avery, ID 83802

Clearwater District
Nez Perce National Forest
Route 2, Box 475
Grangeville, ID 83530
208-983-1963

Emmett Ranger District
Boise National Forest
1805 State Highway 16, Room 5
Emmett, ID 83617
208-365-3811

Fairfield Ranger District
Sawtooth National Forest
P.O. Box 186
Fairfield, ID 83327
208-764-2202

Fernan District
Coeur d'Alene National Forest
Panhandle National Forests
2502 East Sherman Avenue
Coeur d'Alene, ID 83814
208-765-7381

Idaho City Ranger District
Boise National Forest
P.O. Box 129
Idaho City, ID 83631
208-392-6681

Ketchum Ranger District
Sawtooth National Forest
Sun Valley Road
Sun Vally, ID 83353
208-622-5371

Lochsa District
Clearwater National Forest
Route 1, Box 398
Kooskia, ID 83539
208-926-4275

Lowman Ranger District
Boise National Forest
7359 Highway 21
Lowman, ID 83637
208-259-3361

McCall District
Payette National Forest
P.O. Box 1026
McCall, ID 83638

New Meadows District
Payette National Forest
Box J
New Meadows, 83654
208-347-0300

Nez Perce National Forest Supervisor's
Office
Route 2, Box 475
Grangeville, ID 83530
208-983-1950

Palisades District
Targhee National Forest
P.O. Box 398B Route 1
Idaho Falls, ID 83401
208-523-1412

Palouse District
Clearwater National Forest
Route 2, Box 4
Potlatch, ID 83855
208-875-1131

Payette National Forest Supervisor's Office
P.O. Box 1026
McCall, ID 83638
208-634-0700

Pocatello District
Caribou National Forest
250 South Fourth Avenue
Federal Building, Suite 187
Pocatello, ID 83201
208-236-7500

Priest Lake District
Panhandle National Forests
32203 Highway 57
Priest River, ID 83856
208-443-6800

Salmon-Challis National Forest
Highway 93 South
Rural Route 2, Box 600
Salmon, ID 83467
208-756-2215

Sandpoint District
Panhandle National Forests
1500 Highway 2, Suite 110
Sandpoint, ID 83864
208-265-6600

Sawtooth National Recreation Area
Headquarters Office
Star Route Highway 75
Ketchum, ID 83340
800-260-5970

Twin Falls District
Sawtooth National Forest
2647 Kimberly Road East
Twin Falls, ID 83301
208-737-3274

Weiser Ranger District
Payette National Forest
851 East Ninth Street
Weiser, ID 83672
208-549-4200

Appendix B: Bike Shops

Boise
George's Cycles and Fitness
4809 Fairview, 208-376-4526
1109 Broadway, 208-343-3782
1738 West State Street, 208-343-5677
5515 West State Street, 208-853-1964

Idaho Mountain Touring
1310 West Main Street
Boise, ID 83702
208-336-3854

Ken's Bicycle Warehouse
10470 West Overland Road
Boise, ID 83704
208-376-9240

Moo Cycles
1517 1/2 North Thirteenth Street
Boise, ID 83702
208-336-5229

REI
8300 West Emerald Street
Boise, ID 83704
208-322-1141

Screamin' Toad Cycles
3011 West State Street
Boise, ID 83702
208-367-1899

World Cycle
180 North Eighth Street
Boise, ID 83702
208-343-9130

Coeur d'Alene
Vertical Earth
206 North Third Street
Coeur d'Alene, ID 83814
208-667-5503

Fairfield
Claude's Sports
Highway 20
Fairfield, ID 83327
208-764-2319

Grangeville
Holiday Sports
126 West Main Street
Grangeville, ID 83530
208-983-2299

Kellogg
Moon Saddle Cycle
10 West Portland Street
Kellogg, ID 83837
208-786-3751

Ketchum/Sun Valley
Backwoods Mountain Sports
760 Warm Springs Road
Ketchum, ID 83353
208-726-8826

Sun Summit Sports
791 Warm Springs Road
Ketchum, ID 83353
208-726-0707

Idaho Falls
Alpine Schwinn
1352 Holmes
Idaho Falls, ID 83401
208-523-1226

Bill's Bike Shop
805 South Holmes Avenue
Idaho Falls, ID 83401
208-522-3341

Idaho Mountain Trading
474 Shoup Avenue
Idaho Falls, ID 83401
208-523-6679

Lewiston
Follett's Mountain Sports
714 D Street
Lewiston, ID 83501
208-743-4200

Pedals 'n Spokes
829 D Street
Lewiston, ID 83501
208-743-6567

McCall
Gravity Sports
503 Pine Street
McCall, ID 83638
208-634-8530

Hometown Sports
402 West Lake Street
McCall, ID 83638
208-634-2302

Mountain Cycle
212 North Third Street
McCall, ID 83638
208-634-6333

Moscow
Follett's Mountain Sports
410 West Third
Moscow, ID 83843
208-882-6735

Northwestern Mountain Sports
1016 Pullman Road
Moscow, ID 83843
208-882-0133

Paradise Creek Bicycles
511 South Main
Moscow, ID 83843
208-882-0703

Ontario, Oregon
Making Tracks
298 South Oregon Street
Ontario, OR 97914
541-889-5575

Pocatello
Gateway Cyclery
404 South Arthur
Pocatello, ID 83201
208-232-3711

Scott's Ski and Sports
218 Main Street
Pocatello, ID 83201
208-232-1449

Sandpoint
Alpine Designs
312 North Fifth Avenue
Sandpoint, ID 83864
208-263-9373

Outdoor Experience
314 North First Avenue
Sandpoint, ID 83864
208-263-6028

Twin Falls
Blue Lakes Cyclery
621 Blue Lakes
Twin Falls, ID 83301
208-733-9305

Claude's Sports
1239 Poleline Road East
Twin Falls, ID 83327
208-733-2000

Rock's Cycling and Fitness
222 Blue Lakes Boulevard
Twin Falls, ID 83301
208-733-5511

An Index of Rides

Ski Resorts
5. Mores Mountain Loop (limited lift service)
28. Brundage Mountain Elk Trail loop
36. Bald Mountain: Cold Springs Trail
37. Bald Mountain: Warm Springs Trail
52. Kelly Canyon Loop (no lift service)
71. Silver Mountain Nature Trail
72. Silver Mountain–Big Creek Banzai
77. Schweitzer Mountain GRR Loop

Hot Springs Rides
20. Warm Springs Plunge
30. Big Smoky Hot Springs Cruise

Historical Rides
6. Oregon Trail–Bonneville Point–Greenbelt Loop
7. Swan Falls Petroglyph Tour
57. Lemhi Pass Scenic Byway
59. Lewis and Clark Trail/Lolo Motorway

Yurt-to-Yurt Rides
17. Skyline Loop
18. Elkhorn-Alpine Loop
19. Beaver Creek Cabin Gravity Ride
40. East Fork Baker–Coyote Yurt–Adams Gulch Shuttle

Multiday Rides
57. Lemhi Pass Scenic Byway
59. Lewis and Clark Trail/Lolo Motorway

Glossary

ATB: All-terrain bicycle; a.k.a. mountain bike, sprocket rocket, fat-tire flyer.

ATV: All-terrain vehicle; in this book ATV refers to motorbikes and three and four-wheelers designed for off-road use.

Bail: Getting off the bike, usually in a hurry, and whether or not you meant to. Often a last resort.

Bunny hop: Leaping up, while riding, and lifting both wheels off the ground to jump over an obstacle (or for sheer joy).

Clamper cramps: That burning, cramping sensation experienced in the hands during extended braking.

Clean: To ride without touching a foot (or other body part) to the ground; to ride a tough section successfully.

Clipless: A type of pedal with a binding that accepts a special cleat on the soles of bike shoes. The cleat clicks in for more control and efficient pedaling and out for safe landings (in theory).

Contour: A line on a topographic map showing a continuous elevation level over uneven ground. Also used as a verb to indicate a fairly easy or moderate grade: "The trail contours around the canyon rim before the final grunt to the top."

Dab: To put a foot or hand down (or hold on to or lean on a tree or other support) while riding. If you have to dab, then you haven't ridden that piece of trail clean.

Downfall: Trees that have fallen across the trail.

Doubletrack: A trail, jeep road, ATV route, or other track with two distinct ribbons of tread, typically with grass growing in between. No matter which side you choose, the other rut always looks smoother.

Endo: Lifting the rear wheel off the ground and riding (or abruptly not riding) on the front wheel only. Also known, at various degrees of control and finality, as a nose wheelie, "going over the handlebars," or a face plant.

Fall line: The angle and direction of a slope; the line you follow when gravity is in control and you aren't.

Graded: When a gravel road is scraped level to smooth out the washboards and potholes, it has been graded. In this book, a road is listed as graded only if it is regularly maintained. Not all such roads are graded every year, however.

Granny gear: The lowest (easiest) gear, a combination of the smallest of the three chainrings on the bottom bracket spindle (where the pedals and crank arms attach to the bike's frame) and the largest cog on the rear cluster. Shift down to your granny gear for serious climbing.

Hammer: To ride hard; derived from how it feels afterward: "I'm hammered."

Hammerhead: Someone who actually enjoys feeling hammered. A Type-A personality rider who goes hard and fast all the time.

Kelly hump: An abrupt mound of dirt across the road or trail. These are common on old logging roads and skidder tracks, placed there to block vehicle access. At high speeds, they become launching pads for bikes and inadvertent astronauts.

Line: The route (or trajectory) between or over obstacles or through turns. Tread or trail refers to the ground you're riding on; the line is the path you choose within the tread (and exists mostly in the eye of the beholder).

Off-the-seat: Moving your butt behind the bike seat and over the rear tire; used for control on extremely steep descents. This position increases braking power, helps prevent endos, and reduces skidding.

Portage: To carry the bike, usually up a steep hill, across unridable obstacles, or through a stream.

Quads: Thigh muscles (short for quadriceps) or maps in the USGS topographic series (short for quadrangles). Nice quads of either kind can help get you out of trouble in the backcountry.

Ratcheting: Also known as backpedaling; pedaling backward to avoid hitting rocks or other obstacles with the pedals.

Sidehill: Where the trail crosses a slope. If the tread is narrow, keep your inside (uphill) pedal up to avoid hitting the ground. If the tread tilts downhill, you may have to use some body language to keep the bike plumb or vertical to avoid slipping out.

Singletrack: A trail, game run, or other track with only one ribbon of tread. Good singletrack is pure fun.

Spur: A side road or trail that splits off from the main route.

Surf: Riding through loose gravel or sand, when the wheels sway from side to side. Also heavy surf: frequent and difficult obstacles.

Suspension: A bike with front suspension has a shock-absorbing fork or stem. Rear suspension absorbs shock between the rear wheel and frame. A bike with both is said to be fully suspended.

Switchbacks: When a trail goes up a steep slope, it zigzags or switchbacks across the fall line to ease the gradient of the climb. Well-designed switchbacks make a turn with at least an 8-foot radius and remain fairly level within the turn itself. These are rare, however, and cyclists often struggle to ride through sharply angled, sloping switchbacks.

Track stand: Balancing on a bike in one place, without rolling forward appreciably. Cock the front wheel to one side and bring that pedal up to the one or two o'clock position. Now control your side-to-side balance by applying pressure on the pedals and brakes and changing the angle of the front wheel, as needed. It takes practice but really comes in handy at stoplights, on switchbacks, and when trying to free a foot before falling.

Tread: The riding surface, particularly regarding singletrack.

Water bar: A log, rock, or other barrier placed in the tread to divert water off the trail and prevent erosion. Peeled logs can be slippery and cause bad falls, especially when they angle sharply across the trail.

Whoop-de-doo: A series of kelly humps used to keep vehicles off trails. Watch your speed or do the dreaded top tube tango.

Index

Page numbers in *italic* type refer to photographs.
Page numbers in **bold** type refer to maps.

About the Author

Stephen Stuebner is the author of six books, including *Mountain Biking in Boise, Mountain Biking in McCall, Paddling the Payette, Discover Idaho's Centennial Trail,* and *Idaho Impressions.* A professional journalist, he writes for a host of newspapers and magazines such as the *New York Times, Backpacker, High Country News,* and *National Wildlife.* A founding member of the Southwest Idaho Mountain Biking Association (SWIMBA), he serves as the mountain biking representative on the Idaho Trails Council. He lives in the Boise foothills with his wife, Amy, and two children.

Stephen Stuebner enjoys skyline views of the Boulder Mountains on the East Fork Baker Creek doubletrack road, north of Sun Valley.

FALCONGUIDES ® Leading the Way™

FALCONGUIDES ® are available for where-to-go hiking, mountain biking, rock climbing, walking, scenic driving, fishing, rockhounding, paddling, birding, wildlife viewing, and camping. We also have FalconGuides on essential outdoor skills and subjects and field identification. The following titles are currently available, but this list grows every year. For a free catalog with a complete list of titles, call FALCON toll-free at 1-800-582-2665.

Mountain Biking Guides

Mountain Biking Arizona
Mountain Biking Colorado
Mountain Biking Georgia
Mountain Biking New Mexico
Mountain Biking New York
Mountain Biking Northern New England
Mountain Biking Oregon
Mountain Biking South Carolina
Mountain Biking Southern California
Mountain Biking Southern New England
Mountain Biking Utah
Mountain Biking Wisconsin
Mountain Biking Wyoming

Local Cycling Series

Fat Trax Bozeman
Mountain Biking Bend
Mountain Biking Boise
Mountain Biking Chequamegon
Mountain Biking Chico
Mountain Biking Colorado Springs
Mountain Biking Denver/Boulder
Mountain Biking Durango
Mountain Biking Flagstaff and Sedona
Mountain Biking Helena
Mountain Biking Moab
Mountain Biking Utah's St. George/Cedar City Area
Mountain Biking the White Mountains (West)

■ *To order any of these books, check with your local bookseller or call FALCON* ® *at 1-800-582-2665.*
Visit us on the world wide web at:
www.FalconOutdoors.com

FALCON®

FALCON GUIDES® Leading the Way™

FALCON GUIDES® are available for where-to-go hiking, mountain biking, rock climbing, walking, scenic driving, fishing, rockhounding, paddling, birding, wildlife viewing, and camping. We also have FalconGuides on essential outdoor skills and subjects and field identification. The following titles are currently available, but this list grows every year. For a free catalog with a complete list of titles, call FALCON toll-free at 1-800-582-2665.

HIKING GUIDES

Hiking Alaska
Hiking Arizona
Hiking Arizona's Cactus Country
Hiking the Beartooths
Hiking Big Bend National Park
Hiking the Bob Marshall Country
Hiking California
Hiking California's Desert Parks
Hiking Carlsbad Caverns
    and Guadalupe Mtns. National Parks
Hiking Colorado
Hiking Colorado, Vol.II
Hiking Colorado's Summits
Hiking Colorado's Weminuche Wilderness
Hiking the Columbia River Gorge
Hiking Florida
Hiking Georgia
Hiking Glacier & Waterton Lakes National Parks
Hiking Grand Canyon National Park
Hiking Grand Staircase-Escalante/Glen Canyon
Hiking Grand Teton National Park
Hiking Great Basin National Park
Hiking Hot Springs in the Pacific Northwest
Hiking Idaho
Hiking Maine
Hiking Michigan
Hiking Minnesota
Hiking Montana
Hiking Mount Rainier National Park
Hiking Mount St. Helens
Hiking Nevada
Hiking New Hampshire

Hiking New Mexico
Hiking New York
Hiking North Carolina
Hiking the North Cascades
Hiking Northern Arizona
Hiking Olympic National Park
Hiking Oregon
Hiking Oregon's Eagle Cap Wilderness
Hiking Oregon's Mount Hood/Badger Creek
Hiking Oregon's Three Sisters Country
Hiking Pennsylvania
Hiking Shenandoah National Park
Hiking the Sierra Nevada
Hiking South Carolina
Hiking South Dakota's Black Hills Country
Hiking Southern New England
Hiking Tennessee
Hiking Texas
Hiking Utah
Hiking Utah's Summits
Hiking Vermont
Hiking Virginia
Hiking Washington
Hiking Wyoming
Hiking Wyoming's Cloud Peak Wilderness
Hiking Wyoming's Wind River Range
Hiking Yellowstone National Park
Hiking Zion & Bryce Canyon National Parks
The Trail Guide to Bob Marshall Country
Wild Country Companion
Wild Montana
Wild Utah

*To order any of these books, check with your local bookseller
or call FALCON® at **1-800-582-2665**.
Visit us on the world wide web at:
www.FalconOutdoors.com*

FALCON®

FIELD GUIDES

Bitterroot: Montana State Flower
Canyon Country Wildflowers
Central Rocky Mountains
    Wildflowers
Great Lakes Berry Book
New England Berry Book
Ozark Wildflowers
Pacific Northwest Berry Book
Plants of Arizona
Rare Plants of Colorado
Rocky Mountain Berry Book
Scats & Tracks of the Pacific
    Coast States
Scats & Tracks of the
    Rocky Mountains
Southern Rocky Mountain
    Wildflowers
Tallgrass Prairie Wildflowers
Western Trees
Wildflowers of Southwestern
    Utah
Willow Bark and Rosehips

FISHING GUIDES

Fishing Alaska
Fishing the Beartooths
Fishing Florida
Fishing Glacier National Park
Fishing Maine
Fishing Montana
Fishing Wyoming
Fishing Yellowstone
    National Park

ROCKHOUNDING GUIDES

Rockhounding Arizona
Rockhounding California
Rockhounding Colorado
Rockhounding Montana
Rockhounding Nevada
Rockhound's Guide to New
    Mexico
Rockhounding Texas
Rockhounding Utah
Rockhounding Wyoming

MORE GUIDEBOOKS

Backcountry Horseman's
    Guide to Washington
Camping California's
    National Forests
Exploring Canyonlands &
    Arches National Parks
Exploring Hawaii's Parklands
Exploring Mount Helena
Exploring Southern California
    Beaches
Recreation Guide to WA
    National Forests
Touring California & Nevada
    Hot Springs
Touring Colorado Hot Springs
Touring Montana & Wyoming
    Hot Springs
Trail Riding Western
    Montana
Wild Country Companion
Wilderness Directory
Wild Montana
Wild Utah

BIRDING GUIDES

Birding Minnesota
Birding Montana
Birding Northern California
Birding Texas
Birding Utah

PADDLING GUIDES

Floater's Guide to Colorado
Paddling Minnesota
Paddling Montana
Paddling Okefenokee
Paddling Oregon
Paddling Yellowstone & Grand
    Teton National Parks

HOW-TO GUIDES

Avalanche Aware
Backpacking Tips
Bear Aware
Desert Hiking Tips
Hiking with Dogs
Leave No Trace
Mountain Lion Alert
Reading Weather
Route Finding
Using GPS
Wilderness First Aid
Wilderness Survival

WALKING

Walking Colorado Springs
Walking Denver
Walking Portland
Walking St. Louis
Walking Virginia Beach

■ *To order any of these books, check with your local bookseller*
or call FALCON ® *at* **1-800-582-2665**.
Visit us on the world wide web at:
www.FalconOutdoors.com

FALCON®

FALCON GUIDES® Leading the Way™

WILDLIFE VIEWING GUIDES

Alaska Wildlife Viewing Guide
Arizona Wildlife Viewing Guide
California Wildlife Viewing Guide
Colorado Wildlife Viewing Guide
Florida Wildlife Viewing Guide
Indiana Wildlife Vewing Guide
Iowa Wildlife Viewing Guide
Kentucky Wildlife Viewing Guide
Massachusetts Wildlife Viewing Guide
Montana Wildlife Viewing Guide
Nebraska Wildlife Viewing Guide
Nevada Wildlife Viewing Guide
New Hampshire Wildlife Viewing Guide
New Jersey Wildlife Viewing Guide
New Mexico Wildlife Viewing Guide
New York Wildlife Viewing Guide
North Carolina Wildlife Viewing Guide
North Dakota Wildlife Viewing Guide
Ohio Wildlife Viewing Guide
Oregon Wildlife Viewing Guide
Puerto Rico and the Virgin Islands WVG
Tennessee Wildlife Viewing Guide
Texas Wildlife Viewing Guide
Utah Wildlife Viewing Guide
Vermont Wildlife Viewing Guide
Virginia Wildlife Viewing Guide
Washington Wildlife Viewing Guide
West Virginia Wildlife Viewing Guide
Wisconsin Wildlife Viewing Guide

HISTORIC TRAIL GUIDES

Traveling California's Gold Rush Country
Traveling the Lewis & Clark Trail
Traveling the Oregon Trail
Traveler's Guide to the Pony Express Trail

SCENIC DRIVING GUIDES

Scenic Driving Alaska and the Yukon
Scenic Driving Arizona
Scenic Driving the Beartooth Highway
Scenic Driving California
Scenic Driving Colorado
Scenic Driving Florida
Scenic Driving Georgia
Scenic Driving Hawaii
Scenic Driving Idaho
Scenic Driving Michigan
Scenic Driving Minnesota
Scenic Driving Montana
Scenic Driving New England
Scenic Driving New Mexico
Scenic Driving North Carolina
Scenic Driving Oregon
Scenic Driving the Ozarks including the
    Ouchita Mountains
Scenic Driving Pennsylvania
Scenic Driving Texas
Scenic Driving Utah
Scenic Driving Washington
Scenic Driving Wisconsin
Scenic Driving Wyoming
Scenic Driving Yellowstone & Grand Teton
    National Parks
Back Country Byways
Scenic Byways East
Scenic Byways Farwest
Scenic Byways Rocky Mountains

*To order any of these books, check with your local bookseller
or call FALCON® at **1-800-582-2665**.
Visit us on the world wide web at:
www.FalconOutdoors.com*

FALCON®

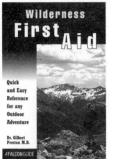

WILDERNESS FIRST AID

By Dr. Gilbert Preston M.D.

Enjoy the outdoors and face the inherent risks with confidence. By reading this easy-to-follow first-aid text, all outdoor enthusiasts can pack a little extra peace of mind on their next adventure. *Wilderness First Aid* offers expert medical advice for dealing with outdoor emergencies beyond the reach of 911. It easily fits in most backcountry first-aid kits.

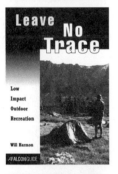

LEAVE NO TRACE

By Will Harmon

The concept of "leave no trace" seems simple, but it actually gets fairly complicated. This handy quick-reference guidebook includes all the newest information on this growing and all-important subject. This book is written to help the outdoor enthusiast make the hundreds of decisions necessary to protect the natural landscape and still have an enjoyable wilderness experience. Part of the proceeds from the sale of this book go to continue leave-no-trace education efforts. The Official Manual of American Hiking Society.

BEAR AWARE

By Bill Schneider

Hiking in bear country can be very safe if hikers follow the guidelines summarized in this small, "packable" book. Extensively reviewed by bear experts, the book contains the latest information on the intriguing science of bear-human interactions. *Bear Aware* can not only make your hike safer, but it can help you avoid the fear of bears that can take the edge off your trip.

MOUNTAIN LION ALERT

By Steve Torres

Recent mountain lion attacks have received national attention. Although infrequent, lion attacks raise concern for public safety. *Mountain Lion Alert* contains helpful advice for mountain bikers, trail runners, horse riders, pet owners, and suburban landowners on how to reduce the chances of mountain lion-human conflicts.

Also Available

*Wilderness Survival • Reading Weather • Backpacking Tips • Climbing Safely •
Avalanche Aware • Desert Hiking Tips • Hiking with Dogs • Using GPS •
Route Finding • Wild Country Companion*

To order check with your local bookseller or
call FALCON® at **1-800-582-2665.**
www.FalconOutdoors.com